JOE ZUKEN

CITIZEN AND SOCIALIST

DOUG SMITH

James Lorimer & Company, Toronto

Front Cover: Painting of Joe Zuken by Glynnis Hardie

Inside Photo Credits: Photos on p. 1-3 of photo section courtesy of Clara Zuken. Photos on p. 4-6 of photo section courtesy of the *Western Canada Pictorial Index*.

Canadian Cataloguing in Publication Data

Smith, Doug, 1954-
  Joe Zuken, citizen and socialist

ISBN 1-55028-305-7 (bound). — ISBN 1-55028-303-0 (pbk.)

1. Zuken, Joe. 2. Winnipeg (Man.) - Politics and government. 3. City council members - Manitoba - Winnipeg - Biography. 4. Communists - Manitoba - Winnipeg - Biography. 5. School boards - Manitoba - Winnipeg - Biography. 6. Ukrainian Canadians - Manitoba - Winnipeg - Biography.* I. Title.

FC3396.26.Z8S5 1990   971.27'4303'092   C90-094006-9
F1060.92.S5 1990   69808

James Lorimer & Company, Publishers
Egerton Ryerson Memorial Building
35 Britain Street
Toronto, Ontario M5A 1R7

Printed and bound in Canada

6 5 4 3 2 1 90 91 92 93 94 95

Contents

Epitaph

There's a dream, which dwells in everyone
At times like frozen ice, at times like warming sun.
One dream, one hope I've harboured long,
It lives within me, as does my heart and song;
When all alone I shall by earth be bound,
When my aged bones shall be in Jewish rooted ground,
Then shall those who pass my place,
Note the grass which is rooted in my race,
Address the living wind and say:
He was a *mensch,* he served his folk in every way.

— *Itzik Feffer,*
translated from the Yiddish by Ben Chudd

Acknowledgements

The writing of any book involves the incurring of innumerable debts.

My greatest debt is to Clara Zuken. She gave generously of her time and her spirit. While this book should in no way be considered an "official" biography, Clara Zuken willingly read and commented on the manuscript in its entirety, providing me with much needed encouragement and enlightenment. I remain eternally in her debt for this support.

I must also express my gratitude to Sheila Moore, who brought Joe Zuken into my life in 1979. Over the years my discussions with Sheila have done much to shape my understanding of Joe Zuken. Sheila also generously shared her own research into the wartime suppression of civil liberties in Canada.

The bibliography of this book contains a full listing of the works I have consulted, but special recognition should be drawn to the writing of Alan Artibise, Roz Usiskin, Reg Skene, Reg Whitaker, Norman Penner, Bob Milan, James Lorimer and David Walker. It is from their work that I have constructed the context for this book, and I thank them most heartily.

Much of my history of Joe Zuken's political career is based on newspaper clippings stored by the *Winnipeg Free Press* and in the *Winnipeg Tribune* archives at the University of Manitoba. In obtaining these clippings I was assisted by Jill Sinkwich, David Kerr, Esme Langer, Orysia Tracz and Michael Angel. I would like to thank Greg Merner for sharing his collection of back numbers of *City Magazine* with me. I would also like to thank the staff of the Provincial Archives of Manitoba in general and Jocelyn McKillop, Barry Hyman and Chris Kotecki in particular.

In the course my research for this book, I interviewed over twenty people — they are listed at the back of the book — and I thank them for their time, cooperation and enthusiasm.

I also owe a debt of gratitude to the following people who read and commented on this book in manuscript form: Reg Whitaker, Reg Skene, Roz Usiskin, Bill Neville, Lawrie Cherniack, Ed Reed, Gary Hunter, Pat Knipe, Robert Chodos, Sandra Hardy, Jean Friesen, Gerald Friesen, Bill Ross and David Carr. I am grateful to them for drawing errors to my attention, but they should not be held responsible for the work or its interpretations.

I will remain forever grateful to Steven Rosenberg for rescuing one of the chapters of this book from the digital purgatory to which my computer had temporarily banished it.

William Gillies and Ed Reed deserve credit for supplying me with valuable information about the 1979 civic election.

I would also like to express my gratitude to James Lorimer for the enthusiasm with which he greeted this project. Curtis Fahey, Virginia Smith and Judith Turnbull have played important roles in shaping the manuscript and dealing with my anxieties. I thank them all.

I wish to express my appreciation to the people of Manitoba for their financial support through the Manitoba Arts Council and to the members of the Joseph Zuken Memorial Society for their support.

I owe two last debts. This book could not have been written were it not for the peace of mind and of household that were provided to me by the staff and directors, past and present, of the Provincial Employees Care for Kids Co-op Day Care. Their underpaid and underappreciated labour is the greatest subsidy this book has received.

And finally, and I fear not for the last time in this book, words fail me in my efforts to thank Sandra Hardy — which leaves me no alternative but to dedicate it to her.

Introduction

I first met Joe Zuken in the spring of 1978. I had asked him to speak on the topic of financial restraint in the public sector at a student newspaper conference I was organizing. A few months earlier I had heard him give an electrifying speech on this potentially stultifying topic. I was hoping he would be able to jolt students who were angry about tuition increases and course reductions to make some links between what was going on in universities and the rest of the world.

Like most Winnipeggers, I was aware that Joe Zuken was a Communist. Like many people who came to hold left-wing views during the Sixties and Seventies, I did not harbour warm views towards the Communist Party of Canada. But Joe Zuken by then was a special case. Everyone sensed that he was at odds with the Communist Party, while his reputation as a defender of the underdog was secure.

The delegates to this conference had come from all over Western Canada, however, and some of them were decidedly put out to discover they were going to be addressed by a Communist. At the workshop Joe was tired, and his speech a little flat. Some audience members were decidedly hostile, and during the question-and-answer session two of them, ignoring the topic and the contents of Joe's presentation, went after him. Their attacks were incoherent and ill-formed, not moving much beyond "Why should we listen to you, since you're a Communist?"

I was embarrassed. But Joe was invigorated. This sort of reception was not unfamiliar to him, and he did not let challenges go unanswered. He stood his ground and defended his career and his positions without apology. After the session he would accept no apologies from me.

A year later I was asked, literally out of the blue, to work as an organizer on Joe's 1979 mayoral campaign. Without giving it a second thought I agreed. Like anyone who has had much to do with electoral politics, I have done many things that embarrass me now, but I am proud of my involvement with that campaign.

Not that Joe Zuken was an organizer's dream. He knew his own mind and was not about to be packaged like a tin of beans. And he was surprisingly shy — he did not want to visit shopping malls and shake the hands of total strangers. He was uncomfortable too with the motorcade the campaign committee planned as a pre-election finale, but he was so withdrawn that he waited until the parade was about to start before telling us that he had no desire to be put on public display.

But in other ways, for all the old-fashioned reasons, Joe Zuken was the ideal candidate. He inspired people to work for him; no one felt they were feeding Joe's ego, and no one worried that they were toiling for someone who would betray their beliefs once elected.

And he brought the city's finest traditions to life — candour, compassion for the oppressed and a sense that we all had a responsibility to try and bring a better society into being.

The night of the election truly was a dark and stormy night. As the thunder crashed and the basements filled up with water, Joe Zuken went down to defeat. We finished in second place, far out of the money, but I don't think anyone ever celebrated defeat the way we did. For many of us, it was the most satisfying, exciting and pleasurable campaign we'd ever worked on.

I did not have many private conversations with Joe during this campaign, but on those occasions when I was driving to or from a meeting, he would spin tales from the city's past. In public he was a formidable debater, but in private he displayed a sly sense of humour and a broadly humanistic approach to everyone he encountered — be they friend or foe. It was during these rides that I formed the desire to write a biography of Joe Zuken — to capture the stories he had in his head and the perspective he brought to public life.

It was apparent to me that this man, who by instinct was the consummate loner, had lived a life that drew together many of the disparate strands of my city's history. Because he was a child of the great age of industrialization and immigration,

his social values were formed in the moral and political transformation that accompanied the First World War. He contributed to the city's cultural life as an actor, a director and an
organizer; his work in the defence of civil liberties has been an
unsung chapter in Canadian legal history. And he capped
these activities, activities that for most people would well and
truly constitute a career, by serving as an elected official for
four decades. During those years his was a courageous voice
raised against the madness of the Cold War, against bigotry,
against those who believed the health of a city is best judged
by the number of its shopping malls, against those who
believed that the role of a municipal government is to provide
services to property.

For me Joe Zuken was also a riddle. Why had someone who
was so uncompromising in his principles, so intellectually
rigorous and courageous in his opinions, remained a lifelong
member of the Communist Party? I felt that a true picture of
Joe Zuken would reveal, not an unbending ideologue to be
either worshipped or scorned depending on one's political
perspective, but a complex human being who spent his life
wrestling at the edges where reality and ideals come into conflict.

The spine of this book is formed by a series of interviews I
conducted with Joe Zuken. From the summer of 1983 to the
fall of 1984 we would meet about once a month in his law office
in downtown Winnipeg. He knew I was interested in writing
a book about his career, and approved of the project. The
pattern of our meetings was always a little stiff at the outset;
neither Joe nor I possessed much of a facility for small talk.
When I went into his office, the radio would be on, since Joe
was always up-to-date when it came to news. A newscast
might lead him to make a few comments, drawing parallels
between some international event and an issue being dealt
with by council, usually an issue which, to my shame, I had
up until then viewed as lacking in substance.

As a journalist I have interviewed many lawyers. Those who
have been in practice as long as Joe was and who enjoy the
degree of public acclaim he did, usually have pretty impres-
sive offices. In Winnipeg their offices are likely to be located
on the top floor of one of a number of high-rise buildings

whose construction Joe opposed. Their desks are mammoth, usually to prevent anyone in the room from getting too close to their egos.

Joe Zuken's office was sparse. There were two portraits on the wall — Abraham Lincoln and Paul Robeson. Both had been lawyers, but made their marks in other fields: one in politics, one in the arts and politics. His desk was a desk, not a statement, and seated behind it Joe seemed approachable. I would set up my tape-recorder, we would briefly discuss what I would be asking him about that day, and then we would begin. He would always have difficulty with the first question. But as he spoke, he would close his eyes and tilt his head to one side. He was a small, frail-looking man, with a bird-like face. The more he concentrated on recreating the past, the more he appeared to relax.

His answers to my questions were long and detailed, for he had given a great deal of thought to his life, to the events that shaped and directed it. He was determined that I understand the importance of the cultural and social values of his parents' generation. It was very important to him that people realize his life was rooted in a tradition and a cultural context — that he was not, as he said once, "someone with two left feet."

He was very generous. He spent much of our interview time discussing the events of another era, his colleagues and the people he respected; he devoted very little time to himself. He was also very private. His personal life, he made clear at the beginning of our interviews, was his own business. We rarely touched on it. When the tape ran out at the end of an hour, it was like surfacing from an underwater swim. Then we could talk freely and easily about the events of the day.

At times it seemed strange to be writing a book about a civic politician, one who never exercised significant power, who was a member of a marginal political party and was a dissident within that organization. As I have been writing this book, each day has brought fresh news about the decay of the Communist movement. I will not pretend to guess how Joe would have responded to the events of the Gorbachev era. But I do reject any suggestion that the recent events diminish Joe Zuken or his accomplishments.

Joe Zuken was fully engaged in the life of his community. His career was spent in solidarity with the powerless. His commitment to social equality was always matched with a commitment to the broadest forms of democracy. The struggle to create a world that is both free *and* equal remains the key challenge for humanity. Joe helped Winnipeggers participate in that struggle. In a city where the Socialists and the Citizens have been at each other's throats for seventy years, Joe Zuken could carry both names with honour and with pride.

ONE

A Child of the North End
1912-1929

*I was part of a generation of child immigrants, with no
recollection of pre-revolutionary Russia except what their
parents used to tell them.*

In 1912 the employees of a small pottery workshop in the town
of Gorodnize in the Russian Ukraine went out on strike. The
union leaders were Jews, members of a working class that
socialist leader Karl Kautsky called "more oppressed, exploited and ill-treated than all others." At the turn of the century, officials of the Socialist International estimated the
working day of the average Russian Jew to be between fourteen and sixteen hours long. Wages in the pottery plant were
low, and working conditions unhealthy. Two brothers-in-law
working at the plant, Louis Zuken and Alec Richman, were to
die of silicosis, a disease their families believed had its roots
in the factory's dusty air. In pre-revolutionary Russia, strikes
like the one in Gorodnize were not uncommon. But successful
ones were. Since the failed uprising of 1905, the czar and his
ministers were suspicious of any activities that even hinted of
radicalism. The pottery workers' strike was quickly crushed
and the leaders dismissed.

One of the strikers left without a job was Louis Zuken. He
had one son, Cecil, and his wife Shifra Leah was expecting a
second child. He had had his fill of czarist Russia. By par-
ticipating in the strike, he had taken his stand and failed. Now
it was time to turn to the opportunities in the New World.
In 1912 he took his place in an exodus that was to bring a third

of the Jews of Eastern Europe to North America. The first wave of immigration was triggered by the anti-Jewish pogroms following the assassination of Czar Alexander II in 1881. Russian Jews, confined to the Pale of Settlement, a 386,000-square-mile area stretching from the Black Sea to the Baltic, were forced to ask themselves if they had a future in Russia. While terror and repression rose and fell in waves, for thousands of Jews, either jammed into the newly industrializing cities or still living in a village or *shtetl*, poverty remained a constant. Letters from relatives who had already made the voyage to North America fed dreams of a life in a world where Jews would be full citizens, where their children could be educated and where their culture would be allowed to develop and flourish.

Louis Zuken chose to keep one foot firmly planted in the Old Country. He left his pregnant wife and young son behind and made the journey across the Atlantic to Canada. He soon established himself in North End Winnipeg, a vibrant immigrant community that was quickly becoming one of the centres of Jewish life in Canada. With the help of relatives, he got a job in a Swift's Canada packinghouse. Soon afterwards an industrial accident sheared off part of the index finger on his right hand, and he was forced to peddle fruit on the streets of North Winnipeg. It was not until 1914 that he had saved enough money to bring his wife and two children to Canada. The family's second son, Joseph, had been born on December 12, 1912.

Louis Zuken had almost waited too long to reunite his family. The First World War broke out before Shifra Leah Zuken and her children left Europe. The family came close to being stranded in Holland, as their ship's departure was continually delayed. Once it left for Canada, it was occasionally shadowed by a German ship. At one point the captain suggested that those who were religious should get down and pray for a safe arrival. With or without prayers, the ship made it to Halifax. The Zukens took the train ride that would end in Winnipeg's Canadian Pacific Railway station, which stood at the east end of the CPR's gigantic marshalling yards. If on their arrival the Zukens had walked to the edge of those yards and looked out over the city, they would have been able to map out Winnipeg's social and economic divisions.

The businessmen who ran the city's government would readily boast that the CPR yards were among the longest in the world. By 1909 they contained 120 miles of track and had room for 100,000 freight cars. Acquiring the yards for the city was one of the business community's proudest accomplishments — in fact it was doubtful that without them Winnipeg would have turned into the mercantile capital of the Canadian West. Originally the CPR was slated to pass through the town of Selkirk, thirteen miles north of Winnipeg. In the grand tradition of the age of railroads, Winnipeg's city councillors virtually bribed the railway into redrawing its plans. The council offered to build a bridge over the Red River and give it to the CPR for free. But the railway upped the ante, demanding $200,000 in cash, free land in the centre of the city for the marshalling yards and a permanent exemption from taxes on those yards. In accepting the deal, Winnipeg's city fathers set the tone for the next century of development. Economic growth was to be given pride of place; the urban environment would come a distant second to the growth ethic.

While the yards were a visible symbol of "Commerce, Prudence and Industry" (virtues so prized by the city's elite that they had the motto emblazoned upon the city crest), they were also an open sore, cutting the city in half, spewing noise, dust and pollution into the neighbouring communities. In Winnipeg there was a literal wrong side of the tracks, and it was north of the CPR yards. On the south side lay the homes of much of the city's skilled Anglo-Saxon working class and its business community. Members of the business class were busy building new neighbourhoods for themselves in the city's expanding South End, on the other side of the Assiniboine River. There, in Fort Rouge and Crescentwood, they created wooded communities far from the smoke and fury of the industrial plants beginning to ring the CPR yards.

In the first two decades of this century, Winnipeg was furiously driven by the twin engines of industrialization and immigration. No other Canadian city took in as many immigrants in so short a period. The population shot from 42,000 in 1901 to 150,000 in 1913. The 1911 census contained disturbing news for those concerned about maintaining a "British" society. No other Canadian city had as high a percentage of

Jews or Slavs, and few had as low a percentage of British-born residents. At the same time, industry was booming. From 1901 to 1906 the output of manufactured goods increased by 125 per cent. In 1906 there were 148 factories in the city, employing 12,000 men and women. And in these factories the immigrant was at the bottom of the employment ladder. In 1910 Winnipeg Presbyterian minister George Bryce outlined what he expected the Slavic immigrants to do in Canada: "dig the sewers, labour on the railways, do the heavy work in the towns and cities," while the women were to be the "invaluable household workers in the cities and towns where domestics are scarce."

The immigrants who made their home in the city's North End were literally cut off from the rest of the city by the CPR tracks. The streetcars did not cross the tracks, and as late as 1914 there were only two bridges and two subways providing North Enders with access to the rest of the city. Property developers had a field day in the North End. Miles and miles of monotonous grid-like streets were laid down; little land was wasted on parks and playgrounds as jerry-built houses were plunked down cheek-by-jowl on twenty-five-foot-wide lots. In 1906 the North End was home to 43 per cent of Winnipeg's population, but they were crammed into less than a third of the city's geographic area. It was a bonanza for builders and developers and a disaster as far as public health was concerned. Sewer and water connections were slow to come to North Winnipeg. In 1905 over 80 per cent of the homes in South Winnipeg wards were hooked up to the city's waterworks, while the figure was less than 45 per cent for the North End. This led to regular outbreaks of typhoid fever in the North End, where the infant mortality rate regularly outstripped that of the rest of the city.

Over the years this cosmopolitan, embattled, resilient community would produce many of Winnipeg's, and Canada's, most prominent artists, professionals, business leaders and politicians. The North End could fairly lay claim to being the cradle of Canadian socialism. And Joseph Zuken — a small, frail, shy, proud and curious child — would be one of its proudest sons and one of the most distinguished leaders of that social movement. His public career spanned half a century, but the values, conflicts, talents and struggles that were to shape his life were already present in this divided city.

The Giants of His World

Although the Zukens and their children would become lifelong residents of North Winnipeg, Shifra Leah Zuken was not an easy convert to one of its most distinguishing characteristics — the sub-zero winters. It became a piece of family lore how, during the first winter in Winnipeg, she broke down one morning, demanding of her husband, "Why have you brought me to this Godforsaken place?"

The answer to this plaintive question was simple enough: they had come to Winnipeg because other Jews from Gorodnize had come there first. These *landsleit*, people from the same village, made up the Zukens' immediate social circle. In 1881 there were only twenty-three Jews living in Winnipeg, mainly of German and English background. The following year the assassination of Czar Alexander II led to the unleashing of a wave of anti-Semitism in Russia, and by June 1882, 342 Jews fleeing persecution in Russia had reached Winnipeg. After that there was a steady stream of Jewish immigration to Winnipeg. This stream would swell in the wake of the failed 1905 revolution, but from then on there was a difference in the philosophy of many of the immigrants. They had become imbued with the secular and radical philosophies that were beginning to percolate throughout Europe.

The Jews of Winnipeg made their homes in the North End. Many went to work in the industries sprouting up alongside the CPR tracks and in the city's garment trade. Others set up small shops along North Main Street and more particularly along Selkirk Avenue, which was to become the commercial centre of the North End. By 1916 over 85 per cent of the city's Jews, or 11,746 people, lived in the North End. In future years it would be a point of pride for people like Zuken to call themselves North Enders. Zuken recalled that "those who went to the South End of the city were regarded as being almost traitors and foreigners, because they were deserting the Jewish community."

Political discussions were a part of everyday life in the Zuken household. In the evenings relatives and fellow immigrants would gather around the fire in the Zuken home at the corner of Alfred and McGregor and discuss the state of the world. The three boys (a third son, Samuel, was born in 1915) would sit by, spellbound by stories of the underground movement against the czar and the adventures of participants in the unsuccessful 1905 revolution. There were tales of the pogroms and the Black Hundreds, and there was humour as well.

And there were stories of work and struggle in Canada. Most of Shifra Leah Zuken's relatives in Winnipeg went into the garment trade and were soon involved in efforts to unionize sweatshop operations. Her brother, Alec Richman, had worked with Louis in the pottery factory in the Ukraine and had fought with the Red Army during the Russian Revolution. When the Russian civil war ended, Alec found himself stranded in Poland and chose to join his sister in Canada. He eventually became an official of the dress makers' union and an important influence on his three nephews. Years later Zuken spoke affectionately of those days: "We spent many fascinating evenings in the winter time in the kitchen listening to these *landsleit* reminisce about the things they had left behind and the struggles that some of them had gone through."

It was through the eyes of these radical Jewish immigrants — the giants of his world — that Zuken formed his first impressions of the Russian Revolution and the Bolsheviks who led it: "In 1917 the Russian Revolution was greeted with joy by the Jewish community here. Now I came in 1914, so I was only five years old. I don't pretend that I could have attended a meeting or understood anything at the age of five that was meaningful. But some of my earliest recollections are of that modest home we had in the North End with my uncle and Joe Gershman [Gershman was from the same part of the Ukraine as the Zukens and was at the beginning of a lengthy career of union organizing and writing for the Communist Party]. They used to discuss some of the experiences in old Russia. And I was fascinated by it. They said the new day had come. It was as if something really great was taking place."

The immigrants did far more though than simply sit around the stove reminiscing. There quickly grew up in North Winnipeg a myriad of self-help organizations. Organizations like the Kiever and the Nikolaiever pre-dated the credit unions and would lend money to newly arrived *landsleit*. According to Zuken: "Their loans were in the range of about $50; a loan of $200 was a big deal. The interest was 3 per cent. As a matter of fact, in one organization the executive raised the interest from 3 per cent to 4 per cent, and there was a great outcry from the general membership. Not only that — each organization had its own doctor attached to the organization. Dr. Ben Victor, who later became prominent in progressive causes in the North End, became the doctor for quite a number of these organizations. When Dr. Victor came into a house that was poverty-stricken, instead of asking his usual fee, of about two dollars, he usually left more than two dollars so they could buy some food."

These organizations were far more than self-help groups; they were also centres of left-wing thought and education. Some members of the Jewish elite joined the old-line parties — in 1910 lawyer S. Hart Green was elected to the legislature as a Liberal, while Moses Finkelstein, an active member of the Conservative Party, became the city's first Jewish alderman in 1905 — but working-class Jews with a taste for radical politics were presented with a wide array of choices. Internationalists, Socialist Zionists, Anarchists and others were vying for their allegiance. At times working together and at other times immersed in bitter factional battles, these groups created vibrant cultural, educational and political institutions, all of which helped ease the immigrant's transition from the village of Eastern Europe to raw industrializing North America.

The foremost of these was the Workers Circle, or Arbeiter Ring. The first Arbeiter Ring was formed by American Jewish radicals, and it spread quickly across North America. It was a self-help organization with a difference — a difference spelled out in one of its convention slogans: "We Fight Against Sickness, Premature Death and Capitalism." There were soon three branches of the Arbeiter Ring in Winnipeg, and as Harry Gale, one of its early members, recalled: "They acquired great influence among the young people because the ideals of freedom, internationalism, brotherhood and working-class unity captured everyone's imagination." The Arbeiter Ring offered its members more than inspiration; there was an Arbeiter Ring Free Loan Association which by 1917 had a working capital of $3,000.

One branch of the Arbeiter Ring, made up of those who called for a Jewish homeland, placed a strong emphasis on education, establishing the first radical Jewish school in Winnipeg. Libraries and choirs were formed along with theatres that produced plays with a strong "social content." Winnipeg was soon an important stopping point for touring radical speakers. The anarchist Emma Goldman visited Winnipeg in 1907, giving five lectures.

In the fall of 1917, on the eve of the October Revolution that would eventually tear apart this vibrant movement, the entire Jewish radical community came together to celebrate the opening of the Liberty Temple. At the corner of Pritchard and Salter in the heart of the North End, the temple was, in the words of the *Israelite Press*, meant to be a home for the Jewish community "where all its cultural and spiritual life shall be centred." It was a meeting place for the various self-help groups, reading societies and youth groups.

As Zuken recalled it, even the synagogues of the day were infused with politics and debate. "I remember being taken on the High Holidays to the little synagogue on Magnus Avenue. And during the break the men would gather and discuss the politics of the city, the province, the world. They were the senate. It was a miniature debating society — everything was being discussed."

The elder Zukens, while never playing leadership roles, were active in that immigrant community. In Joe Zuken's mind they were members of a special generation, and he felt his life was informed by their values: "They did not have much formal education. But there were two things the immigrants of that day did have: a strong passion to see that their children should have a better education than they were able to get and, in their own way, a strong feeling for social justice. I think I was fortunate to get the benefit of that."

For most of the Zukens' early years in Canada, Shifra Leah Zuken was the key family member. Years later Zuken would recall: "My mother was the strong one. She was about five feet tall. But you called her the little general because she was a person of amazing strength and determination."

She was determined that her sons receive an orthodox upbringing. To this end the two older boys were enrolled in a private Hebrew school, which later became known as the Talmud Torah School. "But it was not to be. They taught only Hebrew. They didn't teach Yiddish. Mother said, 'Hebrew, that's all right for praying, if I can ever get my boys to pray, but I want them to learn their language of Yiddish.' " And so the boys were taken out of Hebrew school and enrolled in the most radical school in the city.

In picking Yiddish over Hebrew, Shifra Leah Zuken was choosing sides in a debate that was transforming Jewish culture at the turn of the century. Jewish culture was undergoing a renaissance, and a part of that rebirth involved an elevation of the dignity of Yiddish as a language. Yiddish had long been looked down upon as the language of the poor and uneducated. According to the great Jewish writer Sholom Aleichem, "A man was ashamed to be seen holding a Yiddish book, lest people consider him a boor." But Aleichem and others realized that if they wanted to communicate with the Jewish community as a whole they had to use Yiddish. They were soon turning out books in Yiddish that have become recognized as classics throughout the world.

Yiddish had its defenders in Winnipeg as well. J. Alter Cherniack, one of the founders of the Jewish Radical School, believed that the "Yiddish language and literature with the 'jargon' of nine million Jews in all corners of the earth are our claws and fangs in our desperate struggle against the waves of assimilation."

In reminiscing about the establishment of the Jewish Radical School in 1914, Cherniack said, "We were Jews and socialists in the widest sense of the word. Therefore we had to immediately found a school with a Jewish radical program for the children of the Jewish masses." The school's first lessons were held from five to seven in the evenings in classrooms in Aberdeen School that had been rented from the Winnipeg School Board. When Zuken was attending the school, he was also putting in a full day at Strathcona Public School. In the first year there were eleven students, but enrollment grew to ninety the following year and the school moved to a rented building at Pritchard and McGregor. Two years later the school relocated to a renovated house, finally purchasing a three-storey building on Aberdeen Avenue.

After the death of the prominent Yiddish writer Isaac Leib Peretz in 1915, the school was renamed the I. L. Peretz School. Peretz was a Polish Jew who, through his poetry, stories and novels, became known as the "Prince of the Ghetto." In his story, "My People," Peretz wrote, "We have been chosen for shame and mockery, woe and anguish, blows and pain; we are the weakest and the least ... but that is precisely why my people are spurred on to the farthest reaches of human justice, to the most distant post on the road to human freedom; to the final victory over physical might, over physical coercion."

From its very beginning, the school was not without its opponents among the more orthodox members of the Jewish community. Some synagogue leaders threatened to excommunicate parents who sent their children to an "apostate school." The strength of the Jewish community's commitment to this school can be seen not only in the number of students it attracted but in the educational innovations it pioneered. The *Muter Farein*, or women's auxiliary, of the school managed to establish a kindergarten program there in 1918. The modern concepts of play-and-learn and work-and-learn education were integrated into the kindergarten program. Two years later there was a day program established where children would take a half day of the public school curriculum and a half day of Jewish studies. Music, physical education and art were studied after four o'clock. When Zuken came to serve on the Winnipeg School Board in the 1940s, he was able to look back to the Peretz School for inspiration and example.

Outside of his family, the teachers at the Peretz School probably had the greatest influence on the young Joe Zuken. His brother Cecil felt the school's focus on labour and socialist history helped steer the two of them leftwards. Nor were they the only ones. At least four other members of the school's first graduating class went on to join the Communist Party.

Zuken spoke of the teachers reverentially: "They were radically minded, but they were not [Communist] party people. And they were people who had a great interest in Yiddish culture. They were intellectuals who felt the role of the intellectual is not to be aloof from the people, and that culture was not something that was to be put on the bookcase and simply taken out occasionally." Zuken was an outstanding pupil. When he graduated from the school in 1925 at the age of twelve, he had to write a year-end essay. Looking back, he recalled that "1924 had been the year that Lenin had died. I must have been influenced by those discussions around the fire at home. Because even though I had not read any of his books, I had the *chutzpah* to write an essay called 'Lenin Lives!' And the direction of the school was such that it was permitted to be circulated as one of the graduation essays."

School officials had no problems with Zuken's graduation essay, but they did with his stature. "There was quite a problem, because this was the first time there was going to be a graduation from the Peretz School, whether I should be allowed to graduate. I had passed whatever academic standards they had, but they thought I was too small to go on. Until they were faced with my mother. She marched in on them. And she was a little shorter than five feet. They raised the argument 'He's so small.' She gave them a withering look and said, 'Look. Look at me. How tall do I look?' And she had the voice of a sergeant major. (As a matter of fact, I think that a lot of my speaking ability later must have come from Mother.)"

They caved in, and young Joseph was allowed to participate in the graduation ceremony, where he read what he remembered as a "poem of social significance" by I. L. Peretz.

The keynote speaker at that graduation ceremony was Dr. Chaim Zhitlovsky, one of the leading popularizers of Yiddish in turn-of-the-century North America and one of the key figures in defining Zuken's approach to Judaism. Zhitlovsky's contribution to the cultural debate of the period was his insistence that socialism must have a living, spiritual — though not necessarily religious — component. For the Jew, Zhitlovsky claimed, Marxism must be mixed with Yiddish culture and language to create a social movement that could both sustain the soul and advance human equality. Zuken remembered Zhitlovsky "as a towering figure. He was a philosopher and a writer, and a teacher. He was one who dealt with this question of synthesis, of feeling that one can be a Jew and at the same time not lock yourself into a ghetto. As he said, 'Be a Jew and a *mensch* at the same time.' That is, there is no contradiction between being a Jew and a humanitarian and having a world outlook."

The World of Politics

"Lenin Lives!" might have been a suitable topic for a graduation paper but the Zukens were not interested in having their boys grow up to become radicals. They were not right wing, but Louis Zuken supported the more moderate form of socialism espoused by the Independent Labor Party, a forerunner of today's New Democratic Party. Louis played an active role in ILP election campaigns without ever joining the party, and was present at the victory party celebrating labour leader John Queen's first election to city council. When Joe joined the radical Liberty Temple Youth Club, he decided to keep his membership a secret from his parents. This was no easy task, since many of the fraternal organizations his parents belonged to held regular meetings in the Liberty Temple. On one occasion the younger Zuken was forced to most uncharacteristically hold his tongue. "I remember my father being downstairs at a meeting at the Liberty Temple and I was meeting upstairs with the youth club. And I was keeping quiet because my father shouldn't know that I was on the same premises, but for very different purposes."

One could practise left-wing politics for many different purposes in Winnipeg in the early years of this century. The Jewish radicals of that period were interested in far more than the development and protection of their own culture. They played a central role in the creation of the major national left-wing political parties in Canada. In doing this they reached out and made common cause with leftists and reformers from a host of ethnic backgrounds. The formation of an indigenous Canadian left was not without its birth pains, however. In their most simplistic formulation, these conflicts most often revolved around attitudes towards reform and revolution.

The first major split on this issue took place two years before Joe Zuken was born. The leading left-wing party in the country was the Socialist Party of Canada, a hard-line Marxist party originally based in British Columbia. Its leaders were opposed to trade unions and parliamentary politics, since these activities aimed at merely reforming society. The SPCers were sometimes called "impossiblists" because they believed it was impossible to reform capitalism. Instead they put their efforts into education and propaganda in anticipation of what they viewed as the inevitable revolution.

Nor was reform the only thing of which they were intolerant. At a time when immigrants from Russia, Germany and the Ukraine were changing the face of the Canadian working class, the party's largely British-born leadership refused to grant the so-called foreign-language branches of the party autonomy in their publications and their propaganda. Meanwhile the Eastern Europeans began to see certain reforms as not only possible, but highly desirable. By 1910, Chaim Saltzman, one of the leading figures in the party's Winnipeg branch, was denouncing the "English comrades," pointing out that the "foreign born were more interested in reform work, in progress, in democracy, in immediate demands, which will palliate existing conditions."

The last straw was the SPC's decision to run a spoiler candidate against labour reformer Fred Dixon in the 1910 Manitoba election. The SPC's candidate finished poorly, but managed to grab enough labour support to prevent Dixon from winning. The SPC's rank and file, outraged by the party's move, left to form the Social Democratic Party of Canada. The SDPC's founding membership list reads like a who's who of the Winnipeg left for the next thirty years — Richard Rigg, A. A. Heaps, Jacob Penner, Mathew Popovitch and John Navisowsky.

Recognizing the desire of many immigrant groups to retain their own sense of ethnic identification, the SDPC was organized as a federation of various linguistically based branches. In Winnipeg the Jewish branch of forty members accounted for nearly a quarter of the party's Manitoba membership. In 1911 the party unsuccessfully ran Saltzman for school board. His campaign stressed the need for free textbooks and scribblers for students, evening classes and technical classes for children who have to work during the day, the setting aside of three hours a week for the study of a child's native language, an end to religious instruction and improved salaries for teachers. In 1913 the party elected Richard Rigg to city council, and two years later, when Rigg became the first socialist elected to the Manitoba legislature, he made these comments at a victory celebration organized by the Jewish branch of the SDPC: "For you, the Jews of North Winnipeg — this victory is of great importance. It is in the interest of the working class that all exploited nationalities shall have religious, national and political equality."

That battle was not restricted to the world of politics and elections. The first two decades of this century were filled with fierce social conflict as bare-knuckled capitalists took on a new industrial work force that had been moulded in the crucible of immigration and industrialization, and infused with the still evolving philosophies of socialism and unionism.

Winnipeg's commercial and industrial elite was dominated by men who had risen quickly after coming to the West and who were in no mood to cede the slightest control of their operations to unions. E. G. Barrett, one of the owners of the Vulcan Iron Works, the company whose labour policies helped spark the 1919 General Strike, proudly proclaimed, "This is a free country, and as far as we are concerned the day will never come when we will have to take orders from any union." The machinists union, of course, was not as interested in giving Barrett orders as it was in sitting down and negotiating a contract for their members working in his plant. But even that was more than Barrett was prepared to do.

In 1919 Winnipeg was still very much a businessman's town. All of the city's mayors and most of its politicians had come from the business class, and the political system had for many years been designed to reinforce their power. The franchise was extended only to those who met the very rigid property qualification. In 1906, for example, Winnipeg had a population of a 100,000 and only 7,784 eligible voters.

Industrialization, however, carried with it the seeds of unionization, since many of the skilled workers who immigrated to Winnipeg in the 1880s to work on the railway, telegraph, and printing and construction trades that a new city needed, brought union cards with them. And they were not afraid to strike for their demands. Rail workers engaged in a series of bitter and not always successful strikes. In 1906 street-car employees struck when their union leaders were fired; the privately owned company hired new drivers and the mayor called in the military to protect them against the strikers. By the start of the First World War, there were eighty-two union locals in Winnipeg, representing 10,000 workers.

The war years were to make those workers increasingly radical, particularly in the way they came to view their own unions. The most successful unions of the period had been what were known as craft, or trade, unions, owing to the fact that each union represented an individual skilled craft. Under this arrangement there could be many different unions in one workplace; the railways, for example, had unions for, among others, engineers, conductors, firemen, brakemen, machinists and upholsterers. This could lead to tensions between unions when one local went out on strike and all the others kept on working. As well, the labour movement was not particularly effective in organizing unskilled workers, whose ranks were frequently comprised of Eastern European immigrants. Dis-satisfaction with this elitist form of organization, and with the policy directions taken by national labour leaders on issues like conscription (Western unionists opposed it and the central Canadians supported it) led Westerners to experiment with more radical forms of struggle and solidarity, the most dramatic being the Winnipeg General Strike and the creation of the One Big Union.

The General Strike of 1919 was the final set-piece in a series of ongoing conflicts between labour and capital in Winnipeg. The First World War brought about swift increases in the cost of living and in the profits of many local employers, but workers were urged to forego strikes and wage increases in the name of patriotism. Such appeals were not always success-ful. In the spring of 1918 local unions won a major victory when they all threatened to go out on strike unless the city came to terms with its civic employees. This was the sort of victory Winnipeg's labour leaders were hoping to repeat the following year.

The General Strike was set off in May 1919 when metal trades and construction workers went on strike to protest their employers' refusal to negotiate with them. Strikes of this nature, usually called recognition strikes, were of extreme importance to the nascent labour movement, struggling to assert its legitimacy. The Winnipeg Trades and Labor Council conducted a membership referendum to see if there was support for a general, or sympathetic, strike of all workers in support of the demands of the building and metal shop workers. Winnipeg workers gave overwhelming endorsement to a general strike — the final vote was 8,667 for and 645 against. At 11:00 a.m. on May 15, 1919, 12,000 union members and 12,000 non-union members, walked off the job, bringing most of the city's economic life to a halt.

The support for the strike is not surprising given the events of that spring. In March, Winnipeg labour leaders, meeting with their Western counterparts in Calgary, played an important role in creating what was to become the One Big Union. The OBU aimed to organize all workers regardless of skill, ethnicity or gender, and it adopted a radical political agenda, sending greetings to the leaders of the Soviet government in Russia, calling for the abolition of capitalism and endorsing the use of the general strike as a political weapon.

Although the Winnipeg General Strike was not launched by the OBU (which did not come into formal existence until later that year), many Winnipeggers, particularly the city's business community, chose to view it as a political strike — and a potential revolution. Certainly the rhetoric of some of the strike leaders encouraged that view, although for the most part the strikers were told to stay at home and out of trouble, rather than look for any Winter Palaces to storm. The Citizens' Committee of One Thousand, comprised of the city's leading business figures and their supporters, was created to provide services during the strike and simultaneously work to defeat it. In their paper, *The Citizen*, they argued that "no thoughtful citizen can any longer doubt that the so-called general strike is in reality revolution — or a daring attempt to overthrow the present industrial and governmental system." The Citizens also painted the strike as an "alien conspiracy," asking, "How much longer is the alien to run amuck, insult our flag ... [and] continue his threatening attitude to Law and Order...?"

After six weeks the strike was crushed by the federal government; strike leaders were rounded up in the middle of the night; labour halls — including the Liberty Temple — were raided; and a protest parade was charged by armed Royal North-West Mounted Police officers, leading to a riot that left one man dead and dozens injured. Those strike leaders not in prison called on workers to return to their jobs — if they had not already been fired.

The ending of the strike, and the subsequent crushing of much of the Winnipeg labour movement, did not bring an end to class conflict in Winnipeg. In many ways the strike served to lay the city's social tensions in plain view and set the political agenda for the next fifty years. Even as the leaders of the Citizens' Committee were preparing to prosecute the strikers and as the strikers readied their defence, the same people who had taken on the business establishment in the strike were mapping out strategy for the 1919 civic election. That election was the first of many such campaigns that have been described as the General Strike being carried out by other means.

The Young Loner

Louis Zuken never returned to factory work after his accident at Swift's. The family lived in a few small rooms in the back of a one-storey wood-frame grocery store. There were a number of moves — from McGregor to McKenzie to St. John's, rarely out of the North End and never into a house that did not contain a storefront. Sometimes it was a grocery store, sometimes it was a clothing store, and it was always a family operation. Zuken said, "They never employed anybody. They kept few books, the accounts were marked on the walls, and when there were people who could not afford to pay, my parents simply rubbed out the accounts and extended new credit."

While he painted a picture of a loving and closely knit extended family, Zuken remembered his early years as being "busy but not particularly happy ones." For someone who would act out most of his life dramatically on the public stage of his city, taking controversial stand after controversial stand, Joe Zuken was afflicted with an almost incapacitating shyness. "I always had difficulty talking to people on an individual basis. As a matter of fact, I would cross over to the other side

of the street so I would not have to speak to someone I knew
if I saw them coming down the street."

He was haunted by one lonely memory of a summer camp
he had been sent to by the Methodist Church. "How did I get
there? How did I end up amongst those people? I was probably underweight and the nurse at school detected that I needed
some bodybuilding, so I was a candidate for camp experience.
It was probably the most miserable two or three weeks I have
ever spent. I knew no one there and I was a complete loner."

The loner began to spin some dreams, dreams that inter-
twined the values and aspirations of the evenings spent
around the stove with the *landsmen*, the Yiddish poet's fierce
condemnation of social injustice and the anger of any child
who feels himself singled out and oppressed. "I was about ten,
eleven, twelve — one matured quickly in the pressure cooker
of those events — and one idea began to take form. I thought,
'If I can gain some independence, I won't be pushed around
and I can see to it that other people are not pushed around.'
That led me to have a sort of idea about getting into law, to
see if I could use it as a shield for myself and others."

The rich Jewish culture of North End Winnipeg provided
Zuken with a shield of another sort. "I became fascinated, as
a result of my immersion in the Yiddish language, with Yiddish poetry. To compensate for my personal reserve, I became
active in the Yiddish Theatre and was put on the stage at a
very early age. I was invited to take part in certain cultural
programs at the Liberty Temple and the Yiddish Theatre as
well."

Perhaps the introverted nature of Joe Zuken's personality
can be best grasped by looking at his relationship with his
older brother, Cecil, in these early years. (Samuel suffered
from a weak heart because of a bout of rheumatic fever he
suffered as a young boy. As a result, he did not continue his
education beyond public school. While he remained on friendly terms with his brothers, he did not share their political
involvements.) Both boys were extremely intellectual — Joe
would later win prizes at the University of Manitoba Law
School, while Cecil was accelerated through school and enrolled in university at the age of fifteen. They would go on to
become civic politicians, both of them winning election to the

Winnipeg School Board. And of course they both were leaders in what was for many Canadians, then and now, a pariah organization — the Communist Party of Canada.

Yet according to both of them, they did not spend a lot of time discussing politics — even as they grew up together in cramped quarters in a highly politicized community. As Cecil, years later, recalled, "We talked a bit. Joe was at that time very much interested and involved in cultural work. But we did — there was a year and a half difference in our ages — discuss politics a bit." For his part, Joe said, "It was a very interesting relationship. We did not communicate readily, but we understood each other. I don't think it was necessary for us to sit down and check with each other as to where we stood on each particular issue. There were very few words exchanged between us. But I think we understood each other."

The Peretz School was not the only school that had a formative impact on the young Joe Zuken. Like dozens of other prominent North Enders, he laid particular stress on the importance of the education he received at St. John's Technical School. Like Baron Byng in Montreal and Harbord Collegiate in Toronto, St. John's was the high school that the children of the Jewish and Eastern European immigrants attended. In its classrooms and on its playground, the children of the various ethnic groups studied and played together. According to Zuken: "We did not feel that we were in the ghetto. As a matter of fact, although there was race discrimination against some of us and so on, on the North End issues, somehow the North End united. The foreigners were the people from the South End who came over to play against the North End in some of the games and so on."

To hear the graduates of St. John's tell it, at any one time dozens of young intellectuals could be found dashing up and down the school's hallways. Zuken remembered school debates with Max Freedman, who would later become the *Manchester Guardian's* Washington correspondent — "Max would go down the halls with a book of Macaulay under his arm." Zuken remained impressed by the seriousness and dedication of the teachers he encountered at St. John's, and came away from the school further convinced that quality teachers were the key to any education system. "We had some exceptionally good teachers there, people who opened up the minds of students to literature and history. Those who applied themselves got a lot out of St. John's in those days."

Zuken had particularly fond memories of, of all people, the man who taught the shop courses at St. John's, Richard Johns. Originally trained as a railway machinist, Johns had been one of the leaders of the OBU. In the days leading up to the General Strike, he announced he would be proud to call himself a Bolshevik and made headlines when he told a union meeting, "I say 'Strike today.' This has resolved itself into a question of right. You have the right to demand anything you have the power to enforce. Come on, fellow workers of Winnipeg, we have the power to win." His fire-breathing rhetoric won him a term in jail and lost him his job with the Canadian Pacific Railway. He soon found himself blacklisted in all the machine shops in the city, and it was through the efforts of another former union leader, then serving on the Winnipeg School Board, that he was able to find work as a vocational instructor.

"I was surprised and delighted to discover Dick Johns teaching at St. John's. With me he showed great understanding. I was very clumsy working with my hands. I knew that if I had to make my living with my hands as a tradesman, I would flunk out of life. And there was a bit of a joke between us. He would come around and say, 'Where is the model that you are working on, Joe?' And then he would say, 'Oh, we've lost it have we?' And I would say, 'Yeah.' And he would say, 'Maybe we will find it some day,' and walk away. He gave me a passing mark, and I did not deserve that." Many years later Zuken returned the favour when, as a school board member, he helped hire Johns as the principal of the newly formed Technical Vocational School in Winnipeg in the 1940s.

Although Johns never discussed politics with his students — and his own views were moderating from the days of the strike as he became active in the Independent Labor Party and later the Co-operative Commonwealth Federation — Zuken felt he was "trying to communicate something which had to be communicated, and that was the dignity of work, and he did it very well."

There was one last educational forum for Joe Zuken — the Market Square behind Winnipeg's city hall and the open-air political culture associated with it. The square was site of an agricultural market and was the centre of trade and commerce in the city. It was also the home of a marketplace of ideas. R. B. Russell, one of the founders of the One Big Union and, with Johns, a leader of the General Strike, recalled that when it came to soapbox speaking in the square, "You were competing against the Salvation Army, brass band, silver band, and you were competing against other crowds — Seventh Day Adventists and everything else." Socialist speakers devised all sorts of schemes to get attention. One of them would sell "indestructible" combs to the audience, and after selling his wares, he would snap one of the combs in two, informing audience members they were nothing but suckers. Then he would tell them, "But that is not where you are exploited. You're not exploited as consumers, you are exploited as workers," and from there he would launch into a discussion of socialism.

Zuken remembered: "One could not grow up in the North End without being aware of the Market Square. I would visit the Market Square very often — just walk down there and go from speaker to speaker. I remember listening to J. S. Woodsworth and John Queen. The kind of activity there was very active, very vibrant. That's where I first heard Jake Penner. Once the left brought in a speaker, a man named Olgin, and he was forbidden to speak. The police let him come here from the United States, but he was forbidden to speak. He came out on the platform to show he had arrived, but he could not say anything."

In the Twenties Zuken rarely let a political meeting pass without attending. And he was soon becoming well schooled in the internecine battles of the left. "In the old Talmud Torah you had maybe John Queen and Jack Blumberg [a long-serving socialist city councillor] speaking at an ILP meeting. The Communists would be holding their meeting at the Hebrew Sick Benefit Hall, which is perhaps two or three minutes away. You would have a courier who would run and tell you what the competitor was saying — and then there would be an instant reply. And at the time you would get hundreds of people out to these meetings."

In 1928 a financial crisis gripped the Zukens' small family business. The parents decided to try to make a new start in a new city — this time Toronto. A change in locale would also get the boys away from the influence of left-wing people like their uncle, Alec Richman. The shop was sold and the Zukens strapped their furniture and belongings onto a Model T Ford. But the move to Toronto was a failure on every count. The elder Zukens found the damp weather undermined their health, while the boys found the left-wing climate of Toronto's Jewish community only too agreeable. They met the left-wing activist Annie Buller, whom Zuken would defend a dozen years later, and took a public-speaking course from her.

While in Toronto, Zuken was involved with the Young Pioneers, a left-wing youth group. Despite his painful shyness and introversion, he was assigned the task of going door to door to raise money for the group. It was one of his few efforts at fund raising, and possibly one of his most successful. He chose as his territory the tenements housing the Jewish immigrants. At the door he would announce in Yiddish that he was representing the Pioneers. "Their eyes would light up, and they would say, 'Bless you,' and they would give me a donation. I could not understand why all of a sudden they were blessing the Little Pioneers. Later it dawned on me. They were confusing the Young Pioneers with their own Zionist Pioneer organization in what was to become the state of Israel."

By the end of January 1929, the sojourn in Toronto was over and the family was back in Winnipeg. Cecil Zuken was about to quit university and join the Young Communist League. Joe was finishing high school and preparing for university. And the Great Depression was about to descend on the world. For Zuken the Depression was the great "pressure cooker," the furnace that cast into permanent shape all the influences he had absorbed and dreams he had dreamed growing up in North Winnipeg. By the end of the Depression, Joe Zuken was fully engaged in his life's work.

TWO

A Political Education
1929-1940

You felt that things were happening. They were happening in the Market Square, in the unions, in the mass movements; and then came Spain in 1936 and the people were in motion. And the fact that the left was leading these movements — leading the anti-fascist movements, leading the strike movements, leading the organization of the unemployed. It was natural and logical to go left. And that's how it happened.

To go left. To Joe Zuken the logic of the Great Depression spelled no other alternative. While he did not live in the past, the suffering and the social movements of the Thirties left an indelible mark on his character, just as the immigrant community's thirst for social justice and reverence for learning had informed his childhood. He wrote many decades later that the Depression was not, from his point of view, "ten lost years," as a sensitive oral history of the period had described them. "In the 1930s," he said, "there was mass tragedy caused by hunger and deprivation, but what the Jewish community was able to accomplish, even under those conditions, shows that it was not a lost generation."

It was in this decade, in fact, that Joe Zuken found himself. He became a lawyer, a public figure, an actor and a socialist. And he did none of these things alone — his brother Cecil became a leading figure in the Young Communist League, his future wife, Clara Goldenberg, was a party member, and Jacob Penner, a man Zuken would adopt as a role model for much of his political life, was launching his trailblazing career as a Communist on Winnipeg's city council. Despite its name, the Great Depression was in fact a period of tremendous vitality for the left in Manitoba. Battle lines had never been more distinctly drawn. The need to fight for unions, for a better deal for the unemployed and against the growing dangers of international fascism could not have been clearer. And although it would be two decades before anyone would hear of Joseph McCarthy or Igor Gouzenko, leftists could already feel the chilly breezes of the as yet undeclared Cold War. It was an era of police spies and informers. These were the conditions under which Joe Zuken turned left.

The onset of the Depression forced the Zuken family to make some painful choices. Cecil had been accepted into the University of Manitoba when he was only fifteen and was keen on pursuing a career as an engineer. While it seemed that Samuel was destined to help run the family store, wisdom dictated that "little Joseph" should get a university education if he was going to get on in the world. But in those days education and finances were inextricably linked. Throughout his life Zuken was angered by this. "I felt there was injustice. My mother had to go out at times and borrow money so my brother and I could write exams. You had to pay exam fees. And we did not have the money to buy textbooks; she had to borrow the money to buy textbooks."

Cecil worked summers as a truck driver for an auto-wrecking firm, while Joe taught at the Jewish Radical School. It was work that he loved, which was all to the good, since the pay was not only low but irregular. He kept on teaching even when he was articling, spending the early evenings teaching Yiddish history and literature. The poor state of the family finances forced Joe to take his third year of arts on an extramural basis, studying at home and writing the final exams. It was becoming apparent the family could not afford to keep both sons in school. As Cecil recalled it, "I was physically stronger and more active and contributing to the family. And that led to me dropping out of university." Throughout his life Joe Zuken acknowledged his debt to his brother. "He actually sacrificed his higher education for me. I think he would have made a splendid engineer. But in the end he concentrated on social engineering."

In those days the University of Manitoba's campus was located on Memorial Boulevard in downtown Winnipeg. Every day Zuken would make the long walk over the Salter Bridge from the North End to school. The Depression took its toll on the university as well, and its problems were compounded in 1932 when it was discovered that the chairman of the board of governors, J. A. Machray, had embezzled nearly one million dollars of the university's endowment money. When the administration increased tuition fees to offset the losses created by the theft, Zuken helped to organize a student protest.

For a graduate of the Market Square, the University of Manitoba was a tame place. Although Zuken was always mindful of the sacrifices his family had made to send him there, he chafed at the views propounded by some of the teachers. At the height of the Depression, the economics department clung to theories that sounded to Zuken like "fairy tales." There had been so little change in economic thinking at the university that in one course lecture notes were handed down from father to son (a woman in such courses in those days was a rarity). For one examination, students were asked to explain why socialism would never succeed. Zuken said he spewed back the answers the professor wanted to hear and then, having some time left, proceeded to dispute them.

Zuken did not complete his bachelor of arts, choosing instead, after his third year, to apply for admission to the law school. There was an oral examination that all prospective law students had to take before they were admitted, and Zuken's legal career almost ran aground before it was launched. One of the examining professors suspected that Zuken did not have quite the right attitude towards the law and spent considerable time questioning this student about his growing radical reputation. But in the end he was accepted.

In 1934, while he was still a student, Zuken began to repay his parents for his education under somewhat distressing circumstances. In June of that year, morality officers from the Winnipeg police force raided the Zukens' small combination store and home on Boyd Avenue. The officers found a quart bottle of home brew, and Louis Zuken and nineteen-year-old Sammy were arrested and charged with a breach of the Liquor Control Act. When the case went to court, the *Free Press* was able to report the story under the headline "Law Student Is Successful When Parents Charged." In his first police court appearance, Zuken saved his parents from conviction. Sammy, however, pleaded guilty to having liquor in a place other than a private home. Under his brother's guidance, he told the court that he had found the crock in the garbage can in the back of the building and foolishly brought it into the store without telling his mother or father about it. For his crime he was fined $200 and costs.

Zuken was not excited by the study of law, nor did he have much in common with his fellow students, few of whom would have shared his interest in turning the law into a shield to protect society's disadvantaged. But he did serve as a member of the Law Student Executive and was a member of the U of M Students Union debating team. As such, in the fall of 1935 he helped defeat the McGill-Toronto team on the question "This house refuses to take up arms under any circumstances." Zuken was successful in arguing the pacifist position. He also took part in a debate as to whether Canada should participate in the 1936 Olympic Games to be held in Germany. He used the opportunity to raise the issue of the threat of fascism to world peace and called for a boycott of the games. He also participated in debates against the Oxford Union team and teams from a variety of American universities. Upon his graduation in 1936, he won the E. H. Coleman Prize, while the Gold Medal that year went to one of the few friends Zuken made at law school, Harold Stubbs, son of maverick judge Lewis St. George Stubbs. Years later Stubbs remembered Zuken as a very independent student who did not socialize with his fellow classmates.

The removal of Judge Stubbs from the bench did more to shape Zuken's attitude towards the law than any of the lectures he sat through in his four years at law school. Stubbs started his legal career as a lawyer in rural Manitoba. An active member of the Liberal Party, he stuck with the party in 1917, running as a federal candidate when many Liberals were deserting the party over Laurier's refusal to support conscription. He went down to crushing defeat, but loyalty to the Liberal Party has always had its own rewards. When the party came to power in 1921, Stubbs had the distinction of receiving Mackenzie King's first judicial appointment.

The path from party stalwart to county judge was a well-worn one, even then, and no one expected anything extraordinary from Stubbs. He did a workmanlike job on the bench, and in E. J. McMurray, King's solicitor general and a former Winnipeg lawyer, Stubbs had a good friend in Ottawa. With McMurray's support, Stubbs became Manitoba's senior county court judge in 1924.

His time on the bench led Stubbs to question the fairness of the laws he was pledged to uphold. His daily encounters with the poverty and suffering of so many of the accused who were paraded before him brought him to the rather unoriginal conclusion that there was a law for the rich and a law for the poor. Where countless other judges may have had similar thoughts, Stubbs had the temerity to give them voice.

From the bench he would regularly pass judgement on the law, as well as on the criminal appearing before him. In one celebrated case he gave this warning to a petty thief: "To get away with crimes, you have to be in it on a pretty big scale, steal a million or two, or things of that kind. You have to get to be a real big thief, and then perhaps you will get away with it, and even be rewarded, but not as long as you are a working man."

Where most judges accepted the testimony of a police officer as the gospel truth, Stubbs often wondered aloud if overzealousness led the police to stretch the truth to fit the case at times. In one judgement he accused the police of being "tactless, impulsive and hotheaded" in a situation calling for "patience, restrained and calculated coolheadedness." An opponent of capital and corporal punishment, Stubbs lacked the faith of other judges in the effectiveness of lengthy prison sentences; as a result, the longest sentence he imposed was for ten years.

While this behaviour nettled the police and the provincial attorney general, W. J. Major, Stubbs outraged the Winnipeg establishment in his handling of the will of Alexander

Macdonald. During his lifetime, Macdonald, who had become a millionaire in the grocery business, had freely donated his money to charity and had planned on creating a charitable foundation upon his death. His will, however, made no mention of such a foundation, and the estate went to his family. Stubbs, who as county court judge had the job of probating the will, became convinced it was a fraud. When a superior court judge reversed his ruling, Stubbs launched a public campaign that scandalized his fellow judges.

In 1932 the federal government, at the urging of Attorney General Major, appointed Alberta Superior Court judge Frank Ford to investigate Stubbs's judicial conduct. Stubbs succeeded in having the inquiry opened to the public, and it drew standing-room-only crowds to the Law Courts Building. One of regular attendants of the hearings was the young Joe Zuken. It was little more than a political trial. McMurray defended Stubbs, although the fiery judge often spoke on his own behalf throughout the hearings. Despite the fact there was no evidence of illegal, or even improper, activities on Stubbs's part, Ford concluded he was guilty of judicial misbehaviour and was temperamentally unsuited to hold office. When informed of the decision, Stubbs commented, "Mr. Justice Ford has executed a political mission, he has not made a judicial finding."

The trial of Judge Stubbs was probably the best legal education the young Joe Zuken could have received. He haunted the corridors of the Law Courts Building, soaking in as much of the hearing as he could. When Stubbs was removed from the bench, Zuken drew this conclusion: "There was a lesson there, not only for Stubbs. The establishment was trying to tell people that a line had to be drawn, and the establishment was prepared to draw that line, and to do it without mercy."

Stubbs immediately turned to politics. Within a month of leaving the bench, he announced his candidacy for the newly formed Co-operative Commonwealth Federation's nomination in a federal by-election in the Saskatchewan riding of Mackenzie. By winning the nomination, Stubbs became the CCF's first official candidate, but he lost the election and was soon embroiled in a dispute with party leaders over some campaign expenses. In the 1936 Manitoba election he ran as an independent, choosing as his slogan "Human Rights and Social Justice"; he surprised everyone but himself by winning more votes than any other candidate in the province.

As an MLA, Stubbs often spoke from the same platform as Zuken, raising funds and supplies for the Mackenzie-Papineau Battalion during the Spanish Civil War. They never became close friends. Zuken suspected the cantankerous judge made "few personal friends," but he always retained high regard for Stubbs's courage and forthrightness.

Just as she got him into the Peretz School, Shifra Leah Zuken helped get Joe Zuken into a law practice. Mother and son went from law office to law office looking for someone with whom the young law student could article. They did not get many warm receptions. Zuken's radical views were well known, and in the middle of the Depression even the legal profession was suffering economically — in 1931 there were thirty barristers and solicitors on the public relief roles. However, as Zuken put it, "Mother was very persuasive, and determined." Through a friend of a friend Zuken secured a position with John Mac-Lean, a man who had been Manitoba's first Rhodes Scholar. A literate and learned man, MacLean did not have a particularly busy practice. According to Zuken, the clients were so few in number that MacLean spent much of his time happily reading the Greek and Latin classics. MacLean did not handle the politically charged cases that would later mark Zuken's career, but in MacLean he found an example of integrity and honesty in the practice of law. When Zuken graduated, MacLean offered him a position with the firm until he could find his feet, but the two men soon realized there was no future for Zuken with such a small firm. Money was so tight that Zuken did not apply for membership in the bar until a year after he graduated from university.

The Communist Party

While his brother was getting a legal education, Cecil Zuken was receiving a political one. In 1929, as the world economy came crashing down, Cecil, like many young people in North America, was looking for an explanation as to what had gone wrong. And like many North Enders, he turned to left-wingers for some answers. One evening he went to a Communist Party-sponsored lecture by Scott Nearing. An American economist, Nearing had been fired from his university job for his political views during the First World War. He joined the American Communist Party in the mid-Twenties. The year after he came to Winnipeg, he was expelled from the CP for publishing a book party leaders disapproved of, but on that night in 1929 his critique of capitalism made a deep impression on Cecil.

After the meeting, Cecil went up to Tom Ewen, a colourful and outspoken railway blacksmith who had chaired the evening's talk, and said he would like to join the party's youth organization. Ewen (who sometimes went under the name McEwen) directed him to the offices of the Young Communist League. Cecil joined almost immediately. "I joined because I wanted to know more about the Communist movement, about the theories of socialism and the like."

When he first became involved with the Young Communist League, Cecil Zuken decided he would conduct his political activities under an assumed name. He was still attending classes at the university and suspected he could be subjected to discrimination for his political beliefs. He was mindful as well of the family reputation and the potential damage that could be done to the family business. "I assumed the name of Bill Ross and became known by that name within the Young Communist League." In 1936, when the party decided to run him for school board, a decision had to be made; should the name on the ballot be Bill Ross or Cecil Zuken? "Because the base of my support was in circles around the party, I changed my name legally to William Cecil Ross."

By going left, the Zuken brothers were following the political and social impulses of the North End. But they took their beliefs further than many, and the lives of both men were permanently marked by their decision to affiliate with the country's most controversial social and political movement — the Communist Party of Canada.

At seven o'clock on the morning of May 23, 1921, the founding convention of the CPC was called to order. In keeping with both Canadian and Communist traditions, the chairman of the meeting was an American who was acting on the authority of the Russian-dominated Communist International. Twenty-two delegates from across the country, often under assumed names, had assembled in a barn on the outskirts of Guelph, Ontario, that morning to establish, in their own words, an "underground, illegal organization." The party would dedicate itself to "propagating to the working class the idea of the inevitability of and necessity for violent revolution and prepare the working class for the destruction of the bourgeois state and the establishment of the proletarian dictatorship based upon Soviet power." Communists would only participate in election campaigns for purposes of "revolutionary propaganda and agitation."

Perhaps the party's most significant act, and one that was to exert tremendous influence on its direction for the next sixty years, was the adoption of the "21 points for affiliation with the Communist International as binding upon all delegates present and for its entire membership, without any reservations." The CPC had most firmly hitched its wagon to what it perceived to be a rising star, namely, the government of the Soviet Union. Yet while the possession of the U.S.S.R.'s stamp of approval gave the new party immediate credibility with many radical working people across Canada, blind obedience to the directives of the Soviet government was, in the long run, to lead the party into a sterile sectarianism from which it was never able to fully recover.

Still, it is easy to see why in 1921 the allure of the Soviet Union was so strong. After all, the Russian Revolution had been hailed by moderate as well as radical members of Canada's young socialist movement. The Winnipeg General Strike was only one of the high-water marks of the wave of labour unrest that had rolled across Canada, the United States and Europe in the wake of the First World War. Surely one revolution, particularly in a country like Russia, would be followed by others in the more industrialized world. And to whom should would-be revolutionaries turn for direction if not to the leaders of the world's first successful revolution?

The leaders of that revolution were extremely interested in promoting and directing the affairs of the international socialist movement. Lenin believed the fate of the Russian Revolution was in danger without a subsequent European revolution. And the making of that revolution depended on the creation of left-wing political parties along Bolshevik lines. To this end, the leaders of the Russian Revolution, with the support of a small number of left-wing activists from other countries, created the Communist International in March of 1919.

As noted, the price of admission to the International was a willingness to submit to its decisions and rules. Under any conditions, this would in the long run have turned out to be a foolish requirement, since on countless occasions it led various Communist parties to adopt strategies that may have had some relevance in czarist Russia but were completely out of step with the events in the countries where they were being implemented. Furthermore, the International turned into a far worse bargain after Joseph Stalin rose to power in the mid-Twenties. Under his rule, the CI ceased to be an instrument of international revolution, although it continued to depict itself as such. Stalin cynically used it to advance the interests of the Russian government, sometimes at the expense of the working classes it was supposedly attempting to liberate.

This said, the Communist Party of Canada during the first twenty years of its existence was able to attract and enlist the support of many of the country's most idealistic, talented and committed men and women. Through their examples of sacrifice and solidarity, they played a leading role in the fight for social justice during a long night of reaction, repression and prejudice.

During the Twenties, the CPC's influence in Winnipeg grew partly because of the importance the party placed on organizing unions in the city's garment trades and because of its decision to organize itself into several language federations. By doing this, the party was able to sink deep roots into the various immigrant communities of Winnipeg's North End. Party members played an important role in the creation of Ukrainian, Polish and Finnish labour temples across the country. At the same time, the party — more clearly than any other — articulated the aspirations and the anger of the Eastern European immigrants who found themselves discriminated against, poorly housed, poorly educated and often the victims of wretched on-the-job exploitation. And while the popular image of the Communist Party is that of a rigid and joyless organization — and its history has at times been scarred by ideological rigidity — during the 1930s its members were playing a vital role in the establishment of a series of very popular economic and cultural institutions. Ranging from cooperatively run dairies and lumberyards, to benevolent associations and athletic clubs, to choirs and theatre groups, these initiatives addressed many immediate concerns of the working people of the North End. They also helped Communists win a measure of public esteem as men and women who were serious about achieving real accomplishments on behalf of working people. As the decade wore on, the Zuken brothers came to the forefront of the cultural and political struggles the party was engaged in.

Aside from the representative of the Soviet Communist Party, there was another outside observer at the CPC's founding meeting, an undercover member of the Royal Canadian Mounted Police. In the wake of the Winnipeg General Strike, the federal government began increasingly to use the RCMP as a political police force. The presence of a Mountie in that Guelph barn was a signal that in years to come the Communist Party would be the target of various police operations.

The first wave of legal repression of the CPC peaked in 1931 when, as part of what the Ontario Provincial Police and the RCMP conceived as a "death blow at the Communist Party," eight of the party's leading figures were arrested. They were charged with sedition under section 98 of the Criminal Code — a draconian law passed during the Winnipeg General Strike but never utilized until this instance. The men, including party leader Tim Buck, were given sentences ranging from two to five years in prison.

During this period the Manitoba Provincial Police also kept the party under close scrutiny. The provincial attorney general and the premier, John Bracken, both received regular, detailed reports on Communist activities in Manitoba. These reports appear to have been largely based on the evidence of people who infiltrated the party on the police's behalf. One report, dated February 1932, gave this picture of life inside the Communist Party:

The Communist Party has ceased to meet in its public halls, and has destroyed all its books and papers. Also that all membership booklets have been taken and destroyed; that the meetings are held in small groups which take place secretly in houses; that the names of the individuals have been changed and that they are now using fictitious names; that the meeting places are kept secret and members only notified shortly before a meeting. The material for the meeting is used and then burned at the conclusion thereof.

The police reports gave detailed accounts of Communist involvement in strike support work during a dispute at a foundry in St. Boniface, including lengthy lists of people believed to belong to the party and even information on the activities of their spouses. They also included details on the speeches given at CP meetings and occasionally editorial comments, such as this assessment of one speaker: "This man Marriott is a dangerous man and a convincing talker. There is scarcely a meeting that he does not deliver himself and always his role is that of an agitator." Other reports were signed with coded numbers and included accounts of the party's election plans and the legal strategies being developed following the imprisonment of the party leadership.

The Flin Flon Strike

In the summer of 1934 Bill Ross found himself headed to the northern Manitoba mining town of Flin Flon. There, the members of the Mine Workers Union of Canada (MWUC), an affiliate of the Communist-led Workers Unity League, were engaged in a bitter strike against the the Hudson Bay Mining and Smelting Company. Flin Flon was a company town, developed in the late Twenties to exploit copper deposits along the Manitoba-Saskatchewan border. At the onset of the Depression, HBM&S instituted a "temporary" wage cut of 15 per cent for married employees and 18 per cent for single men. Despite improvements in metal prices, the company was in no hurry to rescind the wage cut.

Earlier attempts to form a union had led to the dismissal of the men involved, so the MWUC had to adopt a secretive approach. The workers were organized into cells of no more than half a dozen men each. Only one person in each cell knew who else was a member of the union. If a cell member were to tell management a union was being formed, only a handful of people would lose their jobs. Union leaders hoped to present the company with a list of contract proposals in July 1934. But on June 27 union activists were dismissed. Management hoped this move would decapitate the union; instead it sparked a full-scale strike. Only 100 of the 800 miners employed by HBM&S stayed on the job. The union proposed an end to the strike in exchange for a return to the old pay rates, an eight-hour day and the reinstatement of the men who had been fired. Management declined to negotiate.

The strike, and the presence of Communists in the union leadership, alarmed the provincial government of John Bracken. His first step was to reinforce the Mounted Police detachment in Flin Flon; by the time the strike was over, there were ninety Mounties in the town. The local business community reacted by establishing the Anti-Communist League, whose membership was restricted to "white males or females 21 years of age who openly avow their opposition to Communism." The league and the company tried to make communism, not wages and working conditions, the issue in the strike. They claimed the miners had been stirred up, and manipulated, by that most fearsome of monsters, "the outside agitator."

As Bill Ross recalled many years later, "It was clear when I got there the town was divided into two camps. And because the miners were isolated hundreds of miles away from Winnipeg, it was going to be a tough battle." Ross's job was to meet separately with younger members of the union and to address union meetings.

The company attempted to break the union by holding its own vote as to whether or not the strike should be terminated. Ballot boxes were set up in the local community hall, but union members surrounded the building while the wives of the strikers blocked the entranceway to the hall. The mayor, a supporter of the company, had sworn in a hundred special constables for the day. It was their job to guide those workers who were against the strike past the striking miners outside the hall. The day turned into a lengthy battle royale. In the words of a *Free Press* reporter, "the whole street was a surging mass of struggling, cursing humanity." The vote was called off by mid-afternoon, and that night the town's mayor was on the phone to Winnipeg demanding that the government take immediate action.

Within days Ross and most of the other strike leaders were in jail. The premier visited the town, and after meeting for just fifteen minutes with the miners (a meeting that MWUC officials were barred from), he announced that the strike was a Communist-inspired affair and that the provincial government would bring it to an end. The RCMP then organized a return to work, a move which effectively broke the strike. In the end the company did have to increase wages, though not up to the old rates.

By then Ross was in the jail in The Pas facing charges of unlawful assembly and intimidation. Years later he remembered the judge as a hanging judge who conducted much of the case while drunk. The charge of intimidation was dropped, but Ross was convicted of being part of an unlawful assembly, namely, the crowd of strikers opposing the company-arranged back-to-work vote. Before passing a year-long sentence on Ross, the judge commented that he could not understand why such a person of such intelligence had got himself mixed up with such a crowd. The sentence was appealed and reduced to six months. He served his time at the Dauphin provincial jail. "Going to jail was one of the risks. It was a common occurrence during that period. This was 1934, a period of sharp struggles." His parents found the jailing extremely disturbing. Ross said, "They were worried, they did not welcome it, but I was not excommunicated." The strike, the trial and the time his brother spent in jail gave Joe Zuken plenty to think about. "It raised," Joe later said, "some very serious questions in my mind about the law and justice. Sometimes the twain did not meet."

The persecution of Bill Ross and the other strike leaders was, quite clearly, part of a larger picture of police harassment of the radical labour movement in Manitoba. During the early years of the Depression, the Communist Party found itself continually under siege. It would be fair to say that at times it brought some of its troubles down upon its own head. At the heart of the problem was the party's relationship to the Soviet Union. In the late Twenties, as he strove to solidify his hold on the leadership of the Soviet Communist Party, Joseph Stalin launched a vicious attack on the party's right wing. Internationally, Communist parties were expected to mimic this attack by criticizing social democratic parties, labelling their leaders as "social fascists" who were propping up capitalism rather than destroying it. In Canada, Communists focused their attention on J. S. Woodsworth, whom they called a "labour misleader" and the labour movement's "most dangerous enemy." The party also attacked the existing labour unions for their lack of militancy, and established the Workers Unity League as a revolutionary alternative.

While some of these criticisms, particularly of the existing union structure, were valid, others were simply ludicrous. And they hurt the party in both the long and short run. During the Flin Flon strike, for example, neither J. S. Woodsworth nor R. B. Russell was anxious to help out union leaders who had accused them of fascism. And later, when the threat of real fascism in Europe led Stalin to attempt to establish a common front with socialists and liberals, the gap created by his harsh rhetoric could not be bridged. This cold war within the labour movement was to be refought for decades. Because of it, people like Joe Zuken would always have difficulty in dealing with the mainstream labour movement or the CCF and its various successors.

Throughout this embattled period, the party's legal arm, the Canadian Labor Defense League, was constantly called upon. The CLDL was led by Albert Edward Smith, a former Methodist minister who had been elected to the Manitoba legislature in 1921 as an Independent Labor Party candidate. Smith soon left the ILP for the Communist Party and moved to Toronto. Created in 1925, during its fifteen-year lifetime, the league defended over 6,000 individuals on charges ranging from sedition to vandalism. By 1933 it had over 17,000 members across the country, who were organized into 350 branches.

In Winnipeg much of the league's legal work was carried out by Saul Greenberg, an accomplished trial lawyer with left-wing sympathies but no attachment to the Communist

Party. It was through the CLDL that Zuken took on his first case with political overtones. In 1934, while still a law student, he was called upon to represent sixteen women facing charges of obstructing a police officer in his duty. The women had been arrested at a demonstration of relief strikers in West Kildonan. Such strikes, staged to protest the low level of relief and the work men had to do in order to qualify for it, were common throughout the Depression. The police had been called out to force the men back to work and a scuffle had broken out. The wives of the strikers had also been on the picket line that day and they had been arrested. The provincial government, viewing the case as one of significant political importance, hired prominent lawyer and former MLA S. Hart Green to prosecute the women.

Zuken's chances, considering that he was up against one of the province's senior lawyers and the testimony of a police officer, were very slim. "But a very interesting situation developed. In the course of the melee the police chief had ended up on the ground and his glasses had become dislodged. When I got to cross-examine him, all he was able to say was that all he saw was that all the women's legs were stepping all over him, but he could not recognize any of the women."

The case was thrown out because of lack of identification. "It was not an earth-shattering case as such, but it was a case of the times. It highlighted the relief struggle and the militancy of the women. And they were not party women. I remember the first time I went out to meet them. I had no office to meet them in, so I had to go to this shabby little working-class hall in West Kildonan. But this was all part of an education."

Clara

On a Friday evening in 1933 Clara Goldenberg reluctantly agreed to accompany an old high school friend to a meeting at the Liberty Temple on Pritchard Street. The eighteen-year-old Clara came from an apolitical, orthodox family, and politics had never much interested her.

"I said to my friend I did not want to go to that place, it was a Communist place. She said, 'Come with me, just to see what it is like.' I was so desperate I did." They got to the meeting hall early, and there sitting on a desk talking to some other club members was Joe Zuken. Clara's friend said, "This is Clara Goldenberg. She is going to join the club." And according to Clara, Joe looked at her and said, "Oh, life is going to be interesting now."

She did join the club and the two of them started going out together almost immediately. At the time, Zuken was teaching Yiddish at the Sholom Aleichem School. Soon Clara was showing up to sit in on the classes with the children. She had been taught Hebrew at home by her father but knew little Yiddish. "Listening to Joe, I got to know and love the Jewish language."

This sudden social life was a surprise to everyone who knew Zuken — he'd never been seriously involved with anyone before — and they soon noted some changes in Joe. According to Clara, "We had a dramatic group that he took charge of. He was very strict and one day we were having a rehearsal and I said something funny and broke up the rehearsal. And Joe laughed, and somebody said, 'If anybody else did this he would give us hell, but because Clara broke us up it is okay.' "

The two of them were married in 1938. At the time, Clara was making more from her sewing machine than Joe was from law and teaching combined. In keeping with their slim means, the newlyweds moved in with Clara's sister Sonia and her husband Bernard Dietch.

They were still living with the Dietches in 1941. Sonia died in the spring of that year. It was a very distressing period for Clara. "It was a struggle for me to continue. I quit work. I was looking after my brother-in-law, Joe and Janice. I was doing everything, it seemed, and it was very difficult for me." Before she died, Sonia had asked Clara to take care of her three-year-old daughter, Janice. Clara quit her garment factory job so that she could devote herself to raising the young girl. A very warm relationship grew up between the Zukens, who were to have no children of their own, and Janice. Janice Dietch thought of Joe Zuken as a second father. "He told wonderful stories. When the Jewish holidays came, I always wanted him to tell me the stories because he told them so well. He could be so funny — there was magic at times."

That evening in 1933, when Joe and Clara met, marked not only the beginning of Clara's romance with Joe, but the beginning of her commitment to the Communist Party. For her it was a time of intense intellectual stimulation. "All of a sudden I felt my mind waking up. I felt as if I was just beginning to think. Someone lent me *The Origin of the Family* by Engels and that really turned me around. It took me a long time to read it, because I was really thinking about it. It was a wonderful period — my mind was growing up."

Clara Goldenberg was born in 1913 in the small village of Pavolotch, about sixteen miles from the city of Kiev. Her father, Nochem Osher Goldenberg, whom Clara remembered as a worldly man, "very well educated in the Jewish traditions," owned a high-quality dry goods store. Her mother came from Kiev, and the two of them were brought together by a matchmaker. They had ten children, but a typhoid epidemic took away three of the sons, leaving them with five girls and two boys.

During the Russian civil war the family had moved to Kiev. There they experienced the White Terror first-hand. Looking back, Clara Zuken said, "I can remember some scenes of soldiers barging into our house and ransacking it. Once in Kiev I remember somebody coming to my mother and hitting her on her bare shoulders. My father being in bed, pretending to be sick, so they should not kill him. An uncle of mine was killed in bed."

Her father had tried his luck in Winnipeg once before, in the years prior to the First World War. But after a brief period in the candy business, he moved back to Kiev. However, as the civil war grew in intensity, the decision was made for the whole family to move to Winnipeg in 1921 and join Nochem Goldenberg's sister.

According to Clara, her father never acclimatized himself to life in Canada. He worked mainly as a private Hebrew teacher, while Clara's older sisters went off to work in garment factories, where Clara joined them a few years after she graduated from St. John's Tech. Her brother worked on a farm in Saskatchewan.

One of her sisters got Clara her first job at the Western Shirt Factory. "The bosses were terrible. It was like working in a concentration camp." In her own view, Clara was a poor and unskilled worker, and because most of the work was paid on a piecework basis, she rarely made much money. She went to work at a different factory, where the forelady had been a friend of her sister's and before her promotion had been involved in unsuccessful attempts to form a union. "When she became a forelady my sister said, 'This is wonderful, because you know what it is like.' 'Oh no,' she said. 'I am on the other side of the fence now.' "

Clara shared Joe's shyness. "I was a very poor worker, I was very timid — a lot of people thought I was stuck up because I was not part of the gang." Nor did she like marches and demonstrations. "But my conscience always bothered me, so of course I marched." But at times she could be outspoken. During the Depression the factory owners could insist that workers stay at their machines even when there was no cloth. That way not a second would be lost once the material arrived. This harsh policy did not cost them anything, since they only paid the machine operators for the work they did, not the time they spent waiting. "One day I sat there from ten in the morning to three in the afternoon. I had my book with me and the forelady would not let us go out in case work came in. I was seething, but I thought I am not going to let her see how I feel. She came up behind me and said, 'What are you reading?' And I showed her. She said, 'You don't think what I am doing is right.' And I said, 'That's right, I don't see why we have to be here.' "

Despite her growing commitment to the Communist Party, Clara was never able to turn herself into a union militant. "A woman came up to me, a Communist organizer, and said, 'Now that you are in the factory, you should try to organize a union." And I said, 'How can I organize a union when I am not even a good sewer? The girls don't even respect me, I am not a good worker.' " But if she was not cut out for leadership, she did not shy away from involvement. When the Workers Unity League tried to organize a union in the factory, she joined up. Unfortunately for her, someone saw her going into the union office and told the boss. "The next day he called me and my sister into his office. He tells my sister he saw me going up to the union office. And so my sister says to him, 'She does not even know what she is doing, she is just a kid. What do you want from her?' So he let me stay."

The Needle Trade Strikes

The garment industry in Winnipeg during the Twenties and Thirties was the focal point of intense labour unrest. It was not a fashion business but concentrated on supplying the work and farm clothes for Western Canada. The factories were often located in the large warehouses that had been built around city hall in the days when Winnipeg was the distribution centre for Western Canada. Many of the city's wholesale suppliers went out of business when the Panama Canal was built and it became cheaper to ship goods to the West by ship rather than by rail. When this happened, the garment industry expanded into the warehouses, which were large but not designed to be used as factories. No single company dominated the local scene; instead dozens of small companies battled for their share of the market, and the key weapons in this battle were low wages and long working days.

The One Big Union, the International Garment Workers Union, the Amalgamated Clothing Workers , the International Fur and Leather Workers Union and the Workers Unity League all took a crack at organizing the garment workers during this period. They came up against bitter opposition from the factory owners — many of whom were former garment workers who had set up their own shops on a small scale. This resulted in a series of bitter and often unsuccessful strikes. From 1922 to 1935, there were twenty-two strikes in the Winnipeg garment industry; most of them failed to achieve their objectives, and most of them were led by the Communist Party's Workers Unity League. The WUL was criticized by its opponents for leading workers into battles they could not hope to win. Most other needle trade unions, however, had simply rolled over and played dead when the Depression hit; they were not winning strikes because they were not even attempting to organize garment workers.

The left was deeply involved in the leadership of one of the most bitter garment industry strikes of the Thirties. The International Fur and Leather Workers Union organized a Winnipeg local in 1935, but the Furriers' Guild, the organization representing the city's various fur companies, refused to meet with the union. After several months of stalling, the guild, under pressure from socialist mayor John Queen, met with union representatives but took the position that its employees did not want to belong to the union and it would not negotiate with the union representatives.

The union had no choice but to call a strike in the summer of 1935. It was one of the longest in the city's history, lasting for nine months. And it was a very bitter conflict. Guild representatives constantly denounced the union, using phrases like "gangster tactics," "foreign agitators" and "New York radicals," the latter referring to some of the union officials from the United States who had come up to assist with the attempted negotiations. Workers who joined the union were locked out if they had not already gone on strike, and others faced on-the-job intimidation. The courts were very protective of the companies' concerns. The Hurtig Fur Company was awarded $2,869.76 in court because union members had ignored injunctions against picketing. The courts also issued a permanent injunction against the picketing of the Hurtig operation.

Through the Canadian Labor Defense League, Zuken was involved in defending many of the workers who were charged with violating the anti-picketing injunctions. Many of them were fined and a few received jail terms. One of them was a young woman named Freda Cooden, who was sent to Headingley Gaol for a year on assault charges that many of her co-workers believed were trumped up. Recalled Zuken, "I knew the family very well. She was a militant trade unionist. She was sentenced to jail because of her work on the Hurtig picket line. To begin with, her health was not very good. Being in jail certainly did not help her health, to put it mildly." While in jail she contracted tuberculosis and died.

Astoundingly, while Joe Zuken was becoming ever more deeply involved in the Communist Party, in the defence of left-wing clients and in work raising money to support the Spanish Republic, he was also able to become a driving force in, of all things, the city's theatre community. Working with the Progressive Arts Club and later with the New Theatre,

Zuken helped bring a breath of fresh and bracing air to the city's intellectual life.

THREE

It Did Happen Here
1933-1940

One day in the spring of 1934, twenty-two-year-old Joe Zuken received a message from Winnipeg's deputy chief of police, Charles McIvor. It was a call he had been half-expecting for some time. Zuken, aside from attending law school, was directing the Progressive Arts Club production of *Eight Men Speak,* which was set to open at the Walker Theatre (now the Odeon Theatre) on May 2. McIvor wanted to see a copy of the script. After all, he said, there had been trouble following the play's premiere in Toronto the previous December. Zuken denied that there had been any problems; as he put it, "There had been a performance, one which was extremely well received." For him to give the chief a look at the script would be to permit prior censorship, something he said he refused to do.

It was a provocative move — and from both a political and an artistic point of view, possibly a wise one. As Zuken later admitted, the Winnipeg production of the play was shaping up as something less than polished. There was only one performance scheduled, and organizers could at best hope for a small but appreciative audience and a short review, buried deep in the papers, noting the energetic but amateurish production. Instead the police decided to halt the production of the play, making it front-page news and attracting thousands of people to a protest rally in the Market Square.

Deputy Chief McIvor was right on one point, there had been trouble following the Toronto production of the play. *Eight Men Speak* was after all the most famous and successful play to emerge from Canada's radical theatre movement of the Thirties. A bold and defiant attack on authority, it sparked

court cases and bannings across the country. The six-act play
was written by Oscar Ryan, Ed Cecil-Smith, Frank Love and
Mildred Goldberg in the fall of 1933 to protest the treatment
of the eight leading members of the Communist Party who
were then imprisoned in Kingston Penitentiary.

Civil libertarians had been outraged by the persecution of a
political party, and a national campaign was mounted to
repeal section 98 of the Criminal Code and free the Communist
leaders. The campaign gathered steam following a riot at
Kingston, where guards fired at least eleven shots into party
leader Tim Buck's cell. Buck claimed that it was part of a plot
to assassinate him. No charges were brought against the prison
guards, but an additional eleven months were tacked onto
Buck's sentence for his role in organizing a prisoners' strike
that preceded the riot.

Eight Men Speak uses blackouts, mass recitations and satire
to outline the trial and the events leading up to the firing of
the shots into Tim Buck's cell. The final scene takes place in a
Workers' Court, where a guard is on trial for the shooting. The
prosecution is carried out by a female lawyer representing the
Canadian Labor Defense League, while the guard is defended
by a bald, red-faced paunchy member of the firm Capitalism,
Capitalism, Capitalism and Exploitation. The key evidence
comes from the eight prisoners who speak directly to the
audience. In unison they urge workers to "smash section 98"
and "smash the iron heel."

The prosecutor makes her final address not to the on-stage
jury but the audience: "Perhaps at this moment a gun is leveled
at Tim Buck. Perhaps tonight a shot will be fired into his cell.
Perhaps, as we sit in this court, bullets are tearing the flesh of
eight men. Perhaps they are succeeding where this man failed."

The judge then calls upon the audience to pronounce the
sentence. In live productions, this brought forth enthusiastic
shouts of "Guilty, guilty."

The play premiered on December 4, 1933, at Toronto's
Standard Theatre. A crowd of 1,500 gave it an enthusiastic
reception, frequently interrupting the performance with cheering and applause. The young cast, made up of members of the
Progressive Arts Club and the Workers' Experimental Theatre,
decided to give a second performance in January. The Toronto

Police Commission moved quickly, threatening to cancel the licence of any theatre manager who allowed the play to be mounted in his hall. The Standard Theatre caved in and the performance was cancelled.

At a meeting to protest this decision, one act of the play, where the eight men all state their case, was performed. Following that, A. E. Smith, the head of the CLDL, charged the federal government with responsibility for the attempted murder of Tim Buck. This brought on sedition charges against Smith. The prime minister, R. B. Bennett, who had come to office promising to crush dissent under the "iron heel of ruthlessness," paid considerable attention to the play. Bennett's secretary, A. E. Miller, wrote in a letter: "Mr. Bennett has read the file [dealing with the play] and thinks that appropriate action should be taken through the attorney general to protect society against these attacks." And in another letter dealing with the play, Bennett himself wrote that he was "of the opinion that we should not permit liberty to degenerate into license."

Given this background, it is not surprising that Deputy Chief McIvor was apprehensive about a Winnipeg production of *Eight Men Speak*. Relations between leftists and the authorities were far from amicable in the spring of 1934. The attorney general was accusing Communists of provoking violence at a packinghouse strike in St. Boniface, the Winnipeg police had refused to give a parade permit for that year's May Day demonstration, and Mayor Ralph Webb was telling anybody who would listen that the best place for reds was in the Red River.

The Progressive Arts Club booked the Walker Theatre, which at the time was owned by C. P. Walker, the city's leading theatrical entrepreneur, who had been presenting big-time touring shows in Winnipeg since the 1890s. In 1906 he built the Walker, a "palatial building" that the *Free Press* described as one "New York or London might be proud of." The theatre was often used for political as well as dramatic purposes. During the drive for women's suffrage, Nellie McClung's *Votes for Women* was staged there, and its walls occasionally echoed to the strains of "The Red Flag" in the tumultuous days leading up to the Winnipeg General Strike. In the days before the PAC was scheduled to take to the boards with *Eight Men Speak*, the

Walker was the scene of a lecture defending the anti-Semitic tract *The Protocols of Zion.*

The police adopted the same tactics which had been used so successfully in Toronto, bringing pressure to bear on Walker. Zuken got the word from C. P. Walker personally. "He told me he had received a call from the police and the performance could not continue. Walker was a decent gentleman, but he was on the spot. In my words, he was being blackmailed by the police department. If he allowed the performance to proceed, his licence would be cancelled. So he gave way; he complied with the police order."

On the day scheduled for the performance, Walker's licence was in fact temporarily cancelled by provincial attorney general W. J. Major. He took the action on the recommendation of the Winnipeg Police Commission, which had concluded the play was "subversive to the public interest." That night hundreds turned up at the Walker Theatre only to be turned away by the police. One rebuffed patron told the *Free Press* that "they can get away with this now, but when Canada is a free country the theatre doors will be open to everyone." Another woman, described as smartly dressed, said, "Well, ain't that something. I thought they were a little more broad-minded here than in Toronto, but it looks like they are all the same."

The cancellation brought the young Joe Zuken into the public eye. He told the papers the police were taking "unwanted and dictatorial action," depriving Winnipeggers of the opportunity to see "an all-Canadian play with a startling stage setting and a compelling social message." The cause was taken up by those who were not normally sympathetic to the Communist Party. *Free Press* editorialist George Ferguson wrote, "The officials' action is an unwarranted interference with liberty and speech and cannot be defended." What risk was there, he asked, in letting the play be performed, since "plays potent enough to lead to public uprisings are rare."

The Progressive Arts Club ran into as many problems in trying to protest the play's banning as it did in mounting the production. Arrangements were made to hold a public meeting in the Civic Auditorium, but after 10,000 leaflets were distributed advertising the rally, the Auditorium Commission cancelled the meeting. Jacob Penner tried to get the city council to reverse the police commission's ban on the play, but he could not get the needed support of the Independent Labor Party aldermen.

A big protest meeting took place, naturally enough, in the Market Square. The speakers included former solicitor general E. J. McMurray, Jacob Penner, Joe Zuken and one of the play's authors, Oscar Ryan. Zuken recalled "that there were thousands of people present. I said that the pretext for the ban — that the play was obscene — was a lot of nonsense. What was obscene was the very arbitrary action by the police of Winnipeg. But the ban was broken because we performed segments of the play at various working-class halls around the city. So if I needed something to cap my activities as a young radical, *Eight Men Speak* did that."

The experience with *Eight Men Speak* only whetted Zuken's appetite for the world of the theatre. Even when he was deeply involved in defending Winnipeg's radicals, his time was increasingly consumed by the Communist Party's cultural organization, the Progressive Arts Club. This arts movement could trace its roots back to the 1913 textile workers' strike in Patterson, New Jersey. Led by the Industrial Workers of the World, the strikers forged a connection between the radical wing of the labour movement and the intellectuals of New York's Greenwich Village. John Reed helped direct a giant pageant staged in Madison Square Gardens. Over a thousand strikers took part in the performance, which dramatized the major events of the bitter strike. The production sparked a decade of cultural experimentation that culminated in the creation, under the Communist Party's careful supervision, of the Workers' Drama League in 1926.

Under the direction of Mike Gold, the league adopted the dramatic techniques being developed in the Soviet Union. There, young Soviet students were performing skits intended to instruct Russian citizens on the principles of communism. Designed to spread political agitation and propaganda, the short, stylized pieces were dubbed "agit-prop." The most successful of these pieces in America was Gold's mass recitation *Strike!* Members of the cast were scattered through the hall, a device later repeated in the far more successful *Waiting for*

Lefty. According to Gold, before the show is over "Everyone in the hall should be shouting: 'Strike! Strike!' "

The league was transformed into the Workers Laboratory Theatre, which, through its Shock Troupe, concentrated on literally taking theatre into the streets. The troupe would appear at picket lines and demonstrations on the shortest of notice. Their skits were often didactic and heavy-handed, and given the fiercely sectarian stand of the Communist Party during this period, as much attention was given to the presentation of the correct political line as to the dramatic delivery of lines.

There was also an effort to develop a national network. In 1932 the League of Workers Theatres was founded. By 1934 it had over thirty member companies across the United States. The following year the New Theatre League was organized with a pledge to develop "the American Theatre to its highest artistic and social level. For a theatre dedicated to the struggle against war, fascism and censorship."

The Progressive Arts Club

Canada's radical theatre movement got its formal start in 1932 with the formation of the Progressive Arts Club in Toronto. The PAC's driving members were the leading intellectual and artistic figures of the Canadian Communist Party — Stanley Ryerson, Dorothy Livesay and Oscar Ryan. The club's theatrical arm was the Workers' Experimental Theatre, an amateur company that marked its debut in the spring of 1932 with the agit-prop production *Deported.* It was not an auspicious beginning — two of the actors failed to show up, while other cast members were nearly an hour late for the performance. The company's next show was marred when the curtain came down early, robbing the play of its moralistic ending.

The PAC was more successful on other fronts, publishing *Masses,* a magazine of radical art, fiction and poetry. By 1933 there were branches of the Progressive Arts Club in Winnipeg, Vancouver and Montreal, all with their own agit-prop theatre troupes. Winnipeg's Workers' Theatre specialized in highly mobile, agit-prop productions staged on picket lines, in working-class halls and in the hotels on the Main Street strip. According to Zuken, these productions were a revolt against the existing culture of the day. "During the Thirties there was a Little Theatre in Winnipeg, which was a very arty kind of theatre. They did fluffy, 'anyone for tennis' sorts of things. We felt the times were such — with mass movements dealing with unemployment and anti-fascism — that the theatre should say something."

Fred Narvey was another young man who was drawn to the Progressive Arts Club. As he recalled it, Zuken was the driving force behind the club's various activities, which included weekly speaker's forums, small-scale productions and skits. Narvey was often responsible for organizing the forums. "We invited all kinds of people, some progressive, some reactionary. It often turned out to be a debate between the audience and the speaker." Once it was arranged to have John Queen, one of the leaders of the General Strike and the then socialist mayor of Winnipeg, attend as guest speaker. Recalled Narvey: "John Queen was a rabid anti-Communist. He spent as much time speaking about the menace of communism as he did in speaking about the menace of Hitler. The people in the audience had a real debate with him, a theoretical debate about the differences between Karl Kautsky and Lenin. Queen knew about the labour movement in England. But about politics and the differences in ideology between the social democrats and the Communists, or differences between the Second and Third Internationals, he was clueless. He said, 'Do you mind if I speak about England?' "

As Narvey remembered the period, Zuken spent most of his time at the PAC's headquarters — at first the recreation room in the basement of a downtown warehouse. "He was always the director of our drama group. He didn't know much about directing — how could he, he was a kid. He had such sincerity. He had such depth of feeling that he inspired the rest of us." Narvey said he once asked Zuken when he slept — the reply was "During the lectures at university."

Zuken also developed a reputation as a hard taskmaster. According to Narvey, he insisted that everybody come on time and not miss rehearsals. "If people did not say their lines properly he would shout blue murder at them. He was so dedicated he could not understand that other people were not as dedicated as he was." Narvey was occasionally subjected to

Zuken's temper himself: "I remember I was supposed to be chairman of a speaker's forum on a Sunday afternoon. A close friend of mine phoned up and said that his father had died and asked would I be a pall bearer at the funeral. The funeral was on Sunday afternoon when I was supposed to be the chairman. I phoned Joe and he said, 'Well, Fred, the forum has to go on.' And that was Joe. Some people resented that. I disobeyed him. I went to the funeral. But this was Joe."

Narvey claimed there was no direct link between the Communist Party and the Progressive Arts Club, but there is no denying the club's members were all either party members or fellow travellers like Zuken. In his recollections of the period, Saul Cherniack, who later became a prominent member of the CCF and the New Democratic Party, said the PAC was seen by others on the left as a creature of the Communist Party. The Progressive Arts Club did not attempt to mount major dramatic productions or to reach into the broader artistic community.

It is doubtful whether the club would have been the scene of some of the debates that one member recalls if its membership had been open to all comers. "I can remember, during the Thirties, during the purges and the big show trials, when Bukharin, Kamenev, Zinoviev, and Radek were all executed, there was tremendous debates that went on. Bitter, bitter debates in the Progressive Arts Club. Particularly between Bill Ross and Joseph Zuken, who happened to be brothers. And no matter what Bill said about these people and their heinous crimes and why they should be executed, Joe said, 'I don't believe it. I don't believe it. These people were giants. They had differences of opinion with Stalin, but they certainly were not traitors.' And no matter what pressure was brought on him, and the Communist newspapers were full of indictment against these people, Joe said, 'I don't believe it, it is a struggle for power.' And he never changed his position. He was a strong character. He fought with his own brother."

The New Theatre
The Communist Party had called the Progressive Arts Club into existence, and it brought it to an end. In the mid-Thirties, finally alarmed by the growing rise of international fascism, Stalin ordered an end to the party's sectarian approach to

liberals and social democrats. Now Communists would seek to form a united front with these once-hated "social fascists." This marked the start of the party's most creative and influential period. Communists often provided the organizational drive for the new unions being created across North America under the banner of the Committee for Industrial Organization.

The coming of the Common Front period saw the end of the more experimental workers theatre, as socialists moved into more mainstream, but still socially conscious, theatre companies. In New York the Theatre of Action included such talents as Moss Hart and Lee Strasberg on its board of directors, while Elia Kazan directed their productions. Clifford Odets, Irwin Shaw and Albert Maltz were both members of the Communist Party and playwrights active in the Group Theatre of the period. They produced *Waiting for Lefty*, *Bury the Dead* and *Rehearsal*, the powerful one-act plays that formed the basic repertoire of any left-wing theatre company in the Thirties. There were even labour musicals — Harold Rome's *Pins and Needles* and Marc Blitzstein's *The Cradle Will Rock* both enjoyed successful runs in New York.

In Canada the coming of the Common Front served to revitalize the Progressive Arts Club. Toronto's Workers' Experimental Theatre transformed itself into the Theatre of Action. In 1936 in Winnipeg, with Joe Zuken playing a key organizational role, the New Theatre came into being. That fall it mounted its first production, Irwin Shaw's anti-war drama *Bury the Dead*.

In the spring of 1937 the New Theatre presented *It Can't Happen Here*, a dramatization of the novel by Sinclair Lewis. Joe Zuken was featured in the lead as the small-town newspaper editor who falls victim to a genial American fascist who wins the presidency. It received a very positive notice in the *Free Press*. Frank Morriss wrote: "Sounding a prophetic alarm to people who believe that dictatorship is a plant that will not flourish away from European soil, *It Can't Happen Here* provides a walloping theatrical evening." Morriss went on to write that the production was "carried forth with an adept touch that is close to professional standards." He singled Zuken out for special praise, saying he played his role with "an appreciation of its warmly human qualities."

In the program for *It Can't Happen Here*, the company addressed the question "What is this New Theatre?"

> The Winnipeg New Theatre aims to establish a permanent repertory group of the best available theatrical talent, for the purpose of presenting such plays of social significance as make for intelligent entertainment.... We feel it never hurt a play to be ABOUT something; that there is no reason why a play with a theme of social importance cannot be both good art and good entertainment if it is well handled, neither is humour excluded from such plays as many seem to imagine. In fact, humour can be one of the social theatre's most effective weapons. Still many cry: "There isn't enough talent in Winnipeg to form a good repertory group! There aren't enough people interested in social plays!" Well, we think they are wrong. We intend to prove that it CAN happen here.

One of the ways the New Theatre tried to make it happen in Winnipeg was by drawing in people who would have been repelled by the overt influence the Communist Party exercised over the Progressive Arts Club. Saul and Sybil Cherniack were among the young CCFers who were drawn to this theatre. Saul Cherniack's father, Alter Cherniack, had played a leading role in establishing the Peretz School and was a prominent figure in the city's social democratic community. Saul had always been involved in theatrical activities in school. "Some of us non-Communists were glad to be involved in a theatre that did work of social significance. It was our opportunity to try and give a message to people about what we believed and what was going on in the world."

Whereas the Progressive Arts Club placed Communist Party politics before all other considerations, the New Theatre struggled to be much more intellectually open. It provided a common ground for radicals to meet and thrash out staging and political strategy. To Zuken it was an ecumenical meeting place for people of various shades of the left. "For example, John MacLean, the man I articled with, was very active in the local chapter of the League for Social Reconstruction. It was the intellectual wing of the CCF. And so I invited him down.

He came and gave us a little talk about the aims and objectives of the League for Social Reconstruction."

The timing for the creation of the New Theatre could not have been better. Bickering within the city's establishment in the mid-Thirties had led to a split within the existing professional theatre community and contributed to the death of the highly successful Little Theatre Company. Since the late Twenties the Little Theatre (or, as it was first known, the Community Theatre) had, under the direction of John Craig, been mounting a series of ambitious and successful productions. One of the company's leading patrons was Lady Margaret Tupper, the wife of Sir Charles Tupper, a local lawyer and the grandson of one of the Fathers of Confederation. Lady Tupper occasionally directed and performed in Little Theatre productions and by all accounts acquitted herself admirably.

The Little Theatre was so successful that it outgrew its facilities on Main and Selkirk. Lady Tupper was able to use her social connections to persuade the James A. Richardson family to make the Dominion Theatre available to the Little Theatre. The Richardsons, the city's premier grain-trading family, had bought the Dominion during the Twenties when they were acquiring land for an office building they intended to erect at Portage and Main. The onset of the Depression had put those plans on hold and the theatre was sitting vacant.

Shortly after the move was made, there was a falling out between John Craig and Lady Tupper. Tupper felt the Little Theatre should attempt to improve its national image and reputation by focusing its efforts on winning the Dominion Drama Festival, a contest Tupper had helped establish. For his part Craig felt the theatre should devote its resources to satisfying the Winnipeg audience. He was in part frustrated by the fact that the Dominion Drama Festival was restricted to one-act plays, since he wanted the Little Theatre to tackle far more ambitious productions. As a result, in 1933 Lady Tupper resigned as the president of the Little Theatre to form the Player's Guild. She was quick to attract the support of most of the city's establishment — the guild's board of directors included the provincial chief justice, a leading King's Counsel and a couple of former members of the Citizens' Committee of One Thousand.

The Little Theatre soon fell victim to its own success. The company's productions of *The Taming of the Shrew* and *Peer Gynt* demonstrated that theatre could pay its own way. The Richardsons evicted the Little Theatre and imported a professional company from Eastern Canada, the John Holden Players, as a resident theatre company. This stock company was under instructions to see that of all its expenses the rent was paid first. Not surprisingly it filled its playbill with remounts of successful Broadway productions. The Little Theatre attempted another season, but financial pressures forced the company to cancel the final production. After she had arranged to have the Dominion Drama Festival held in Winnipeg in 1938, Lady Tupper seemed to lose interest in theatre, choosing to switch her patronage, and that of the Richardson family, to the ballet.

One result of this bickering was that a large number of talented amateurs in the city were looking for a theatre company which would challenge them intellectually. The New Theatre was custom-made for this purpose and provided many people who had, ironically, cut their theatrical teeth with the Little Theatre with an outlet for their talents. Just as ironically, it was to be the New Theatre, founded and led by people who were anathema to the city's establishment, and not the Player's Guild, that would go on to win national acclaim at the Dominion Drama Festival.

The New Theatre attracted a wide cross section of people, and some of them went on to careers within the Canadian Broadcasting Corporation, the National Film Board and the professional theatre. The New Theatre's alumni included Mercer McLeod, Tommy Tweed, Frances Goffman, George Werier, Bernard Latham and Gordon Burwash. The program for one of its 1941 reviews lists a young Monty Halparin as one of the performers — now better known as Monty Hall.

While it provided a creative outlet for some at a time when the city's theatrical fortunes were sagging, it also gave a large number of politically aware young people an avenue to express their dissatisfaction with the age. For many people, politics, culture and the joys of youth were intermingled in an experience that was all-consuming. Sybil Cherniack's reminiscences of the period are typical: "I just think it was total involvement. I don't think it happens very often, where you just think about it, you're involved in it and you are enjoying it. It was exciting, it was lovely. We did not ask people if they were Communists, or if they weren't. None of us had any money and everybody seemed to be working together. At one point there were many of us who spent maybe five evenings a week at our headquarters. We had rented headquarters, we washed the floor, we had skits, we had classes and we had children's classes. It was fun."

The New Theatre also organized play readings for interest groups. Saul Cherniack and his brother-in-law used to do readings from the works of John Dos Passos for example. And there were dozens of chores that had to be performed in advance of a performance. Sybil Cherniack recalled typing each script out up to ten times so there would be enough copies for all the cast members.

The range of activities organized by the New Theatre becomes clear with a quick reading of its newsletters and programs. Even the advertisements say something about the period. The 1936 production of *It Can't Happen Here* was sponsored by, among others, the Youth Committee to Aid Spain, the Winnipeg Fur Workers, and Perth's Cleaners, while the program for the 1942 production of Friedrich Wolf's *Professor Mamlock* contained greetings from the Rosa Luxemburg Bridge Club, Northern Taxi and City Hydro and an announcement of an upcoming talk — at the Walker Theatre — on the "Soviet Union at War," featuring Anna Louise Strong.

According to the newsletters, there were weekly meetings during 1939 and lectures on early Canadian theatre by Tannis Murray and on Scandinavian Theatre by Esse Ljungh. Aside from its own regular play readings, the New Theatre did readings for the Young Men's Hebrew Association, the Young Communist League, the League for Peace and Democracy, the Russian Club, the North End Cultural Club and the Yiddish Culture Verband. It also provided actors for other local productions — Frances Goffman, Jim Klady, Joe Zuken and George Werier all appeared in a theatrical evening mounted by the Jewish Dramatic Club to raise money for German refugees.

The North American New Theatre Movement, centred in New York, not only provided companies with plays like

Waiting for Lefty and *Bury the Dead*, it also supplied directors. In 1940 Max Glandbard hitchhiked from New York to take up work with Winnipeg's New Theatre as its director. According to Saul Cherniack, the theatre paid Glandbard fifteen dollars a week and sold his services to the YMHA for five dollars. Narvey remembered him as a "clever young man," and he would have had to be to live on fifteen dollars a week. But, according to Narvey, he was not clever enough to make the method system of acting work in Winnipeg: "Glandbard made us read two of Stanislavsky's books. One of them was called *My Life and Art* and the other one was called *An Actor Prepares*. *An Actor Prepares* was our bible. We had classes where we would study it, chapter by chapter. And Stanislavsky would teach how you should gesture, how you should speak, etc., etc., etc. Get your mental processes in order, you should learn fencing, and so on. So we study Stanislavsky."

Even though most of the theatre's work was consciously left wing, the audience was not necessarily working class. Saul Cherniack recalled with some pride how he once sent Lady Eaton's chauffeur away empty-handed when he came to the theatre early in an attempt to buy an advance ticket to one of the productions, which was against the company's policy. In retrospect, his wife felt the theatre's audience was largely made up of friends and relatives, but Saul believed the company had a larger influence. "Winnipeg was thirsting for cultural plays. And we had built a reputation as being pretty good actors. We had people from the cultural literary circle, the Winnipeg Little Theatre people would come. We had skit evenings where people would come in large crowds — large crowd means a hundred to two hundred." Joe Zuken, however, who devoted much of his time during this period to the New Theatre, sounded a cautionary note to those who would romanticize its influence: "Those who say this was naturally adopted and picked up by the working class are sadly mistaken. We had to sweat to get people out to see New Theatre performances. It was a problem because it was very new, and very new to them, the idea that they would go to a theatre and see something that had a message."

While the Communist Party did not formally control the New Theatre, it did try to pull some of its strings from behind the scenes. Although Zuken was not a formal party member at the time, his brother was rising in the party ranks. Some party leaders felt Zuken should help implement party policy in the theatre company. According to Zuken, he resisted party efforts to have him make the New Theatre hew to the party line. "There were no holds barred. The New Theatre was not under the control of the party. As a matter of fact, I got into trouble with the Communist Party because as the chairman of the general meetings I did not allow any individual or group to try to give the line, as it were, to the organization. I remember making the remark 'Well, no one here is the repository of all wisdom.' I must have been an opinionated little bastard, but I would not stand for anybody trying to tell me or the organization what to do. There may have been members of the Young Communist League who may not have been too happy, who thought that maybe I was trying to do things without consulting the YCL. So be it."

But at the heart of the New Theatre experience was not sectarianism, but real camaraderie. Much of this came out in their "evenings of social significance," evenings where the word social was given numerous interpretations. Stressed Zuken, "We had a sense of humour. It wasn't all dull, heavy pretentious stuff." The evenings of social significance were in reality beer and skit nights, where scenes and recitations were put together to satirize local events — and the pretences of the theatre company itself. As Sybil Cherniack recounted, Joe Zuken was often at the centre of this merrymaking: "The curtain parted and Joe Zuken was sitting on the back of an upright piano. He was not very well dressed, and there was a big announcement from backstage, in a voice as loud as the 'March of Time' used to do: 'Ladies and Gentlemen, the Voice of Labour 1939.' And Joe Zuken then cackled like a chicken and pulled forth an egg. That was very funny. Especially after a few glasses of beer."

As Fred Narvey recalled, it was seen as a sign of maturity for the company to make fun of itself — "Such as when Frances Goffman comes out covered in a robe. And she lets the robe fall and she is standing there covered in a bikini and says, 'Workers of the world, tonight!' Looking back, I think it was terrible, but at the time, we thought it was funny."

The sense of self-satire also comes across in *Three Stage Struck Jennies*, where three young members of the company lament:

> Oh, they fill me on conflict and contact and crisis and climax
> and change and Stanislavsky's development
> Why can't there be
> A chance for me
> In the drama department?

Five years after the Winnipeg police department forced the cancellation of *Eight Men Speak*, Winnipeg's radical drama company achieved national celebrity, this time for a play that was actually produced. The New Theatre entered its production of the one-act play *Rehearsal* in the 1939 Manitoba Drama Festival, and it took first place. In reporting the victory, the *Free Press* twice referred to the work as a "propaganda play." The festival adjudicator, George Skillan, also attempted to put some distance between himself and the New Theatre. According to the press, "He pointed out that in picking the play, his duty was not in connection with politics or religion, but simply had to do with staging and acting."

The victory gave the company the right to compete in the 1939 Dominion Drama Festival in London, Ontario — if the members could afford the trip. At the time, most of the cast were unemployed. Fred Narvey, who had a minor part in the production, recalled, "I don't think anybody had to leave their job to go to the drama festival. Hardly any of us had jobs." Fortunately, John Queen was still the mayor of Winnipeg, and he came up with the funding necessary to send the company down to London.

Rehearsal was a sign of how far left-wing drama had come since the days of *Eight Men Speak*. It was written by Albert Maltz, one of the numerous playwrights who had been attracted to the Communist Party during the Thirties. Maltz would later write a successful wartime novel and move on to Hollywood as a scriptwriter. From there it was a short step to becoming one of the Hollywood Ten, the black-listed writers and directors who were driven out of Hollywood for their political beliefs. *Rehearsal* was directed by a professional, Mercer McLeod, who was a regular radio drama producer with the CBC, and the leads were played by people who were to pursue professional careers in the arts — Gordon Burwash and Frances Goffman.

As with many of the social-content plays of the period, it made a virtue of necessity, using no props or scenery. As the name suggests, it is a play within a play. A group of young actors are rehearsing a play, and according to Zuken, "there is a great deal of trouble getting the young lady who plays the lead into the role." Zuken played a comic part, the frustrated playwright who sees his lines mangled and changed. It turns out the actress is unable to commit herself because she is romantically involved with a labour leader and her mind is preoccupied with a local strike. Implicit in the production was a criticism of the Little Theatre movement of the day and its lack of social commitment. Like *Waiting for Lefty*, the play ends by breaking down the barriers between the cast and audience, urging the audience to make a commitment to social change.

Rehearsal was based on a real incident, the killing of a number of picketing workers during a strike at a Ford Motor Company plant in the United States. This fact only heightened the tension at the Drama Festival in London, which was the Canadian headquarters for Ford. According to Zuken, the festival organizers were a little concerned about the contingent coming from Winnipeg. "They were expecting that we would come down with flags furled and singing the 'Internationale.' " For their part, the New Theatre cast members were apprehensive about the reception they would receive. Sybil Cherniack recalled that while the other participants were being put up in private homes, they were going to stay at a hotel because people "were afraid of these Communists."

Much to the cast's surprise, the New Theatre won the prize for the best one-act play in the English language. Said Sybil Cherniack, "There were three one-act plays in London and we were on first. We came into the audience after we had taken off our make-up and changed out of our costumes and they were still applauding. There were many bravos and people were standing up. It was an experience for them; they had never seen anything like it." Zuken was the company's president that year, and he took full advantage of the opportunity to deliver himself of a political speech when he came to accept the prize. "I made the dire prediction that this would be the last Dominion Drama Festival for a long time because Hitler was loose in Europe. Unfortunately the prediction was right on."

Zuken's gloom did not cast a pall over the company's victory celebration, or its brief ascent into the world of the London establishment. The cast was invited to celebrate the victory at the home of a local judge. Narvey said the indigent cast members lost no time stocking up on the cigarettes displayed at the doorway. "One at a time we came along and shook hands with the judge. When he came to Joe, he said, 'You were pretty damn good, you little Communist.' "

Ironically, the play's success led to the New Theatre's only major labour problem — not with performers, but with the playwright. Zuken said, "We were naive, or penniless, or both. But one day I got a letter from a lawyer, and the lawyer turned out to be Sam Freedman, who later became the provincial chief justice. Sam was very merciful and made no accusations. In a very gentle way he said, 'You know the author is entitled to be paid some royalties.' And finally we settled it over a period of time."

Volpone

Max Glandbard's most venturesome and successful production was the February 1940 performance of Ben Jonson's *Volpone,* which featured Zuken in the title role and Saul Cherniack as Mosca. Zuken recalled Cherniack's performance as magnificent. In discussing the production, both men stressed that the play, which is a condemnation of human avarice, dealt with enduring and contemporary issues. Recalled Cherniack, "You can find people like that in today's society. It was a very progressive play. And all reports were that we did it very well."

It was indeed very well received. Writing in the *Free Press,* Frank Morriss noted that the "Winnipeg New Theatre took a stride forward in its enterprising career when it presented a modern adaptation of Ben Jonson's *Volpone.* The production had a glitter, bite and a very real understanding of the robust treatment Jonson's comedy needs. Director Max Glandbard has pointed up the action with satirical jests and seen to it that characterizations are given with broad strokes."

In the show's program Glandbard explained that the production was meant as an answer to those critics of the New Theatre who "complained that its choice of plays were limited and chosen for social bias, rather than their own worth. The New Theatre has consistently claimed that it was interested primarily in good plays, preferring those which combined good writing with an intelligent appraisal of society. The production of *Volpone* is a vindication of this claim." For the Winnipeg production Glandbard had abandoned Jonson's blank verse, whose "artificial tone was foreign to our time," in favour of a contemporary script.

The German-Soviet non-aggression treaty and the outbreak of the Second World War threw the New Theatre into a state of confusion. While the theatre had long been warning of the dangers of fascism and raising concerns about the gathering storm, when war came, the Canadian Communists, though initially supportive, followed the line laid down in Moscow and opposed the war effort. Many people left the party over the issue, while those who were not Communists found themselves at bitter odds with fellow theatre members.

In the spring of 1940, however, with both Communists and non-Communists, the company was able to mount three one-act plays: Bertolt Brecht's *The Informer*, Ben Bengal's *Plant in the Sun* and James Macauley's *Lo! The People* — the latter a dramatization of the trial of Sacco and Vanzetti, two American anarchists who were executed by the American government in 1927 on what many observers believed to be trumped-up murder charges. In his program notes for this production, Glandbard took the opportunity to comment on the relationship between art and propaganda. In the past, he said, the New Theatre had been accused of using propaganda to distort truth and reality, but the outbreak of war had brought about a change in the company's critics. "It seems that these true lovers of art have left the citadel of vacuous purity and now strain every sinew for the new 'cause' [the war effort].... How can these people who criticized our work in the past as propaganda, carry on their present activities without misgivings?" The only lesson to be drawn from this turn of events, Glandbard concluded, was "if the other fellow doesn't say what you believe, then he is a propagandist."

The theatre's fortunes began to rebound in 1941, when, following Hitler's invasion of the Soviet Union, Communists were able to commit themselves whole-heartedly to the war. It is fitting that the company's last major production in the spring of 1942 was Friedrich Wolf's *Professor Mamlock*, the story of a Jewish surgeon driven to suicide following Hitler's rise to power. An attack on fascism, it outlines the extent of Nazi racial persecution. Prominent in the cast were future Manitoba attorney general Roland Penner and Leon Mitchell, who helped organize Winnipeg civic workers and went on to become a prominent labour lawyer. The Winnipeg productions were used to raise money for prisoners of war in Hong Kong. In his review, Frank Morriss called *Professor Mamlock* one of the New Theatre's finest efforts. "It proves," he wrote, "that a propaganda play does not have to be blind in one eye."

The political pressures within the company took a new form. Where once the Communists were critics of the war, now they claimed the Allies were not fighting hard enough. The Cherniacks felt that the CP was forcing the company to toe the party line. "What we objected to was that they [the Young Communist League] were holding meetings before and after our [New Theatre] meetings in order to review our decisions. When I was told our meetings were being discussed by the Young Communist League, I was resentful because I felt differences could be discussed openly."

Zuken's personal involvement in the New Theatre started to decline in the summer of 1940. The federal government had begun to intern dozens of Communists and left-wing activists. As their lawyer, Zuken soon found himself at centre stage in a real-life drama involving the suppression of civil rights, one that far overshadowed the cancelling of one production of one play. He was up against the powers of the War Measures Act.

FOUR

The Defence of Canada
1940-1942

On the morning of July 6, 1940, a loud knock at the door woke the family of Andrew Bilecki, a Communist member of the Winnipeg School Board and the manager of the People's Co-operative Dairy. A Winnipeg police officer stood at the front door. There was another officer at the backdoor and a third policeman watching from the street. "One man came in and told me I was under arrest. My older daughter, who was six, woke up. I said goodbye to her, lightly kissed my youngest daughter, who was still sleeping, and left."

On that July morning, dozens of Winnipeg police officers were engaged in a series of raids across the city. Over twenty leading members of the Communist Party were taken into custody. Most of them were soon to be whisked off to a camp in Kananaskis, Alberta, where they were interned with German prisoners of war and Canadian fascists. These men were to be held without trial for over two years.

The raids marked the beginning of the Canadian government's latest "death blow" aimed at the Communist Party. The party was outlawed, its papers were shut down, and its leaders either arrested or driven underground. Until the Nazi invasion of the Soviet Union on June 22, 1941, the party reeled under a relentless legal onslaught. It was a period of mass arrests and mass trials. For Joe Zuken, a young lawyer at the start of his career, it was a baptism by fire.

It was only as the Depression was drawing to an end that Joe Zuken had finally decided to go into private practice. He bought some cheap furniture and hired a secretary — it was difficult to say who was more frightened of whom — and opened an office in the Confederation Building, which was, as he put it, "crawling with lawyers." He set himself some high standards. "I would try to practise law with a social conscience. I would try to see if I could do so without being pushed around. I would decide what sort of case I would handle and be very tough on ethics. I would regard it not as a cash register or a business. As long as I could pay my rent and pay my secretary, I could somehow get by. I was afraid clients wouldn't come. And if they did, what was I to tell them? How was I to help them?" The government soon provided him with plenty of clients.

The official reason for the government crackdown was the Communist Party's opposition to the war effort. Actually, when war was declared in September 1939, the CP was one of the first organizations to rally in support of a conflict it had long been predicting. The *Mid-West Clarion*, the party paper in Western Canada, trumpeted, "This is OUR war, workers and farmers of Canada! Close ranks in invincible unity of the entire nation for the defeat of Hitler." William Kardash, a party member and a veteran of the Mackenzie-Papineau Battalion, wrote to the commander of Military District 10 (Manitoba), "offering to join in an expeditionary force to fight once again to preserve world democracy and peace."

Since the mid-Thirties, Communists had been sounding the tocsin about the dangers of fascism. In 1934 the Canadian party had organized the Canadian Congress Against War and Fascism and had managed to attract a number of prominent non-Communists as conference participants. The conference gave birth to other important organizations in the Thirties, including the Canadian Youth Congress and the Canadian Committee to Aid Spanish Democracy. And Communists were well represented in the Mackenzie-Papineau Battalion, which they helped organize and send to fight on behalf of the Spanish Republic.

Fascism was not merely a European problem. On September 23, 1933, at a Winnipeg meeting hall decorated with Union Jacks, William Whittaker, a retired British army officer, stepped forward to address the first public meeting of the Canadian Nationalist Party. He and his followers were dressed in khaki shirts, light brown riding pants, and boots. Whittaker announced the party intended to fight communism "tooth and nail," but the party paper was soon retailing the anti-Semitism that characterized fascism.

Communists often attended, and attempted to disrupt, Nationalist Party meetings. The most famous of these encounters was the 1934 "Battle for Market Square." Whittaker's decision to hold a fascist rally on June 5 in the square — long the home turf of a variety of left-wing speakers — was a deliberate provocation. The local Communists made sure their supporters were there in number. A *Free Press* reporter gave this description of the affair: "Knives flashed in the fast-waning sunlight, heavy clubs crashed against cap-protected skulls, and huge slabs of wood were torn from the stalls of the market gardeners and used as battering rams against the tightly pressed wall of snarling humanity."

Among those present in the Market Square that day was Bill Ross: "They came marching down William Avenue in their brown shirts and swastikas and leggings and they were going to plant their flag on the square. They sure beat a hasty retreat. It was a good healthy reaction on the part of the workers. Because they did not buy the argument that the fascists have the same right as the workers to speak from the square. They recognized that fascism was a threat to workers and a threat to all others who were in opposition to a fascist dictatorship. After that the Whittaker organization went into a decline. There were still remnants, but their public role was cut down to size."

Communists and CCFers in Winnipeg's Jewish community overcame long-standing differences to battle the rising tide of local anti-Semitism. After J. Alter Cherniack attracted a degree of public attention by attending an anti-Semitic lecture and asking the audience to leave, he was visited by a number of local Jewish Communists. According to Cherniack, they "suggested we work together to organize an anti-fascist league." The League to Combat Fascism and Anti-Semitism issued newsletters and distributed labels urging people to boycott German-made goods. It also organized a number of successful public meetings.

The Communist Party dropped its initial support for the war when on September 18, 1939, Stalin, through the office of the Comintern, issued a startling directive. "The present war," he wrote, "is an imperialist and unjust war for which the bourgeoisie of all the belligerent States bear equal responsibility. In no country can the Communist Parties or the working class support the war." These orders were the logical conclusion of the non-aggression pact that the Soviet and German governments had concluded on August 22, 1939. By September 20, 1939, the Canadian Communist Party had a new slogan: "Withdraw Canada from the War!" For the next two years opposition to the war — and the capitalists who were profiting from it — was at the centre of the party's platform; one party pamphlet suggested people might enlist in the army, but only with the aim of helping to turn "the war into a civil war against the bourgeoisie."

In 1982 Zuken wrote the introduction to *Dangerous Patriots,* an oral history of the Communists who were interned during the war. In it he argued that for the Soviet Union the non-aggression treaty was "an act of desperation to gain time to build up its own military strength for the expected Nazi invasion." He also suggested that the Canadian Communist Party dropped its initial support of the war because "the western powers sat back and made no effort to fight."

In a subsequent interview Zuken said he had been "shocked" when he heard of the Hitler-Stalin pact. "I remember talking to some people who were working in the shops, and they had to go through hell the day after the news broke." He said that because he was not a CPC member in 1939, he was not called upon to publicly defend the pact — "And perhaps it is good for me that I was never called upon to defend it; I would have had a most difficult time."

The Defence of Canada Regulations
Rather than defending the Russia-Germany non-aggression treaty, Zuken was to spend the next three years battling on behalf of left-wingers who ran afoul of the Defence of Canada Regulations — a draconian assault on civil and political liberties that the federal government had promulgated under the authority of the War Measures Act.

That act, passed in August 1914 at the start of the First World War, provided the government with almost unlimited powers. Cabinet was empowered with the authority "to do and authorise such acts and things, and to make from time to time, such orders and regulations, as [it] may by reason of real or apprehended war, invasion or insurrection, deem necessary or advisable for the security, defence, peace, order and welfare of Canada." It was a blank cheque; the House of Commons did not even have the right to review the orders or regulations that were issued under the act.

On September 3, 1939, on the advice of an interdepartmental committee, the King government declared the Defence of Canada Regulations. These sixty-four regulations gave the government the power to intern without trial, to ban political and religious organizations, to seize property and to severely abridge freedom of the press. Historian Ramsay Cook called them "the most serious restrictions upon the civil liberties of Canadians since Confederation."

The most sweeping and dangerous provision was Regulation 21. It allowed the federal justice minister to order the internment of anyone who might act "in any manner prejudicial to the public safety or the safety of the state." There was no provision for either the right to trial or habeas corpus. For governments this was a highly convenient regulation, and it remained in force until the war's end. Over 1,200 people were interned under its provisions.

Regulation 39 was little more than a frontal assault on freedom of speech and freedom of association. It prohibited statements liable to be "prejudicial to the safety of the state or to the efficient prosecution of the war." It was amended in 1940 to proscribe sixteen organizations, including the Communist, Nazi and Fascist parties. The following year, groups as disparate as the Jehovah's Witnesses and Technocracy Incorporated were added to the list. The regulations allowed for a very broad interpretation of what constituted membership in one of these banned organizations: "in the absence of proof to the contrary," attending a meeting, publicly supporting the cause of an illegal organization or distributing the organization's literature was taken as proof of membership. In other words, guilt by association was the rule and the presumption of innocence a thing of the past.

While the justice minister had the right to intern anyone for as long as he wanted without trial, there were provisions in the regulations for courtroom prosecutions. However, once the accused found themselves in court, the proceedings were stacked against them. Usually the accused are allowed to choose between trial by jury or a trial before a judge; under the Defence of Canada Regulations, it was the provincial attorney general who made the decision. In most cases attorneys general declined to put these cases before a jury. According to Zuken, only twice had the Manitoba attorney general authorized such trials and "in both those cases, the accused were arrested on their way to a jury trial and interned. That is the closest any accused has ever got to a jury trial under the regulations."

These then were the regulations. What was their impact? After two years of defending people charged or interned under them, Zuken delivered a lengthy speech to the National Council for Democratic Rights in Ottawa. He pointed out that regulations and restrictions in wartime were nothing new:

> However this merely adds to the argument that as a democracy, and a young democracy at that, Canada should be exceedingly careful in the regulations which it imposes on the people and how this democracy is or is not limited, because not only do these Regulations affect the civil liberties and lives of the Canadian people, but they may distort and stunt the institutions of democracy.

He maintained that the regulations "contain in themselves the germs of future and greater oppression."

> Perhaps the most astounding feature is that there has been throughout this country so little public discussion of the Regulations under which we live, and this is to be particularly regretted in Manitoba, because of all provinces Manitoba has the doubtful distinction in that more people have been interned in this province under the Regulations than in any other province, and that Manitoba

has witnessed the first example of a mass trial under these Regulations.

Having ceded that wartime required certain limitations on communications to prevent espionage and sabotage, he said, "no war-period, particularly when this war effort is conducted for the sake of democracy, is sufficient excuse for regimentation insofar as civil liberties are concerned." And he pointed out that in none of the left-wing cases involving the Defence of Canada Regulations had there been any evidence of sabotage or espionage.

He also suggested that the regulations fostered the use of informers and spies. "The foreign born sections of the population may be terrorized by the exercise of repressive measures. What is to prevent petty animosities and personal hatreds and political hatreds [from] being used in order to inform on certain people and remove them from the community?"

Under the regulations, the police "have set themselves up as constituted censors and literary critics." Not only were the police seizing books, he said, but they "have sometimes gone so far as to demand explanations why people read certain literature." This power was, in his opinion, carried to extremes: "We hear of books being seized, books innocent in themselves, seized simply because they happen to be written in a foreign language." He said this was a true reflection of the spirit of the regulations, since "in the eyes of the police anything that is foreign may well become synonymous with subversive." A list of such dangerous books included *The Official Proceedings of the Trades and Labour Congress in Canada*, a novel by Maxim Gorky, a book opposing Japanese fascism, a brochure distributed by the Winnipeg Committee in Defense of Spanish Democracy, Sidney and Beatrice Webb's *Soviet Communism — A New Civilization* and the official *History of the Communist Party of the Soviet Union*. Derisively Zuken speculated: "If it would ever occur to the people conducting the searches to walk into the public library, they might find to their amazement that the public library is well stocked with what the authorities choose to call 'subversive literature.'"

But it was Regulation 21 that drew Zuken's strongest fire, the section allowing the federal minister of justice to order the arrest and internment of anyone he felt to be a danger to society. "Section 21 does not defend Canada but actually puts Canada along the road to totalitarian control.... In fact under these regulations he [the federal justice minister] can do almost anything except 'change a man into a woman and a woman into a man.' "

He noted there was an appeal process designed to alleviate the harshness of Regulation 21. However, aliens were denied appeal, and he said the process in reality was "pretty much of a farce" — he later described it as "trial by file." Internees never received the particulars of the charges against them — they were simply told that information had been received that they were a member of this or that illegal organization. In such a case, all the internees could do was deny the charge: they could not dispute the specific evidence because it remained unknown to them. Zuken summarized the procedure as being one where the crown says, "We know that you are guilty and we have the evidence in this file to prove that you are. Now we won't tell you what evidence we have, but you go ahead and convince us that you are innocent." And even in cases where the advisory committee recommended that people be released, its decision could be, and on occasion was, overturned by the justice minister.

The regulations could, he feared, be used in the shaping of postwar policies. "Much," he wrote, "is being said and written these days about the new world order. This new world order is being determined by events of today and tomorrow. There are powerful forces in Canada today who are most interested that this new world order should actually be a maintenance of their present private vested interests."

He was particularly disturbed by the lack of national opposition to the regulations "because obviously if democracy is smashed at home today, democracy will be smashed for today and tomorrow, and unless reconstruction begins in our local and national life and takes place continually, it will lack the atmosphere and the prerequisites necessary for a sane social construction." He saw no value in making amendments to the regulations, for in his opinion they were irredeemable.

It is a fundamental question of recognizing that this battle at home for democracy is a decisive and important one, and that while no air-raids are taking place in Canada, raids and attacks are taking place on democratic institutions and on the leadership and organizational strengths of the working class. It would seem that the reactionary forces in Canada are certainly conducting a war on all fronts.

Zuken always maintained that the government used the Defence of Canada Regulations to settle long-standing scores with the the left-wing movement. "The war gave them the opportunity and the Defence of Canada Regulations gave them the instrument to settle that score." The regulations were, he felt, a continuation of the policies the government had pursued during the Thirties and would continue to pursue after the war itself ended.

On this, the facts bear him out. In the days prior to the Nazi-Soviet pact, RCMP officials paid far more attention to Communists than to domestic fascists. Senior liberal-minded government officials, like Norman Robertson, found themselves waging a lengthy battle to get the police to to focus their undercover work on the various pro-fascist organizations in the country. The head of the RCMP Intelligence Section, Charles Rivett-Carnac, saw communism as a much greater threat than fascism, since the latter did not involve the "overthrow of the present economic order." As late as 1939 he was arguing that fascism was simply a middle-class reaction to the threat of communism. Even before the war broke out, Rivett-Carnac was making plans for the mass detention of Communist Party officials. During the war, 133 Communists were interned by the federal government.

The Crackdown

Even before the Communist Party was officially outlawed, Zuken found himself defending people who were being prosecuted under the Defence of Canada Regulations. In February 1940 two young men, Anthony Leniew and John Kurba, were arrested and charged with distributing a pamphlet deemed likely "to be prejudicial to the efficient prosecution of the war." They were the first Manitobans to be charged under the Defence of Canada Regulations. And they were in all likelihood the luckiest. Zuken took on their case and was able to win them an acquittal because the prosecution witnesses could not make positive identifications.

The assault on the party did not begin in earnest until after June 6, 1940, when, following the fall of France, it was outlawed by the federal government. Five days later Jacob Penner, a member of the Winnipeg City Council for the past seven years, was arrested. The papers announced that other leading Communists, among them James Litterick, who had been elected to the Manitoba legislature in 1936, had gone underground. On July 6, nineteen leading Communists, including Andrew Bilecki, were arrested. Three days later the papers were able to report that, without any court appearances, all nineteen were on their way to Kananaskis. It was left to the families and friends of the interned men to pick up the pieces. Jacob Penner's son Norman, Joe Zuken and alderman Joe Forkin were instrumental in founding the Committee to Release the Labour Prisoners.

Zuken recommended that the committee challenge the legality of Penner's internment. Saul Greenberg, who had handled many cases for the Canadian Labor Defense League during the Thirties, took on the job. He soon discovered just how broad the powers of the War Measures Act were. Greenberg argued in court that while the regulations permitted the justice minister to order internments, he could not intern Penner simply because he was a Communist. The internments, Greenberg claimed, had to be preceded by individual investigations. The crown, however, successfully made the case that an order given under the War Measures Act was beyond the review of the courts.

The committee hired E. J. McMurray to defend William Kardash. At the trial McMurray lectured the court on Kardash's accomplishments during the Spanish Civil War, concluding, "You ought to take your hat off before this man. He fought against fascism before you ever heard the word or knew there was such a thing." Kardash was one of the few leading Communists acquitted of charges under the Defence of Canada Regulations who was not subsequently interned.

The Zailig Case

The fall of 1940 saw another round of raids and arrests. Zuken referred to this as the period of the mass trials. Although there were no formal group trials, the courts and the jails were crammed with Communists and alleged Communists. And their trials took place in rapid order. On October 24, 1940, for example, a dozen people appeared before Magistrate R. B. Graham in the city police court on Rupert Avenue. They included some big and some little fish — the biggest was Tom McEwen, a member of the Canadian Communist Party's national executive; the smallest were a number of young men who had been nabbed with a few party pamphlets in their pockets.

These cases were handled largely by Zuken, McMurray and Harry Walsh. McMurray had developed his reputation as a civil libertarian twenty years earlier when he defended many of the leaders of the Winnipeg General Strike. This reputation served him well, and in 1921 he successfully contested the North Winnipeg federal riding for the Liberal Party. He was made solicitor general in the King government but only served one term. After his return to private practice, McMurray concentrated on criminal law and became one of the leading criminal lawyers in the country. During the Thirties a young law student, Harry Walsh, joined his firm. Walsh, later to emerge as one of the country's best-known criminal lawyers, played a key role in the Defence of Canada cases. According to Zuken, it was Walsh who "found the smoking gun" that led to the overturning of a number of convictions for distributing subversive literature.

The attitudes of the judges and the harshness of the regulations severely restricted the effectiveness a defence lawyer could have. Zuken, Walsh and McMurray found themselves regularly pointing out that there was no conclusive evidence proving their clients were CP members, that being at a meeting was not proof of membership, and simple possession of a book or pamphlet was not sufficient evidence to warrant a conviction. Zuken and Walsh both recalled Magistrate Graham making the comment that when it came to charges based on the Defence of Canada Regulations, he forgot all about the principle of reasonable doubt.

Graham's zeal in convicting and sentencing Communists was to bring him to grief. On November 13, 1940, Abraham Zailig was convicted on charges of possessing subversive literature. Graham handed down a sentence of twelve months with hard labour. Norman Penner recalled being in McMurray's office the following day: "He called in Walsh and told him to sit up all night and find out what was wrong with this judgement. And he came in the next morning with sixteen flaws." The first flaw was sufficient. Graham had exceeded his authority; there was no provision for hard labour in the Defence of Canada Regulations. McMurray took the case to the Court of King's Bench where he got a sympathetic hearing from Judge W. J. Donovan. Donovan was so angered by the illegal sentence that on November 28, 1940, he quashed the conviction and set Zailig free.

The Bass, Bilinsky and Corley Cases

The decision in the Zailig case provided Zuken with the opening he needed to have a number of other convictions overturned. In the process, Zuken discovered the illegal measures that court officials, including magistrates and prison governors, were prepared to take to prevent suspected Communists from being released.

In October 1940 the Winnipeg police searched the Young Street home of Alfred Bass, an unemployed railway worker. They found a number of scraps of paper, including a newspaper clipping from — according to court records — the *Saturday Night Financial Post*, in a suit of clothing hanging in the closet. A number of leaflets were located stuffed in between the sofa cushions. The officers also searched the upstairs apartment, which was rented out to two leading CP members, Tom McEwen and Mitch Sago. There they seized several cartons of papers and a typewriter. Bass was arrested, charged with continued membership in the Communist Party and had his bail set at the then astronomical sum of $10,000. Zuken intervened on this point and convinced the magistrate to let Bass free on his own recognizance.

When Bass was brought before a magistrate, the main evidence against him was two receipts he had initialled and given to Sago, the pamphlets found in his suite and the documents taken from Sago's suite, none of which gave any direct indication that Bass was a CP member. However, during the course of his trial, Bass gave evidence contradicting statements he had made during the trial of Mitch Sago. At the Sago trial he denied having signed the receipts, but this time he acknowledged initialling them. In a memorandum written after the trial, Zuken said, "In our opinion the Crown actually failed to establish the case and it was only Bass' shifty manner of giving evidence and the fact that he foolishly contradicted himself on certain points which were actually not fundamental to the issue, that led to his conviction."

This opinion was reinforced by the judge's decision. Magistrate R. B. Graham said, "His whole attitude in the witness box, coupled with the admitted falseness of his statement with regards to the receipts, compels me to take his story that he was not or did not continue to be a member of the Communist Party for what it is worth, which is nothing. I am convicting." Bass was sentenced to a year in jail.

On October 18, 1940, the Winnipeg police searched the North End home of Michael Bilinsky. In a clothes cupboard they found copies of CP publications, some dating from the fall of 1940. The officers also found a pamphlet written by Bill Ross entitled *Fight for Your Civil Rights* and a number of other Communist booklets. After conducting the raid, the officers proceeded to the Main Street barbershop where Bilinsky worked and arrested him.

Bilinsky was charged with continued membership in the party and distributing banned literature. At his hearing Bilinsky said he was given all of the literature by a man he did not know while he was making his way home from work a few days before his arrest. He denied party membership and even denied having read any of the literature. The crown produced evidence indicating that Bilinsky's named appeared on a list of "literature agents" kept by a local CP leader. On the basis of this evidence Bilinsky was sentenced to a year in jail.

Also in October 1940 the Winnipeg police raided the North End home of Angus and Amy Corley. Among the things they seized were twenty-eight sealed and addressed envelopes. Each contained a letter attacking the government war effort and a copy of the *Manitoba Farmer*, a CP publication. Amy Corley told the police the letters might belong to her daughter, Ida. The police returned the next day and arrested Ida. Bail for this young woman, who had never been in trouble with the law before, was set at $10,000. Eventually her parents and her brother James were also arrested under the Defence of Canada Regulations.

Zuken represented Ida Corley in court on November 8, 1940. She was charged with continued membership in the Communist Party and having in her possession literature that was detrimental to the war effort. She denied ownership of the envelopes, but she did admit to bringing them into the house. She said they were given to her by Margaret Mills, a local CP member. She said that Mills was ill and had asked her to address the envelopes and mail them for her. Corley denied ever being a member of the CP, or being on party salary. Beyond the fact that she had addressed the envelopes, the only evidence presented by the crown was the fact that her name and address appeared on a number of party lists that had been seized by the police. After thinking on the case over night, the magistrate convicted Corley and sentenced her to a year in jail.

In all three cases, Magistrate Graham had meted out the stiffest possible sentence allowed under the Defence of Canada Regulations. But when he prepared the actual warrants of commitment, the documents that accompany a convicted person to prison, he went one step further and added the phrase "at hard labour" to the sentence. This was exactly the same thing he had done in the Zailig case.

McMurray and Zuken decided to use the Zailig appeal as a test case. Before the Zailig decision came down, Zuken had conducted a search of the court records in the Bass, Bilinsky and Corley cases and confirmed that all of them had hard labour included in their sentence. The Zailig decision threw the magistrate's court into a frenzy. On December 2, 1940, the clerk of the Winnipeg Police Court wrote the governor of Headingley Gaol, providing him with a new warrant of commitment. The clerk wrote, "You will note that the provision for hard labour has been struck out."

Two days later Zuken asked the clerk for all the documentation in the Bilinsky, Corley and Bass cases. The clerk said it was all in the hands of the crown attorney. When Zuken was finally able to examine it, he noted "a very suspicious fact," namely, that the sentences had been tampered with and that the provisions for hard labour had all been stroked out. Zuken and McMurray went to Headlingley to examine the warrants of committal there. Zuken wrote at the time that the "warrants simply confirmed my original suspicion because although they were dated November 13th and November 8th, 1940, respectively, they appeared to be too new to be authentic and had all the earmarks of being freshly typewritten."

McMurray then telephoned Graham and asked if he had been substituting warrants in these cases. According to McMurray, Graham admitted this is what had happened, but he said he did not know what had become of the original warrants. After Zuken and McMurray brought this information to the crown's attention, the attorney general's department furnished the two lawyers with a copy of the December 2, 1940, letter in which the police court official asked that the warrants be substituted.

It was clear the substitute warrants had been issued following the decision in the Zailig appeal and were an effort to make sure that Bilinsky, Bass and Corley were not released on what the magistrate apparently viewed as technicalities. In a letter outlining these cases, Zuken wrote, "Had I not made a search of the court records before the Zailig decision was given and compared this information with what appeared on the Court records searched by me after the Zailig decision, the deception would not have been discovered."

As a result, Zuken and McMurray filed a motion calling for a quashing of Bilinsky's conviction. In the motion they argued that not only had the crown failed to prove a case against Bilinsky but that in open court Magistrate Graham had sentenced Bilinsky to a year and then in his chambers had added the hard labour provision. Graham had further compounded this by deleting the hard labour provision without dating the changes to the warrant of committal. The lawyers claimed the conviction was "void for duplicity and multifariousness."

When the case came to the Court of King's Bench, Bilinsky was represented by McMurray and Walsh. Justice Donovan upheld the motion and quashed the conviction. In his decision the judge wrote, "I have assumed the magistrate's motive was to a predominant degree to see that a person who he believed to be guilty should suffer the full penalty imposed on him. In doing that he apparently gave no heed to the illegal commitment."

But the decision did not bring much pleasure to Bilinsky (or to Bass and Corley), since it was made on June 12, 1941 — after they had served most of their sentences. During that period both Bilinsky and Bass wrote Zuken a number of letters complaining about the length of time it was taking to get the case heard. On April 30, 1941, Bilinsky wrote Zuken to express his dismay, pointing out that he had now served more than half of the original twelve-month sentence. He wrote that "my sentence is an absolute disgrace on the basis of the evidence upon which it was made, this is even more doubly true in view of the fact that my wife will be confined in child-birth almost immediately, and the whole burden of my imprisonment to suffer as well, since circumstances prevent me from giving her the assistance and comfort that common decency prompts." The three were released following the judge's decision in the summer of 1941. (Zuken billed the Defence Committee a total of ninety dollars for handling all three cases.)

The Sago and McEwen Cases
At least it could be said that Bilinsky, Bass and Corley were freed once their convictions had been quashed. The events surrounding the case of Mitch Sago and Tom McEwen were more sinister and disturbing.

On October 22, 1940, police apprehended both Sago and McEwen in a raid on Alfred Bass's home. McEwen, the man who had helped recruit Cecil Zuken into the Communist Party eleven years earlier, was charged with continued party membership and publishing a subversive newspaper. Sago, who was one of the party's leaders in the Ukrainian community, was brought up on similar charges. Zuken was called to the North End police station where the two men were being held. "I had never personally met Tom McEwen before. I walked in and there was a man with a rather fierce moustache and a military bearing. For the first ten or fifteen minutes we sparred until we established that he was really Tom McEwen and I satisfied him that I was Joe Zuken the lawyer."

Sago and McEwen made their first appearance in court on October 24, 1940. The crown opposed bail for the men. In the case of Sago, the magistrate agreed, and in setting McEwen's bail at $20,000, he was virtually refusing bail. The case went to trial on November 7, 1940, and concluded the following day. Both men were convicted for their participation in the publication of *Manitoba Worker*, a party newspaper. McEwen pleaded not guilty to continued membership in the Communist Party, but according to a letter Zuken wrote at the time, McEwen made a lengthy statement "in which he dealt with his record in the labor movement and justified his right to belong to the Communist Party."

As in the other cases at the time, McEwen and Sago were sentenced to a year in jail, and once again Graham added hard labour to the sentence. They continued to serve their sentence while the lawyers dealt with the Zailig and related cases. On July 28, 1941, Zuken went to Headingley Gaol and asked the turnkey to show him the warrants of commitment for Sago and McEwen. He was shown warrants that had the phrase "with hard labour" stroked out. When he asked the turnkey if there had been a substitution, he was told no, these were the original warrants. Zuken then went through the police court files and found copies of Graham's letters of December 1940 requesting that the original warrants in the McEwen and Sago cases be returned and new ones, with no provision for hard labour, be substituted. Armed with this, he confronted the governor of the jail, who admitted that there had indeed been a substitution and that the same thing had occurred in other cases.

With this information as support, Zuken and Walsh launched a motion of habeas corpus on behalf of Sago and McEwen. When the case came up before the judge for the first time on September 5, 1941, half a dozen RCMP officers in the judge's chambers were ready to take action should the judge order the two men's release. But it was not until October 10, 1941, that Judge Donovan brought down his decision. In the judge's chambers that day, along with Walsh and Zuken, the court reporter and the crown attorney, were two members of the Mounted Police. Donovan was unsparing in his criticism of both Magistrate Graham and the prison officials. He wrote that once the men had been delivered to jail, the magistrate had no jurisdiction to amend or substitute the warrants of commitment — even if he had exceeded his jurisdiction in handing down the sentence. The judge wrote, "It seems contrary to the proper administration of justice for the fact of substitution or attempted substitution of warrants to be kept secret from the prisoners affected thereby." What is interesting in this case is that Sago and McEwen had been kept at hard labour even after that provision had been struck from their sentence.

As in the Zailig case, Donovan quashed the conviction and ordered the men released. In concluding his judgement, Donovan made his anger clear by stating that he would not be making the usual order protecting the magistrate or the administration of the jail from any charges of false imprisonment that McEwen and Sago might consider bringing forward.

Zuken's account, recorded in a letter, of what happened next paints a gripping picture:

> Later that afternoon [October 10, 1941] a formal Order of Discharge was drawn and signed by Mr. Justice Donovan and at about four o'clock in the afternoon, Mr. Walsh and I served the Order of Discharge upon the Gaoler at the Detention Home. He took a long time reading the Order and it was obvious he was merely stalling. He drew me aside and he told me that the R.C.M.P. were here. I informed him that I knew that. McEwen and Sago then walked towards the front door of the Gaol. Walsh and I followed. Just before they reached the front door two R.C.M.P. stepped from a room just off the front door and walked ahead of McEwen and Sago. Just outside the Detention Home, one of the R.C.M.P. produced a Detention Order for McEwen and Sago. I examined the Detention Order. McEwen turned to one of the R.C.M.P. and said: "I hope you are proud of what you are doing for Canada today."

Even the *Winnipeg Tribune* found this turn of events troubling. The paper editorialized:

The authorities in charge of the Defense [*sic*] of Canada regulations would do well to consider that they cannot have it both ways except at the risk of creating serious public alarm and inviting a sense of injustice. This procedure of attempting to get convictions in the regular courts reflects the Dominion government's timidity in the handling of one of its most important wartime problems. It is unfair to the courts to use them as a "first resort" and then, if the court's action fails to meet the unrevealed desires of the Defense authorities, make use of the "last resort" of holding for internment a person whom the court has just found not guilty.

Though the *Tribune* editorialist clearly disapproved of what happened in the McEwen and Sago cases, his solution seems to have been to have the government avoid the appearance of unfairness by simply interning all those it suspected without ever making use of the courts. He failed to draw the reasonable conclusion that the real unfairness was not to the courts but to the acquitted men who found themselves back behind bars.

When Sago and McEwen were interned, Zuken launched a court case against the magistrate and the prison authorities, suing them for $20,000 in damages. The case appears to have been dropped when the men were finally released from internment in 1942. During their internment their case was reviewed by a tribunal. According to Zuken, the hearings would usually unfold along these lines: "I would get up and say, 'My name is Joseph Zuken, I am a member of the bar of Manitoba, entitled to practise both as a barrister and as an attorney. I am representing Mr. McEwen and Mr. Sago at this hearing.' I would pause and the chairman of the tribunal would then say, 'Well, we will hear what these men have to say.'

"I would then ask, 'Mr. Chairman, I ask that witnesses be produced, documents produced and tendered as exhibits so that I may have the opportunity to cross-examine the witnesses. I am asking that witnesses be produced to show why these men should have been detained and why they should be detained in the opinion of the minister of justice.'

"There was absolute refusal. I then, as agreed in a previous conference between myself and McEwen and Sago, said, 'I regret very much gentlemen, but we cannot be part of such a hearing. This is not a hearing which protects the rights of Mr. Sago and McEwen. As far as Mr. McEwen, Mr. Sago and myself are concerned, this hearing can be terminated now.' "

In the fall of 1942 McEwen, by then free from detention, wrote Zuken to thank him for the efforts he had taken on his behalf. "I am not forgetful that in the darkest days of this period you had the courage to accept the hard and unpopular task of defending men of my political faith. For this alone I will be forever thankful." In a responding letter Zuken said, "It is I who should be thanking you and your colleagues, whom I defended before the Courts and the Advisory Committees, because my experiences in these Defence of Canada Regulation cases have given me a deeper understanding and hastened my development as a labor lawyer."

The Doukhobors

In the fall of 1940 at the height of the mass trials in Winnipeg, Zuken received a letter from Alexander Sturgeoff, a Saskatchewan Doukhobor. Sturgeoff had been on the editorial board of *Kanadsky Gudok*, a Russian-language publication that had been banned under the Defence of Canada Regulations. Sturgeoff was interested in starting a new magazine and wanted legal advice as to whether the magazine should be registered with the federal government.

Zuken wrote back that there was no need to register the magazine but that since it would in all likelihood come to the eventual attention of the authorities, he might as well send them a copy. In describing the way the federal government enforced the Defence of Canada Regulations, he wrote, "It is impossible to be a prophet in these matters."

It would not take great powers of prophecy, however, to predict that Sturgeoff was going to run afoul of the federal government. The Doukhobors had come to Canada at the turn of the century, having been driven out of Russia, primarily for their refusal to perform military service. The Canadian government of the day, eager for agricultural immigrants, had been quite willing to grant the Doukhobors a permanent exemption from military service. When the King government decided in 1940 to register men for military service, it ran headlong into a conflict with the Doukhobors. Efforts were made to provide a form of service that could not be directly linked to the war effort — mainly road construction. But many Doukhobors opposed the plan, claiming this strategy was intended to draw the Doukhobors into the war effort. In particular, they objected to the fact that it would be compulsory and that, because it was aimed only at twenty-one-year-old men, it could only be seen as an alternative to military service. In their minds, performing the alternative was the same as performing the service.

In his new magazine *Vremia* (Time), Sturgeoff published an article by his cousin Fred Rozansoff criticizing those Doukhobor leaders who advocated cooperation with the War Services Board. "After all," Rozansoff wrote, "what harm will the Doukhobors bring the country if they continue toiling on land, or in other occupations to secure their means of livelihood. Production of grain, production of commodities in factories is not produced at a loss to the country."

This article and the comments made by Sturgeoff, Rozansoff and a third man, Fred Konkin, at a series of public meetings in the spring of 1941 prompted swift official response. All three were arrested and charged with attempting to persuade the Doukhobor community to "resist the operation or enforcement of the National War Services Regulations." The three men were held in jail for a week before bail of $5,000 a piece was granted.

Zuken was hired to act as their lawyer. The trials took place on July 11 and 12, 1941, in the Canadian Legion Hall in Kamsack, Saskatchewan, and was presided over by Magistrate S. H. Potter. Years later Zuken recalled: "When I arrived, the Doukhobors were all lined up. And as I approached, a murmur went through the crowd. I was later told that what they were asking was 'Is he for us or against us?' " The hall was full, and the windows were left open so that those who could not fit into the hall were able to view the proceedings. The men pleaded not guilty to the charges. In an account of the trial Zuken wrote:

> The article complained of in *Vremia* was merely a discussion article of all questions of public discussion amongst the Doukhobors. It was argued by me that at most the article constituted a criticism of certain members of the Doukhobor community and a criticism of the War Services Regulations, but that criticism of the War Services Regulations was not an offence and indeed was vital to a democracy. As an illustration I said that Mr. Hanson, the Conservative leader, in advocating conscription was going much further in criticizing the Regulations and in impeding the enforcement and operations of these Regulations.

The crown was unable to present the slightest evidence against Konkin, and consequently the case against him was dismissed — but not before Magistrate Potter had given him a piece of his mind. He asked Konkin where he came from, but before the man could answer, the judge said, "So you were born in Russia. Why did you come here? Why don't you go back where you came from? If you think you can make a Russia out of Canada, we are going to make things so unpleasant for you that you will want to go back to Russia."

Things did not go as well for Sturgeoff and Rozansoff. They were sentenced to a year in jail and fined $100. When Zuken indicated there would likely be an appeal, Potter said he would immediately write to Ottawa and see to the internment of the men.

The government's victory in court did not appear to have the desired impact on the Doukhobor community. The day after the trial concluded, it was learned that thirteen Doukhobor men had been arrested for failing to register for road work.

As the case developed, Zuken found himself in the strange position of having to recommend that his clients not appeal the conviction or even pay the fine. The appeal would not only be expensive, but Zuken feared that if it were successful, it could end up creating additional problems, since the men would probably be interned upon their release. While additional time would be tacked onto their sentence if they did not pay the fine, an early release might also lead to their internment. And internment could last until the end of the war. The two did not appeal and were released after serving a little less than a year in jail. Zuken's charge for representing the three men was thirty-five dollars, "as low as I could ask and as high as people interested in Sturgeoff's and Rozansoff's cases could pay at the present time."

The Case of Annie Buller et al.

On the evening of February 28, 1941, the Winnipeg police carried out one of their most successful raids of the wartime period. Swooping down on a home in Winnipeg's core area, they captured four leading Communists who had been underground for nearly a year. Caught that evening were Annie Buller, her husband, Harry Guralnick, rail unionist Jock Mc-Neil and Louis Guberman. When the four first appeared in court, bail for McNeil was set at $10,000, at $20,000 for Buller, who had been the business manager of the *Mid-West Clarion*, and at $10,000 for Guralnick, who had been active in the city's anti-fascist movement prior to the war.

Buller had been in hiding for the past year, ever since the other editors of the *Clarion* had been interned. She faced fourteen charges, including continued membership in the Communist Party and publishing statements likely to cause disaffection to His Majesty. The statements at issue were made in two editions of the *Clarion* published in February 1940. The paper supported the Soviet invasion of Finland while denouncing the Canadian war effort.

She was no stranger to conflict or trouble. For over a decade she had been one of the CP's leading figures. She helped organize needle trade workers and had participated in the Bienfait Coalminers' Strike of 1931. In 1933 she was sentenced to a year in prison for the role she played in that strike. According to the *Free Press*, when she made her first court appearance after being arrested in 1941, Buller "sighted someone she knew in the courtroom and gave the Communist salute by holding up her right arm with fist clenched."

Zuken had taken a few public-speaking lessons from Buller when the family lived in Toronto. Now he represented her in magistrate's court. Detective David Nicholson, the head of the Winnipeg police's Red Squad, gave evidence against her, and the ever-obliging Magistrate Graham quickly convicted her on charges of publishing a paper "likely to impede the war effort." But the crown was having difficulty proving any ongoing membership in the CP. Nicholson maintained he had caught the four of them holding a secret meeting of the Communist Party and that a variety of notes found on them were proof of it.

But Graham concurred with Zuken that the documents provided by Nicholson were not evidence of ongoing membership, although he did feel they indicated the meeting was for "furthering the interests of the Communist Party." As the crown's case started to bog down, Graham interrupted the prosecutor: "It seems to me there is an awful lot of beating around the bush in this case." He turned to Buller and asked, "Miss Buller, were you ever a member of the Communist Party?"

Zuken and Buller had prepared for this possibility. He responded on her behalf: "Your worship, my client is prepared to answer that question if you will give her the opportunity to make a statement to the court." Graham agreed, and Buller addressed the court: "I am privileged to be a member of the Communist Party which has defended the best interests of the working people today. It may be illegal or otherwise, but it is a party which will lead the whole Canadian working people to victory and socialism."

The magistrate may have appreciated Buller's candour, but he did not reward her for it. He sentenced her to two years in jail and, in passing sentence, remarked, "I feel this woman is a danger to the country. I have no assurance that she will be interned so I propose to keep her out of circulation as long as possible." When she heard herself described as a danger to the country, Buller reportedly looked at Zuken and laughed.

One of the most revealing exchanges of this whole period took place on May 30, 1941, when, during the trial of Jock McNeil, E. J. McMurray cross-examined Detective Nicholson. The officer indicated that he was very familiar with McNeil's career. He had heard McNeil speak over the radio numerous times on behalf of the CP and had witnessed him addressing at least two May Day rallies in the Market Square. Nicholson was also intimate with McNeil's political career, pointing out that he had made six unsuccessful runs for city council.

McMurray asked Nicholson if he believed that all those people who had been members of the Communist Party at the time of its being banned had continued their membership. The detective replied that "I have not known of one instance where they have been that they are still not continuing." McMurray then asked what the officer meant by Communists, and Nicholson replied, "Do you mean actual members of the party?" When McMurray suggested there could be no other answer, Nicholson said, "No, there are a lot of Communists besides the actual members." In short, in the eyes of the man whose word Magistrate Graham willingly accepted as gospel truth, anyone who was a member of the CP when it was banned was guilty of continued membership in the party unless there was some contrary evidence — although it is difficult to imagine what form that evidence would have had to take. Further, even if someone had not been a party member at the time of the banning, Nicholson thought it was possible that he or she could be guilty of membership in the party. Not surprisingly McNeil was convicted.

The Case of the Talkative Watchmaker
One gets a sense of the extremes to which the government enforced the Defence of Canada Regulations when one examines the case of Boris Sachatoff. He was charged with making comments likely to cause disaffection to His Majesty in the spring of 1941. Born in Tula, Russia, in 1871, Sachatoff came to Canada in 1906 and became a citizen in 1925. He moved to Winnipeg from Saskatchewan in 1940 and opened up a shop as a watchmaker. At the time of his arrest he was sixty-nine years old. His bail was set at $5,000.

The circumstances surrounding the charge are remarkable. In April of 1941 a Winnipeg police officer in civilian clothes visited Sachatoff's shop in order to have his watch repaired. In the course of conversation, Sachatoff complained that he suspected the police would not be successful in arresting whoever had recently robbed his store. From there he decried the general state of society, claiming that Justice Minister Ernest Lapointe was no better than Hitler, since Lapointe was throwing labour leaders in jail without right of counsel. He then worked his way up to the war effort, claiming that "this is an imperialist war." The officer went back a few days later and once more engaged Sachatoff in conversation. This time the watchmaker said that "revolution is the only way to get pure socialism" and "capitalistic people have to be done away with." And he went on to point out that the Canadian army was being "cut to ribbons."

A few weeks later an RCMP officer from the intelligence branch went to the repair shop and conversed with Sachatoff. Sachatoff made a number of negative remarks about Hitler and then offered the officer a copy of the *Canadian Tribune*, the CP's weekly paper. According to the officer, Sachatoff said he bought half a dozen copies of the paper at a time and gave them to his friends. The *Tribune* had been banned under the War Measures Act, but by then the ban had been rescinded. It was after this meeting that he was arrested.

When Sachatoff was put on the stand, he admitted that he had likely criticized Lapointe for interning people without trial, but he denied having compared him with Hitler. On the question of imperialist war, Sachatoff said he believed that Germany's, not Canada's, war program was imperialist. He also pointed out that he was a supporter of the War Savings Drive. As the case proceeded, Sachatoff revealed that he was a former Doukhobor who had split with the organization because of their pacificism. He said, "I could not agree to that. We must fight Hitlerism. And I left because of that." He indicated he was a vegetarian and a follower of the moral teachings of Tolstoy.

He was convicted and sentenced to four months in jail. Zuken appealed the case. In a memorandum prepared for the appeal, Zuken wrote, "No evidence was tendered by the Crown that the accused is in any way connected with a political group or organization, nor is he charged with that." Zuken pointed out that there was no concrete evidence Sachatoff's comments had caused the two police officers to become disaffected with His Majesty. He examined the various comments his client was said to have made, and noted that even if he had compared Lapointe to Hitler, it was not with the intention of causing disaffection. Zuken noted: "Just the other day, Mr.

Hepburn [the premier of Ontario] sent a telegram to Ottawa and it was reported generally in the press throughout Canada that Mr. Hepburn accused Mr. King of Hitler tactics. If this is disaffection, it is certainly disaffection in high places." The appeal was heard on November 7, 1941, and was a mixed victory. The conviction was upheld, but Sachatoff was given a suspended sentence. When Zuken billed for the case, he reduced his estimated fee of one hundred dollars to sixty.

Life in the Underground

Zuken's brother, Bill Ross, was one of the few members of the party's provincial leadership who managed to go underground and escape arrest. When the party was declared illegal, Ross was the secretary of the Young Communist League and a school trustee. Like Bilecki and Penner, he was stripped of his elected position for non-attendance. Over a twenty-eight-month period, from June 1940 to October 1942, Ross lived the life of a political fugitive. During that time he lived in twenty-four different places. The police were convinced he had left the country for Mexico, but he was only out of Manitoba for one brief period. "It was gratifying," he said many years later, "that there were so many people, both party and non-party people, who were prepared to take the chance to afford me accommodation during that period." It was a time of tension and secrecy. "Your public movements were restricted, you did not go out in the day time, you only went out in transportation that was carefully arranged for, you were in touch with other people through couriers, and you were separated from your family."

There were occasions when he and his wife Ann were able to get together. Once when he was hiding in a suburb where he thought there was little chance of anyone recognizing him, they decided to take in a film. Ross had dyed his hair and made a few other changes to his appearance, but still they decided to wait until the show had started to enter the theatre. There was a double bill and it was Ross's intention to leave while the second show was on. To his horror, after the first show the house lights came on for the drawing of a series of door prizes. "Here I was sitting in the middle of the theatre with the lights on. Fortunately no one recognized me and I got away with it."

Another time a car in which he and his wife were travelling through rural Manitoba was stopped by the RCMP. "I said, 'Well, it looks like this is it, boys.' But they were carrying through a safety check of cars; they told us to go into the restaurant in the town and they would check the car."

Throughout the period Ross was underground, he maintained contact with the Workers Election Committee and once managed to travel to Eastern Canada for a party conference. He also appeared at a couple of Manitoba party conferences that were held "under strict and controlled conditions. So that was the way I was able to function. Certainly I was restricted in many ways, but still able to carry on."

One person who was never arrested or interned during this period was Joe Zuken. Although he was not officially a member of the Communist Party during this period, he was certainly identified with the party in the public mind. Once in a courtroom hallway he had a conversation with the Red Squad's Detective Nicholson. The officer told Zuken, "We were looking for your name, Mr. Zuken, but we could not find anything." Zuken simply smiled back and said, "Maybe you did not look well enough."

The Left Ukrainians
In his reminiscences Zuken noted that there appeared to be a deliberate attempt on the part of the authorities to make it appear "that the foreigners were the troublemakers here." The authorities did in fact concentrate much of their attention on the radical Ukrainian community — a third of the Communists interned were of Ukrainian background. Once again it appeared police were using the power of the War Measures Act to crush a centre of radical dissent. In 1939 the Ukrainian Labour-Farmer Temple Association (ULFTA) had 10,000 members and between 200 and 300 branches across the country. There were over 100 temples and over 50,000 people participated in their activities. There is no denying that the CP played a large role in the founding and leadership of the association, but the branches of the association were far more than mere front organizations. Their activities included music, folk dancing, poetry readings and language education.

When the ULFTA was outlawed in June 1940, its leaders attempted to comply with the law. By mid-June the association had boarded up the three labour temples in the city, but within a month the buildings were raided by the police, their contents hauled away and the leaders of the organization interned. As a result, Zuken found himself not only battling to help secure the release of the people arrested or interned, but fighting the federal government for the return of the property confiscated from them. The most significant — and the most successful — of the cases involving the left-wing Ukrainians was that of Michael Ukas.

On February 6, 1941, the Winnipeg police raided the North End home of Michael Ukas, a former organizer with the Ukrainian Labour-Farmer Temple Association. Under the direction of Detective Nicholson, they seized some Ukrainian-language left-wing publications and arrested Ukas. He was charged with possessing, in quantity, a variety of banned publications, continued membership in the Communist Party of Canada and continued membership in the ULFTA. It was the first time the government had claimed that the ULFTA was still operating. Many within the Ukrainian community feared the trial would lead to charges against others who had been active in the ULFTA.

The case came to trial on March 13, 1941, and Zuken was successful in getting Magistrate Graham to drop the charge of "possession in quantity." He argued that while Ukas did indeed possess a quantity of radical literature, except for five copies of one paper he had only single copies of a variety of publications. The crown then entered a stay of proceedings on the question of Ukas's continued membership in the CP, since the only evidence it had of his membership was the publications taken from his residence.

But the crown proceeded with the charge of continued membership in the ULFTA. As evidence it introduced a variety of ULFTA documents which showed that Ukas had enrolled in a ULFTA course in 1938, that he was considered a valued association organizer and that his name appeared on the ULFTA membership list for 1938. In addition, the crown introduced as evidence some handwritten notes dealing with the American, French and German revolutions.

In his cross-examination Zuken was able to establish that the police had no evidence of Ukas paying dues to the ULFTA after 1938 and that in the various searches conducted at the homes of radical Ukrainians they had been unable to find any publications they could link to the ULFTA that had been published after the organization was banned on June 6, 1940. At this point Zuken called for a dismissal of the charges, arguing that "the Crown had not proved that the Ukrainian Labor-Farmer Temple Association continued to exist." Graham denied this motion.

Then Ukas took the stand. He said that he had remained a member of the association up until May 1940, but once the ULFTA had been banned, he felt he ceased to be a member. Since June 1940 he had paid no dues and attended no meetings; as far as he knew there was no longer an organization to pay dues to. The crown attempted to link the CPC and the ULFTA by pointing out that Ukas was in possession of a variety of Communist Party publications at the time of his arrest.

But the key evidence in the crown's case was five handbills that protested the fact that the ULFTA's buildings and presses had been handed over to what were referred to as "pro-fascist elements." The crown also produced a letter written by Ukas protesting the seizure of the ULFTA property — Ukas said he planned on sending the letter to the local newspapers and the *Canadian Tribune*. On the basis of this evidence, Graham reached his judgement quickly and bluntly: "I don't think this organization ceased to exist and I find the accused is still a member and I find him guilty." The sentence was a year in jail.

Zuken immediately announced his intention to appeal. Unless the verdict was overturned, he wrote in a memorandum, "anyone whose name appeared in the membership ledger of the Ukrainian Labor-Farmer Temple Association would be in danger of being arrested and charged with being a continuing member." Bail for Ukas was set at $2,000.

The appeal was heard on December 5, 1941. Appearing before Judge D. A. Stacpoole, Zuken argued that the discovery "of materials in the Ukrainian language in the home of the accused was not proof of the existence of the Ukrainian Labor-Farmer Temple Association." He also pointed out that there had been no evidence produced indicating the association still existed. The judge agreed and quashed the case without even asking the defence to present evidence. During the course of the proceedings, the judge turned to the crown and said that there was nothing wrong with former members of the ULFTA protesting the way the government had seized and disposed of their property. He said that if his property had been treated in the same way, he would be protesting. He said the existence of such protest did not in any way establish the continued existence of the ULFTA, merely the continued existence of its former members. Stacpoole concluded that from what he could see, the evidence suggested that the association had, in fact, ceased to exist.

The Civil Liberties Associations

As Joe Zuken noted, during this period the federal government was able to place severe restrictions upon civil liberties with very little opposition. At the start of the Second World War, there was no national civil liberties organization, although Montreal, Toronto and Vancouver had local organizations. In Winnipeg two United College professors, A. R. M. Lower and David Owen, joined forces with two CCFers, Lloyd Stinson and Alistair Stewart, to write the prime minister in the fall of 1939 to protest the Defence of Canada Regulations. The following year they helped to create the Provisional Committee on Civil Liberties, which prepared a critique of the regulations.

In 1940 the Winnipeg Civil Liberties Association was created. The association did much to publicize the dangers inherent in legislation like the War Measures Act, but its members were leery of being associated with the far left. Association members believed involvement with Communists would be an "embarrassment." In a letter to King, the association boasted that its supporters were "without exception people who do not stand for extreme views of any sort, but on the contrary represent the sober common sense of our community." To protect that image, the association on occasion shied away from protesting the treatment Communists were receiving because the cases involved "extremists" with "ulterior motives." For its part, the RCMP did not appreciate such fine distinctions; police officials wanted to have the civil liberties associations banned as little more than "respectable communist fronts."

The Communist Party formed the National Council for Democratic Rights, which held two conferences, one in Ottawa and one in Toronto. The council was headed by that old war horse of the Canadian Labor Defense League, A. E. Smith. Zuken was the council's Manitoba president and was a featured speaker at its conference in Ottawa. Because it was seen as an arm of the CP, it was not able to attract much public attention to its views.

The *Winnipeg Free Press* made editorial space available to opponents of the regulations. At times the paper expressed concern about the stringency of their application but in the main supported them. In 1941 the paper editorialized: "There does not appear to be much ground for the apprehension that under cover of these regulations Mr. King, suddenly emerging as a Hitler with Mr. Lapointe transformed into a Himmler, will pull the foundations from under the Canadian democratic system." The paper's Ottawa correspondent, Grant Dexter, took the extraordinary position that in time of war "special precautions are needed to safeguard the state. These cannot be provided by the courts because in many cases no evidence exists to warrant detention. Yet the risks are so great that no chances can be taken."

On June 22, 1941, Hitler invaded the Soviet Union, and in the language of Communist Party members, "the character of the war changed." Communists were again 100 per cent behind the war effort. Those party leaders who were underground made it clear the party line had been once more reversed, and many in the federal government were hoping the internment could be ended. Lester Pearson, for example, wondered, "Why should we keep Communists interned when their views toward the war which necessitated such internment must now be changed?" Even so, it took a year before the Communists were freed. Before they could gain release, they were required to swear they would not engage in Communist Party activities or in "any organization over which the party exercised control." A parliamentary committee recommended in 1942 that the ban on the party be lifted, but the government, with the full support of the RCMP, refused to act on the suggestion. The Mounties maintained the ban was important, since Communists still aimed for an "all-out class war for the defeat of Capitalism in Canada." In late 1942 those party members who had gone underground began to surface.

One of the first to do so was Bill Ross. In September 1942 Ross walked into the Communist-Labor Total War Committee headquarters at 980 1/2 Main Street in Winnipeg. Along with party supporters and well-wishers, there were a number of reporters present who had been tipped off that he would be turning himself in to the authorities that day. Ross told reporters, "I am coming out to work publicly. My intentions are to devote all my time and energies to the task of helping win the war. I have only one desire — to serve Canada in whatever capacity I can contribute most to the war."

Ross was briefly interned. He then spent a short spell with his family and enlisted in the army. In this he was followed by many of the Communists who had been interned or forced underground. Joe Zuken also attempted to enlist at this time, but he was rejected for military service by a recruiting officer who was doubtless commenting on both Zuken's 116-pound physique and his unorthodox politics when he said, "Oh, oh, we've got Gandhi from the North End." The War Measures Act crisis, at least for the Communist Party, had come to an end. By then Zuken had begun his career as an elected politician.

FIVE

The School Board Years
1942-1962

On November 27, 1941, Joe Zuken was elected to the Winnipeg School Board. Running as a candidate for the Workers Election Committee, Zuken topped the polls in the North End's Ward Three. No one at the time knew it, but it was the beginning of a forty-two-year political career. Years later Zuken said, "I thought, 'I'll serve a few years and that will be it.' But like *The Man Who Came to Dinner*, it went on and on." He sat on the school board for two decades, years that were witness to a brief renaissance in Communist Party popularity, then the Cold War and the splintering of the Communist movement in the wake of the turbulent events of 1956.

It was during these years that Joe Zuken emerged as a public figure, and his image was a controversial one. To the Winnipeg establishment, Zuken symbolized the Communist threat in its most dangerous incarnation — he was intelligent, quick-witted and industrious. As a result, he came under regular attack both at the board and in the media. He did not shy away from conflict, and few of his political opponents from this period would have thought him shy or introverted. At twenty-eight years of age Zuken was unshakable in his political beliefs and loyalties; for the next four decades those beliefs were often to place him at the centre of public attention.

Zuken's election to the school board, rather than a breakthrough for the Communist Party, was a recapturing of lost ground. From 1933 onward Communists had held public office in Manitoba. When the party was banned in 1940, Joseph Forkin and Jacob Penner were members of the Winnipeg City Council, Zuken's brother Bill Ross and Andrew Bilecki were school trustees, and James Litterick was a member of the provincial legislature. The repression of the early war years wiped out all these gains, as Penner and Bilecki were interned and Ross and Litterick went underground. In the midst of defending the men who had been arrested and interned, Communists found they also had to fight for their right to participate in public life.

In the fall of 1940 Winnipeg City Council revoked Penner's aldermanic standing. On October 9, 1940, the Winnipeg School Board, by a unanimous vote, stripped Andrew Bilecki of his seat on the board. It then passed a resolution calling on the provincial attorney general to ban Communists from running for positions on the board. A week later aldermen C. Rhodes Smith and Garnet Coulter introduced a resolution petitioning the province to ban Communists from seeking election to city council. At the end of the month, Mackenzie King announced that the Defence of Canada Regulations were being amended to prohibit internees from seeking public office.

With the German invasion of the Soviet Union in the summer of 1941, party fortunes began to mend. In the 1941 provincial election William Kardash, in a campaign that was managed by Zuken, won election to the provincial legislature. And by the time the fall 1941 civic elections rolled around, the Communists were able to mount a strong enough campaign to send Zuken to the school board and allow Forkin to once more take his place on city council. In its weekly "Security Bulletin," the RCMP noted, "Another Communist Elected to Office," commenting that "through the indifference of 70 per cent of the 31,000 eligible voters who neglected to use their franchise, Forkin defeated his three opponents, having a majority of 578 in the final count."

In January 1942, Zuken found himself walking across the Salter Bridge to attend his first meeting as a school trustee. Prior to his election he had never attended a school board meeting, but he had strong views on some of the changes he wanted to see made in the public school system. Despite the efforts of the CP and the CCF, in 1942 there were no kindergartens and little vocational training, and the burden of numerous fees for textbooks and examinations fell heavily on working-class families. In looking for a model for reforming the educational system, Zuken would draw heavily on the egalitarian Jewish schools that he had attended and taught in. But first he had to establish himself in the political arena. "When I walked into my first meeting of the Winnipeg School Board, there was nobody else from the Workers Election Committee on the board. I was met with cold but curious stares. People were saying, 'I've heard about this fellow, what is he going to be like?'

"I remember what I said: 'I am very glad to be here. I expect that I am going to try to play a very active role as a school trustee, but I deal with issues and don't get involved with squabbles about personalities. So, we shall deal with the issues.' "

And issues there were aplenty. The postwar years were a period of tremendous stress and strain on the public school system in Winnipeg. During the Depression there had been virtually no new investment in public schooling. Between 1937 and 1948 only one new school, River Heights Junior High, was built by the board. Eight of the schools still in use in 1947 had been constructed in the 1890s.

The Depression and war years had been tough ones for school teachers as well. In 1931 Winnipeg teachers were forced to accept a 10 per cent pay cut, and two years later the school board introduced a special wage reduction for female teachers, who were already making less than their male counterparts. It took the teachers until 1941 to win back all that had been lost in 1931.

In Manitoba in 1941 only 42 per cent of the adult population had completed up to eight years of school — and in the coming decade this only fell to 39 per cent. During the Forties 31 per cent of the children in the province between the ages of five and nineteen did not attend school. In Winnipeg only 53 per cent of the students who enrolled in grade one in 1945 were in grade ten by 1955.

The end of the war brought about tremendous changes in Winnipeg. Between 1946 and 1950 some two hundred new industries sprang up in Winnipeg, 30,000 immigrants moved to Manitoba (mostly to Winnipeg), and the process of rural depopulation got under way, as rural Manitoba lost people during a time of provincial growth. And on top of it all was the baby boom, spurred by the return of soldiers from overseas. In Manitoba the boom peaked in 1947 at 20,136 births or 27.4 births per thousand. Educators were under pressure to modernize, to expand and to keep down costs. These conflicting pressures made education a very political issue, one that in the Fifties was to lead to the defeat of a provincial government.

As he made his way to his first board meeting in the winter of 1942, Zuken, like other Communists who enjoyed success in Winnipeg politics, knew he was travelling a path blazed by Jacob Penner. For much of Zuken's political career, Jacob Penner was a touchstone for him. "I [chose him] for obvious reasons: his personal integrity, his honesty and his dedication to his work. Jake was incorruptible. And I think he brought something new to city hall — a working-class point of view. I would constantly ask myself, 'What would Jake do on this question?' And that was a pretty good test."

Jacob Penner was born in 1880 in a Russian village on the banks of the Dnieper River. His parents were German Mennonite farmers who tried, unsuccessfully, to interest their son in pursuing a career as a farmer. While he was studying land surveying in college, he was exposed to anti-czarist literature. His movement to the left accelerated when he witnessed the brutal suppression of a metal workers' strike in 1902. Years later he told his son Norman, "All this impressed me to such an extent that I came to the conclusion that it was wrong to have these factories privately owned." Eventually the young man joined an underground discussion group, secretly distributing their leaflets.

In 1904 his parents decided to move to Canada and take their son with them; among their reasons was their fear that his involvement in left-wing circles would eventually land him in Siberia. There must have been winters on the Manitoba prairie when Penner wondered why his parents had chosen such a cold and desolate plain as an alternative to Siberia.

Not long after his arrival in the country, Penner plunged into the world of North Winnipeg politics. He joined the Socialist Party of Canada, but then left to help found the Social

Democratic Party when he became convinced the SPC was merely spouting rhetoric rather than "dealing with the issues of the day." Penner was a member of the General Strike committee, and in the aftermath of the strike his house was raided by the police and most of his library confiscated.

It was at this point that Penner was drawn to the Communist Party. In 1921 he contested the federal riding of Winnipeg North for the party, and although he placed poorly, he took enough votes to help deny victory to General Strike leader R. B. Russell, who was running as a socialist candidate.

Penner was elected to city council in 1933 at the high-water mark of the CP's most sectarian period. While his political speeches were often full of the rhetoric of class struggle, his work on council was very much rooted in the concrete concerns of the people of North Winnipeg. With CCF alderman Jack Blumberg, he exposed the city's practice of threatening relief recipients with deportation. He was also successful in getting council to drop its policy of prohibiting people on relief from picketing. While most of his fellow councillors felt Penner took too dogmatic and Marxist an approach to most issues, the local CP leadership held a different view. Party leaders felt that Penner, by concentrating on specific reforms, was not doing enough to promote socialism and revolution. According to Norman Penner, "He got hauled up several times before the party in Winnipeg and was told, 'Look, this is not what you are supposed to do. You are supposed to fight for socialism.' " But the tide was turning in Penner's favour; by the mid-Thirties, party policy had changed completely and his approach to the issues became the model for Communists in political life.

Upon his release from internment in 1942, Penner was re-elected to council, and he held his seat until his retirement in 1961. His political popularity, like Zuken's, withstood the battering of the Cold War. *Winnipeg Free Press* reporter Michael Harris covered North End politics for that paper for years and gave these reasons for Penner's success:

[The] working people had a lot of problems with the City Council and they could not get anywhere. Some aldermen wouldn't say anything, wouldn't do anything, or had no time — they always had some excuse, but when they see Penner, well he never refused a single one: a request to him to do something whether it was their homes or their jobs or anything like that.

Harris recalled covering a meeting of the Ukrainian Conservative Party where a man was advised by the president of the association to take his problem to Jacob Penner, since "Jake Penner will do anything you want if it is possible."

Constitution of the Board: Left vs. Right

Zuken was on the school board for two decades. During that period the faces around the board table were to change regularly, but the alignment of power remained constant. The board was controlled by a loose majority of Liberals and Conservatives, most of whom ran with the backing of the Civic Election Committee (CEC), the political successor to the Citizens' Committee of One Thousand, which had put down the General Strike. Facing them were four to five CCF trustees. These included a number of men who, like Saul Cherniack, Phillip Peturrson and David Orlikow, were to go on to make their mark in national and provincial politics. There were a number of prominent trade unionists (also members of the CCF), including Harry Chappell of the Canadian Brotherhood of Rail Employees and future Manitoba Federation of Labour president Len Stevens. In addition, there was generally a clutch of independents who would usually supported the CEC but on any given issue might take a more progressive position.

And there was Zuken. For all but two of his terms on the board, Zuken was the only Communist member. In 1947 he was joined by Margaret Chunn, who made electoral history by being the first of Winnipeg's civic Communists to win an election outside of the North End's Ward Three. Chunn had come to public attention as a leader of the Manitoba Housewives Association, a Communist-sponsored consumers' association that lobbied for day cares, the maintenance of price controls and a public-housing policy. In Winnipeg its members attempted to organize a boycott of Coca Cola when local prices when up. Chunn met with defeat in the 1949 municipal election. In 1960 Mary Kardash, the wife of Bill Kardash, began her career on the school board — a career that would run intermittently until her retirement in 1986.

In 1953 the *Winnipeg Tribune* published a series of verses written by Edith Tennant, one of the CEC members of the board. The rhymes paint brief portraits of the various trustees. In writing of Zuken, she focused on his controversial proposal to extend kindergarten education to four-year-olds:

> *He'd take the little four-year-olds*
> *And right to school they'd go,*
> *They'd be a nuisance to the teachers*
> *But their moms would just love Joe.*
> *He says he's often lonely —*
> *The reason's plain to see,*
> *That's bound to be the fate of those*
> *Who join the LPP.*

Another verse profiled Andrew Robertson, one of the few close friends Zuken was to make in political life. Wrote Tennant:

> *Another Scot is Andy,*
> *A C.C.F.er true,*
> *He has three little echoes*
> *And he tells them what to do.*
> *He'd talk from morn to midnight*
> *If his speaking wasn't timed.*
> *And so we made him chairman —*
> *I hope he does not mind.*

Zuken and Robertson were a most unlikely pairing. Where Zuken was small, bookish and shy, Robertson was huge, athletic and outgoing. But both of them were always happiest when in the midst of a political fight.

As with Zuken, Robertson's radicalism was rooted in Old and New World experiences. Born in Glasgow, Scotland, in 1906, Robertson grew up in a period of political turmoil. The local shipyards earned themselves the name of the Red Clyde for the militancy of the local unionists. One of Robertson's older brothers worked in the Clyde yards as a painter and was involved in a local socialist party. He would take the young boy to the parades and demonstrations that gripped the city in the wake of the First World War. Robertson was left with vivid memories of how these were often broken up by the police. As exciting as postwar Glasgow was, it was also a place of decreasing economic opportunity. One of Robertson's brothers had died from injuries suffered during the war, his father was no longer living at home, and older brothers and sisters were heading across the Atlantic in search of work. In 1921 Robertson and his mother followed suit, joining relatives in Winnipeg.

Robertson was not in Canada long before he made contact with the local labour movement. On one of his first Sundays in the city, he attended a lecture at an inner-city labour temple. The speaker that day was J. S. Woodsworth. Never one to hang back, the young Robertson asked a question or two. "After the meeting J.S. said to me, 'You're not long from the old land, are you?' It was the understatement of the day. I was broad Scotch then and still am." Woodsworth invited the fifteen-year-old home for lunch and a fast friendship was formed. Robertson soon found himself at work on Woodsworth's first federal campaign and virtually became an additional family member. At one point Woodsworth offered to send him to study with Frank Scott at McGill University, but the proposal offended Robertson's pride — he had recently married and felt a man should take care of himself and his family.

Robertson became a professional bookbinder and was fiercely proud of his skills. He also maintained his involvement in the CCF. In 1941 when the ailing J. S. Woodsworth was making out his political will, he convinced Robertson to run for school board, not that it took much encouragement. Robertson won an easy election in Ward Two and went on to serve on the board for two decades before he made the jump to municipal politics.

According to Robertson, Zuken once tried to recruit him to the Communist Party. The two men were walking home from a meeting at the board's old offices on Ellen and William when they passed the Leland Hotel. As Robertson recounted: "Joe says, 'Well how about having a beer, Andy?' I looked at him and thought, 'He's going to give me a jaw, see if I won't join the Communist Party.' And I said, 'Alright.' So we went in. Of course, I've played the pipes and played soccer and all that —

I can drink all the God-damn beer they could give me. We went in there and Joe orders two beers and sat down. Sure enough, soon as we got into conversation, Joe says, 'You know, since I've met you, there hasn't been much time to talk. So I thought it would be a good idea to come here, have a beer and talk things over. You're from Glasgow.'

"And I said, 'Sure, Commies are no strangers to me, I know them, all kinds of them.' So the talk went on and he said, 'With your background, you don't want to be with the CCF. Why don't you come to the Communist Party?'

"I says, 'No, Joe. I have an admiration for the Communists. They state their case and they don't make no bones about it. But I know the Communist Party. I come from Glasgow and they are strong on the Clydeside. And they are too bloody dictatorial. I am not used to someone telling me what I've got to do and what I have to think and so on like that. I prefer the Labour Party idea of freedom of movement.' So Joe asks the waiter to bring another couple of beers. I don't think Joe ever drank more than one glass of beer at a time in his life, you know, but he struggled on. I was going to order another couple of beer, but I didn't. Ever since we have been good friends."

According to Robertson, there was always tension within the CCF caucus over whether or not members should support, or even second, Zuken's proposals. Robertson claimed that provincial leader Lloyd Stinson pressured CCFers on the school board not to support Zuken's positions, since such support gave ammunition to those who claimed there was no difference between the CCF and the Communists. Robertson's response had been blunt. He had said, "If Joe Zuken moves a motion that I think is for the benefit of the kids in the schools, I don't care who moved it, I'll second it. And I'll vote for it."

Zuken and Robertson had no difficulty, however, expressing their differences with one another. In April 1958 they took part in a public debate over which country had the best school system, Canada or Russia. Zuken argued for the superiority of the Soviet system, saying, "Russia was the first country to develop free schooling at all levels for all who have the ability. We have no equality in our system." Admitting he never thought he'd defend the Canadian system, Robertson claimed that its freedom of expression and diversity made it the better of the two.

From the point of view of the Workers Election Committee, Zuken's first term on the school board was successful. When he ran for re-election, the committee was able to list over a dozen resolutions introduced by Zuken that had been adopted by the board. These included a retroactive wage increase for caretakers, the investigation of a hot-lunch program and the creation of a committee to help organize home and school associations. In 1945 Zuken was one of a number of trustees who successfully steered through the board a proposal for evening music lessons for between 150 and 200 grade three and four students in eighteen city schools.

In 1943 he was in the news attacking the conservative members of the board for blocking the appointment of Fred Tipping as the principal of Riverview School. Tipping, one of the leaders of the 1919 General Strike, had just won the CCF federal nomination in Winnipeg South and was being punished for his political activities. Zuken told the *Winnipeg Tribune*, "There is no place in our school system for such an attitude of political witch-hunting. I bitterly opposed the action of the Civic Election Committee trustees at the management committee meeting." In 1945 the provincial government established a Special Select Committee on education to examine the issues the province would have to face in the postwar era. In September Zuken appeared before the committee. His recommendations give some idea of the issues he had been pushing at the board level: "a minimum salary for teachers of $1,500, abolition of all examination fees, extensive scholarships, free textbooks for all grades, increased vocational training and technical institutes, extension of adult education, provision for the deaf and the immediate opening of the Tuxedo School."

All of these were sound proposals for reform. Over the years, in one form or another, they have all been instituted. While they did not bear much surface resemblance to the class struggle or Marxism, they did reflect Joe Zuken's attitude to politics: "You don't walk in there," he said years later, "with *Das Kapital* under one arm and the *Communist Manifesto* under the other. You walk in there bringing with you — as I think every trustee brings with them — a summary of his or her experience as a human being. And I walked in there with what I had learned from my folks, and what I had learned from the immigrant generation, and what I had learned from the Depression. I think I am not a prisoner of those days, but one would be stupid not to draw certain conclusions — political conclusions as well as economic conclusions — from those days. And this may be the main thing, a feeling of the need to find a working-class position in politics and stick to it."

One issue that he was to successfully pound away at for two decades was the introduction, expansion and maintenance of public kindergartens.

The Battle for Kindergartens

German educator Friedrich Froebel was the originator of the underlying principles of kindergarten education in the late 1800s. Froebel held that each child contained the "germs" of what they would grow into; what was needed was a garden to help these seeds properly develop. "Only through the exercise of self activity" would children reach their full potential. Froebel felt this self activity would grow "through imitation to free creativeness." By 1895 there were Canadian Froebelian societies in Winnipeg, Toronto, London and Ottawa.

From its beginning the kindergarten movement had two goals. Some people saw kindergarten as another weapon in the arsenal of social reformers; members of the Winnipeg Free Kindergarten Association, for example, believed that wholesome early childhood education would do "much to reduce poverty and crime in any community." To others, kindergarten was a challenge to the then current philosophies of education. These critics claimed that pubic schools buried a child's originality and initiative, rather than allowing them to flower.

The spread of kindergartens across the country has been uneven. The Toronto School Board opened the first public kindergarten in 1883. Ten years later there were sixty-six such classes across Ontario. Despite this early start it was not until the Second World War that kindergartens became common across the country (even now the level of public support for kindergartens varies widely across the country).

According to Zuken, it was during the debate on the board budget that he was able to introduce the motion that eventually led to the establishment of local kindergartens. "I asked that there be an increase in the budget of one thousand dollars, which enabled a few teachers to inaugurate kindergarten classes for a few months."

The meeting where the proposal finally went through was a dramatic one. Andy Robertson felt the turning point came when a young woman whose son was attending a kindergarten organized by the United Church made a brief presentation to the board. "She came up to the rail and she said, 'I haven't much to say. All I know is I live in one room with by son. My little boy goes to the school. I don't know what I would do without that school. He is so wrapped up in going to school. He comes home and he has his lessons and there is some time for me to do something. Oh, I think it is the most tremendous thing there could be for the kids.' You could have heard a pin drop."

In the 1942-43 school year there were four kindergarten classes established across the city with twenty-five students in each class. Two years later Zuken stirred up a new controversy when he suggested the program could no longer be considered "experimental" and should be greatly expanded. "Even with 20 classes," he said, "we won't be able to handle all five-year-old children in Winnipeg." Dr. Mindel Sheps, a CCF trustee and a long-time supporter of kindergarten, backed up Zuken's proposal, noting that the school board "should not always follow demand, but sometimes must be the proponent of progressive principles." The board's majority cut the proposed increase in half, reflecting the view of board chairman Dr. F. E. Warriner that "[I would rather] creep before I walk."

Zuken also voiced an early call for public day care. In the summer of 1943 he got the school board to agree to a motion that called on the provincial government to enter into an agreement with the federal government to establish day nurseries. Created during the war as a response to the needs of the growing number of women working in war-related industries, the day nursery program provided care for children two to six years of age. Zuken was angered that only two provinces, Ontario and Quebec, had entered into the cost-sharing agree-

ment with the federal government to establish day cares. He
warned against thinking that the demand for day nurseries
would only be temporary. "The emancipation of women is
here to stay. The women of Canada didn't want the old slogan
to be dragged out after the war that they must stay in the
home." Day nurseries, he felt, should be part of the school
system. Unfortunately for the day-care movement, Manitoba
never took advantage of the federal day nursery program,
which itself was abolished after the war.

Even after they had been in operation for a decade, kindergartens were far from accepted by all members of the board.
Late in 1952 it became apparent that falling enrollments might
force the Winnipeg School Board to lay off ten kindergarten
teachers. As an alternative Zuken proposed extending the program to include four-year-olds as well as five-year-olds. At the
board meeting where he proposed this, trustee Peter Curry
chided Zuken for seeking to introduce his "socialist ideas" into
the school system. The *Winnipeg Tribune* picked up on this
argument in an editorial on December 12, 1952:

> The suggestion by Joseph Zuken, Communist member of
> the Winnipeg School board, that Winnipeg kindergartens
> should be opened to four-year-olds is not surprising. The
> Communist philosophy demands that a child be taken
> from its home and from parental control as soon as pos-
> sible. Mr. Zuken was merely promoting the party line.

Zuken's proposal was not acted on, and three years later
kindergarten came under direct attack, both from the *Tribune*
and a number of trustees. In February 1956 trustee Hugh
Parker, a member of the CEC, called for an abolition of the
kindergarten program completely, thus saving the board
$400,000. At that point, 72 per cent of the students eligible to
attend kindergarten were enrolled in the program. The *Tribune*
echoed Parker's argument, and after reiterating the charge that
Zuken only supported kindergarten because it was part of his
"leftist philosophy of state control of family life," the paper
suggested that while there may have been some need for
kindergarten during the war, there was no justification for this
"costly baby-sitting service." When the matter came to a vote,
the level of support for kindergarten was clear. Only one

public delegation favoured abolishing the program, and the proposal, which Zuken termed "the most destructive and ill-advised in recent school board history," was defeated 14 to 1.

Over a decade later Zuken, then a Winnipeg city councillor, was still trying to expand the range of pre-school programs open to Winnipeg children. In December 1969 he supported a proposal that the city establish day nurseries that would be funded by the city and the provincial welfare department. He called the idea "a long-neglected step, but a first step," adding that he hoped that local schools could be used to house such facilities.

Rebuilding the School System

In 1948 the scope of the literal rebuilding job facing the school board was brought home by a special report conducted for it by Professor William C. Reavis of the University of Chicago. Reavis called for the demolition of fourteen "obsolete" schools, indexing teachers' salaries to the cost of living, reducing classroom size from thirty-five to twenty-five pupils, and improving teacher training. Reavis also suggested that the board be reduced in size from fifteen to nine members and that it be elected at large —a proposal heartily endorsed by the *Winnipeg Tribune*:

> At present the board has representatives of both the CCF and the LPP [Labor Progressive Party], acting and working as political groups. Clearly this cannot be in the best interest of the school children of the city as a whole. If the school board were chosen from the city at large the CCF would probably retain its present quota of seats. The probable disappearance of LPP members would not be generally regarded as alarming.

While there was general support for the bricks-and-mortar improvement in the school system, in many circles there was no great desire to modernize provincial education. As early as 1946 R. O. MacFarland, the provincial superintendent of education, characterized the curriculum then in use as having been designed seventy-five years earlier for the instruction of children intended for the medical, ministerial or teaching

professions. A decade later Neville Scarfe, the dean of education at the University of Manitoba, resigned his post, claiming
the provincial government of Douglas Campbell was completely reactionary in issues of educational reform. It was a
sentiment that Zuken heartily endorsed: "We have a horse and
buggy attitude toward education in the age of Sputnik. The
greatest obstacle to education reform in Manitoba is the minister of education. He should be fired. Public opinion has to get
just as aroused about education as about a Canadian pipeline
or the Blue Bombers."

For Zuken and the CCF members of the board, the major
battle in the postwar years involved getting the board to expand the range of programs it offered and to improve the
teachers' wages. In December 1947 Zuken managed to have
the board adopt a resolution of his that would provide
teachers with a $15-a-month cost-of-living bonus. When trus-
tees Peter Taraska and Campbell Haig warned that the increase would create budgetary problems, Zuken leapt to his
feet, saying, "You can't expect school employees to bear the
brunt of balancing the budget." He also pointed out that the
increase was a compromise from the $300-a-year increase the
teachers were asking for. At that time the division budget was
just under $5 million.

Zuken and Mindel Sheps also fought a long battle on behalf
of the women who taught for the Winnipeg School Board. At
the height of the Depression, the board imposed a far greater
wage cut on female teachers than on male teachers. This move
caused a split in the provincial teachers' federation, resulting
in the establishment of male and female locals. (Long-time
socialists like Fred Tipping were so appalled by the complicity
of the male teachers in implementing the cuts that they trans-
ferred their membership to the women's local of the teachers'
union.) In 1943 Sheps proposed the differential be eliminated,
along with the rules restricting the hiring of married women.
When her resolutions were defeated, Zuken commented,
"Boy, Hitler would love you guys." When pressed by the
chairman for a retraction, he settled on "these anti-democratic
practices are best exemplified by the actions of Mr. Hitler."

Zuken also felt the board had trouble separating policy matters from administrative work, with the consequence that
policy development suffered. He recalled one instance where

"a desk had to be picked for use in the schools. So here you had all the high-priced help in the administration at a school board meeting, together with all the trustees, gathered around a sampling of desks. They were going around each desk trying to determine which one would be suitable. My goodness. It was an administrative question which should have been left to the administration."

The board administration was the source of many proposals for curriculum improvement, proposals that could usually count on Zuken's support. In 1956 the assistant superintendent, Gordon MacDonnell, prepared yet one more devastating critique of the provincial curriculum. In MacDonnell's opinion, the curriculum was "restrictive," did not allow schools to "strike out boldly on new paths," discouraged teachers from experimenting "with new methods" and from grade eight up "provincial examinations aggravate the situation." The rigid provincial guidelines, which stipulated the number of minutes to be spent on each subject each week, led to a situation where "the actual objectives in a high school may well be to pass the Grade 11 departmental examination" — and nothing more.

This sort of criticism was music to Zuken's ears. His experience at St. John's High School had convinced him that teachers were the key ingredient in a good education. Because Manitoba schools were so tradition-bound, he felt, "very few teachers, as a whole, dared to come out and do any prodding and prying and opening of minds. In many cases we had too many teachers who were textbooks wired for sound."

Zuken's opinions relating to MacDonnell's study were quoted in the press:

No one is arguing that we chuck out all examinations, but it is a question of cramming for exams. The pressure is on the teachers and the students, and it is a crammed course, the student spills it out on the paper and if you gave the student the same paper 12 months later the student would not have the first notion of how to deal with it. This is an abuse of the educational process. If that is general, and our high schools are examination ridden, we should do something about it.

Zuken, and the Communist Party itself, was not immune to some of the social conservatism of the Fifties. Ironically, while the guardians of law and order saw Communists as a dark and alien force, subverting the young, Zuken stood foursquare for the more traditional values of the period. In the fall of 1954 he was calling on the federal government to "exert more rigid control over the import, publication and sale of crime and sex comics," which he termed the "real educational institutions among our children." He said, "In every city drugstore is a library of the worst kind of material. The effect on the youngsters is poisonous." Over the years he was to propose or defend hot-lunch programs, high school football, music and swimming lessons and evening classes for adults.

In the fall of 1955 Zuken raised an issue that in later years would become central to him. He walked out of a closed-door session of the board to protest the lack of public scrutiny of a $3-million insurance proposal. He told reporters:

> I should have done this long ago. The board has been meeting in camera on too many questions the public should know about. This is a matter that should not only be done right but that should appear to be done right. The public has a right to know what we are doing on a matter that not only is concerned with three million dollars of its money but also a group contract that is being dealt with for the first time. I want to warn the board I will not be a party to such a discussion. I won't sit in on any hush hush meeting where a matter of such importance to the public is being talked over.

Racism and Religious Intolerance in the Schools

Long before the days of multiculturalism, Zuken was arguing that schools should be used to combat racism and cultural conflict. He moved one resolution in 1945 that schools "make a greater contribution towards the achievement of racial friendship and cooperation and thus make a great contribution to the removal of racial prejudice in our community." Some trustees opposed this because they felt children knew nothing of racial prejudice, which was simply a problem for adults. Zuken criticized the board policy of identifying students according to their racial and religious background when they enrolled in school. "I'd like to see boys and girls enter our schools as little Canadians, not as a group divided into racial categories. They shouldn't have to specify the racial origin of their mother, the racial origin of their father, and their religious denominations as well."

The early Forties witnessed an at times intense debate over religious exercises in the school system. CCF trustee Meyer Averbach proposed that the board ask the provincial government to repeal a section of the Public Schools Act that would allow for religious instruction in the school system when such was requested by the parents of any twenty-five students in a school. Averbach was particularly disturbed by a section in the act that said such instruction would "be conducted by any Christian clergyman whose charge includes any portion of the school district." When Zuken rose to Averbach's support, Peter Taraska accused him of simply believing that "religion was the opiate of the masses." The board adopted the proposal, only to reverse itself a month later. Trustee George Macleod argued, "I don't want the board to remove Christian education from our national institution." He said he was glad the act prevented instruction in the "Jewish religion, the Mohammedan religion or any other religion." In response Zuken suggested Macleod himself was guilty of more than a little racial prejudice. Zuken concluded, "I wish this country would stick to Christian principles. Christianity speaks through actions, not words." Like many controversies Zuken was involved in, this one did not go away. In 1960 he was the author of a resolution opposing any extension of religious instruction in public schools, a move that had been proposed by a recent provincial royal commission. His motion passed 9 to 4, with strong support from CCFers Robertson and Dr. Isadore Wolch.

Throughout his years on the school board, Zuken regularly raised concerns regarding the treatment and depiction of minorities in school textbooks. In December 1952 he asked that Charles Dickens's *Oliver Twist* be withdrawn from the high school curriculum because of anti-Semitic remarks made by the book's chief villain, Fagin. He made it clear he did not suspect the book's author of anti-Semitism, noting, "Mr. Dickens is a

very fine author and another of his works could be substituted."

Four years later, in the wake of a Toronto decision to drop
Little Black Sambo from the school curriculum, Zuken was
calling for a similar move in Winnipeg schools. At the time,
the board superintendent said, "While it is recognized that
attention is directed to skin color, the whole point of the story
is to make a hero out of Little Black Sambo. It is considered
unlikely that the story tends to raise any problems in the
popular [mind], and it is therefore suggested that no action be
taken and nothing be done to draw any further attention to
this story." This recommendation was accepted — with a number of trustees joking that if they pulled *Little Black Sambo* they
would have to eliminate *Black Beauty* and that the Humane
Society ought to be protesting the fate of the tiger in *Little Black
Sambo*. In defeat Zuken noted that "sarcasm" did not befit the
school board and stuck to his position that "Sambo was a
carryover from slave days and the name was a caricature."

In 1959 he protested the use of the *Club Song Book for Boys*
in Winnipeg schools because of the version of "Polly Wolly
Doodle" that appeared in the book. Zuken said that the verse
"Oh, I came to a river and I couldn't get across, / So I jumped
on a nigger cause I thought it was a hoss" was shameful. "It
points out the danger of left-over racist connotations within
our schools." He said that he had been told by a parent that a
twelve-year-old student had refused to sing the verse because
it was derogatory to another race and the teacher said, "I'm
three times your age and I'll put you out of the classroom."

But it was in the naming of Andrew Mynarski School that
Zuken scored his most public victory in this campaign for a
more pluralistic society.

For many decades in Winnipeg, school names were part of a
general campaign to "Canadianize," or assimilate, the foreigners of the North End. George Bryce, a leading Presbyterian
minister at the turn of the century, wrote in an article entitled
"Our Happy Ruthenian People" that Ukrainian boys and girls
"should remain at school until they are able to do what business they have to do at the store, or the bank, or the taxpayer's
office, or in buying horse's or cattle or sheep, or reading a

newspaper." But beyond that he doubted they could be taught all that much. Education Minister Robert Thornton went one step further in outlining what he saw as the main object of the Manitoba educational system when it came to the residents of North Winnipeg. It was not "to teach children to read and write but to make good citizens out of them." And good citizens would love a Protestant god, an English king and a British empire — these characteristics would mark them clearly as Canadians.

It was in this spirit that, in the years prior to the First World War, the Winnipeg School Board embarked on a scheme of naming North End schools after "men of eminence" — meaning English nobility. It was hoped this would help the immigrant children learn of these men and "their significance." And so King Edward, Lord Aberdeen, Lord Selkirk, Cecil Rhodes and Lord Strathcona schools came into being. Given the ambiguous role the Canadian Pacific Railway had played in the lives of many of the residents of the North End, one wonders how they felt about sending their children to a school named after the railway's president, Sir William Whyte. From 1900 to 1949 there were forty-one schools built in Greater Winnipeg — all but four of which were named after people of Anglo-Saxon background. The four were named for people of French ancestry.

In 1955, therefore, when the Winnipeg School Board began casting around for a name for its new school on Machray in the North End, the board was inclined to look with favour on the name of former governor general Baron Tweedsmuir. Tweedsmuir is better known as John Buchan, the author of spy novels more than faintly tinged with anti-Semitism.

Zuken had an alternate proposal in mind. He introduced an amendment, calling on the board to name the school after North End war hero Andrew Mynarski. At the same time he suggested that three other new schools all be named after Canadians, including Louis Riel. "It was a natural. Mynarski was a V.C. winner, a North End boy, and he had gone to the same school that I had. What more could you ask for than that?"

Mynarski had been posthumously awarded the Victoria Cross for his efforts to save one of his comrades when the Lancaster bomber they were flying in was shot down over

France. He could have successfully escaped from the plane, but chose instead to try and release the rear gunner, who was trapped in the tail section of the plane. In his efforts Mynarski's parachute and clothing caught fire, and he died from burns and injuries. Miraculously the gunner survived the plane's crash landing and testified to Mynarski's heroism.

Zuken's motion was defeated. At the meeting, trustee Herbert Moore explained that the Manitoba Historical Association had vetted the recommended names and concluded that the name Mynarksi "does not lend itself to the name of a school." According to Zuken, Moore's comments sparked a furore in the community. "And that's the first time I really saw citizen participation at the school board level. People from the Polish community, the Ukrainian community, they came down and they literally stormed the school board. I felt proud of the people of the North End; they really rose to the occasion."

More than fifty people, including veterans, leaders of various ethnic organizations, Mynarski's former teachers and school principal, packed the school board meeting room on April 19, 1955. They were there to protest the board's previous decision, and they brought a petition bearing 400 names to back up their demand that the new school be named for Andrew Mynarski. According to the *Tribune*, "the words 'discrimination, slur, racism and snobism' were tossed at the uncomfortable Board." William J. Sisler, the former principal of Strathcona and Isaac Newton schools, said, "It is a bit of arrogance to anyone to say the name Mynarski does not lend itself to a school." By this time Moore was claiming the papers had misquoted him and was more than willing to back the new name. In the end Mynarski was adopted by an all but unanimous vote; trustee George Frith said he felt that for "policy reasons" Tweedsmuir was still a much better name.

The story of the naming of Mynarski School was one Zuken never tired of telling: "The establishment was embarrassed that it had been forced to retreat in a shameful way. So what started as simply the naming of a new school became a fight against bigotry and racism. And from that point of view it was significant."

Education and the Cold War

It should not be surprising that the school system was seen as one of the key battlegrounds of the Cold War. Despite this, when one surveys the havoc red-baiters caused in the American school system, what happened in Manitoba is mild by comparison. During the 1950s a wholesale purge of Communists and leftists was carried out in the New York City school system. While such systematic discrimination did not occur in Manitoba, even as mild and moderate an organization as the Manitoba Teachers Society, which willingly gave up the right to strike, found that in the postwar years union involvement could lead to unemployment. According to MTS general secretary Thomas McMaster, "These people are being dismissed solely and simply because of their interest in the work of the society."

The predominantly rural Manitoba Association of School Trustees played a leading role in conflating unionism and communism. One issue of the MAST newsletter editorialized: "Shall teachers form unions and affiliate with labour organizations?? The answer is emphatically NO — if teachers value the future of their profession and country."

The 1951 issue of the *Manitoba School Trustee* carried an article headlined "Marxism Discredited in One Easy Lesson." The article noted that the "Marxist thought of 'taking from each according to his ability' and giving 'to each according to his need' " looked to many students "like a pretty shiny idea." The article suggested that a teacher could combat this by proposing to take 20 points away from a student who received 95 points on a test and give them to a student who received 55 points. By the end of the lesson the students would come to realize that socialism "would eventually turn all the people, except the 'authorities' and a few of their favourites and lackeys, into sheep."

As late as 1959 the *Manitoba School Trustee* was running articles like this:

Right within our own borders communism works to beset and bedevil the cause of freedom. One of the chief ends of the communists and their world plan is to blot out freedom as we know it. Yet they work right in the midst

of our free society towards their purposes. Unscrupulous-
ly they take every possible advantage of the very principles of freedom which their own doctrines sneer at.

Not only was the Manitoba school system fully enlisted in
the anti-Communist crusades of the Fifties (the author of one
study writes he was hard pressed to find *any* facts, let alone a
balanced presentation of the facts, about Marxism, socialism
and communism in the Manitoba school curriculum of this
period), but educators saw little to criticize in the integration
of the American and Canadian economies. According to *The
Geography of Our American Neighbours,* a grade seven textbook
used in the early Fifties in Manitoba, "The United States needs
our raw materials for its great industries and we in return
require its manufactured goods. It can truly be said that both
countries are good neighbours dependent on each other."

During the Fifties, the Cold War directly injected itself into
the politics of the Winnipeg School Board whenever two interrelated subjects came up for debate — civil defence and
military training for students. For many Winnipeggers these
topics were simply beyond discussion: students should be
preparing to defend God, Queen and Country, and given the
fact that the godless Soviets had exploded an atomic weapon
in 1949, civil defence was simply a sensible precaution. National civil defence planning was given considerable impetus
when the St. Laurent government organized the federal-
provincial Civil Defence Conference in 1951. The government
also published a variety of pamphlets advising citizens what
to do in the event of a nuclear attack. As well, a number of
plays with titles like *Bombed Out, Emergency Feeding in Disaster*
and *Civil Defence in Schools* were staged across the country.

Zuken saw the phenomenon as a sign of resurgent
militarism, a militarism that could only be aimed at the Soviet
Union. Certainly the Canadian Peace Congress, which drew
much of its inspiration and policy direction from the Soviet
Union, focused its efforts on criticizing civil defence programs.
And these programs were deserving of much of this scorn,
since they increased young people's fears about the bomb
while simultaneously providing them with a sense that there
was some way to survive a nuclear attack. If the dangers of a
nuclear war with the Soviet Union were underplayed by the

Communists, the effectiveness of civil defence as a way to rationally deal with the threat of such a war was greatly exaggerated by Western politicians.

These issues were often to bring Zuken into conflict with military figures. In 1950 at a forum on school cadet training, Zuken accused the Canadian Infantry Association of red-baiting. He made the charges after the association had claimed that Communists had prevented the Winnipeg School Board from going ahead with a cadet training program. According to Zuken, the association was planning to establish military institutions in the schools.

These sorts of attacks drew a response from the *Free Press*, which pointed out that

> not once did he mention his spiritual home, where children of eight are dragooned into real military organizations. Mr. Zuken might spend his summer to better purpose denouncing such activities in the Soviet Union. He would undoubtedly be given all the facilities, including the use of Moscow radio and perhaps a soap box on Red Square.

In December 1951 Zuken warned his fellow trustees that civil defence might make children "hysterical." He said that similar programs in the United States had "operated to the detriment of children's health and well-being." And he characterized a plan that had been proposed by Major-General M. H. S. Penhale, the director of the Metropolitan Civil Defence Board, as being a "military proposition directed by a military man."

Zuken was the centre of a chaotic debate the following year when a trustee tried to reduce the rent the school board charged the Civil Defence Board for the use of classrooms to provide civil defence training for adults. In making his proposals, trustee S. M. Carrick said, "Civil Defence is just being opposed by Communists like Mr. Zuken." Zuken jumped up and demanded a retraction, and when he could not get one, he called Carrick a liar. Carrick continued his speech, referring to "groups like the Peace Council that are disloyal to this country." Zuken was at this point heard to shout, "You're an ignorant drunkard." When the chairman was unable to restore order, Saul Cherniack succeeded in having the meeting adjourned.

In 1952 Zuken distributed a pamphlet opposing civil defence programs in the schools:

> Civil defence is not peace preparedness or insurance for the children. It is harmful to the mental health and welfare of the students. Emphasis on war in our schools can cripple their young minds emotionally and intellectually. It is dangerous and foolish to instil the idea that hiding under desks and in school corridors will defend the students against atom bombs.
>
> It is dangerous and brutal to have children subjected to the fear, tension and hysteria that an atom bomb attack is inevitable and may come at any time.

During the 1953 provincial election, Zuken told a radio audience that the Civil Defence Board's request to erect air-raid warning units on three schools was part of

> the psychological warfare against the people of Winnipeg, designed to promote hysteria and panic. Precisely at a time when the armistice in Korea is so close and new hopes are rising for settling differences, people will not accept such perverse reasoning. At a time when St. Joseph's hospital is in danger of closing for lack of funds, why should money be spent for air raid units when there is no danger of attack.

As the Fifties turned into the Sixties, more people became doubtful about the effectiveness of civil defence procedures. But at one of the last board meetings Zuken attended, there was a proposal that local teachers be sent to attend a survival course being offered by the Department of National Defence. Zuken's speech would, by then, have been familiar to all but the most junior of trustees. "Let's not kid ourselves," he said. "There is no hiding place, no safe building in the Winnipeg school system. Our buildings are built for education not megaton bombs."

As the years wore on, it became apparent, even to those trustees who violently disagreed with Zuken's political views, that he was one of the more capable and informed members of the board. Despite this he was continually prevented from playing a national role on the educational stage. In 1957 he complained the board had failed to send him to a national trustees conference in Fredericton because he was a Communist. He was particularly irritated by this, since he had been responsible for "raising the need for co-ordinated research on teacher recruitment," one of the issues that would be discussed at the conference. The following year the CCF members of the board nominated Zuken as a delegate to a federal education conference in Ottawa. But the Civic Election Committee majority overrode this, choosing to send the head of the finance committee, Catherine Stewart. An angry Zuken said the decision was not made on the basis of merit but on "vicious political discrimination." He noted that it was a motion of his, put before the Canadian School Trustees Association Convention the previous year, that "set the wheels in motion for the conference." These charges were substantiated by trustee Nina Patrick, who told the *Free Press* she thought "Mr. Zuken would doubtless be the best choice but his 'political affiliation' forced her to vote against him."

Under the headline "No Place for a Communist," the *Winnipeg Tribune* backed up this view:

> The board would have been open to severe censure had it succumbed to Joseph Zuken's eagerness to journey to the national capital on its behalf.
>
> Regardless of Mr. Zuken's ability he is an avowed Communist. It would be a black eye to Winnipeg to send such a man to represent this community and to make suggestions for the "improvement" of education in Canada.

The issue came up again in 1959. This time, after Zuken had been nominated by the board's policy committee to attend the annual convention of the Canadian school trustees in Victoria, the board as a whole voted 8 to 6 to strike out Zuken's name, sending Andrew Moore in his stead. Trustee Ross Little moved the substitution, noting that "Mr. Zuken has announced to this board he is Communist. His personal qualifications are without exception but his declared membership as a Communist makes him unsuitable to represent this board." Said Zuken, "I'm completely fed up with being kicked around as a political football.... As a school trustee I am not entitled to be favoured but neither to suffer rank discrimination." To her credit on this occasion, Nina Patrick overcame her political objections and did vote in favour of sending Zuken to the conference.

It was not until May 1961, Zuken's final year as a trustee, that by a 9 to 5 vote the board agreed to send Zuken to a national education conference. Catherine Stewart opposed the move, saying, "In my opinion a Communist should not represent Winnipeg at a national convention." But Michael Baryluk, who rarely agreed with Zuken on anything, demonstrated how, slowly, establishment thinking about Zuken was starting to change. "I think," he said, "it's wrong when Miss Stewart says we are going to send a Communist to a convention. We are sending a trustee. I think he can be relied on to represent the Winnipeg school district. It's time we grew up."

SIX

The Cold War in Manitoba
1945-1962

In August 1943 Zuken was one of 600 delegates to attend the founding meeting of the Labor Progressive Party in Toronto. In his speech to the convention, the party's leader, Tim Buck, made it clear that the creation of a new party was necessary because the "King government insists upon maintaining a ban on the Communist Party in Canada." In the years to come, editorialists would denounce the LPP as a clever disguise for the Communist Party, but there is little doubt the Communists would have preferred to go back into business under their old name — which they did in 1959. Even though numerous senior civil servants and an all-party committee of the House of Commons had recommended lifting the ban on the CP, King, in keeping with his general approach to controversy, declined to act. This dilatoriness was in no small part due to the fact that both wartime justice ministers, Ernest Lapointe and Louis St. Laurent, took much of their political direction from the archbishop of Quebec, Cardinal Villeneuve. In 1942 Villeneuve wrote St. Laurent a letter of praise for his "firmness and courage against the efforts of those who would restore communism to a legal position in Canada."

Despite the fact that he had been active in the left-wing movement since his teens and publicly associated with the CP for the better part of a decade, it was not until he participated in the 1943 founding convention of the LPP, close to two years after the party had engineered his election to the school board, that Zuken officially became a Communist. There appear to be few satisfactory explanations for this seeming anomaly. Certainly his social democratic and establishment opponents viewed him as a Communist prior to 1943, and he had done little to hide his political sympathies. When asked if he thought it odd that he delayed joining the party for such a long time, he replied, "Not really. I was in the left. I regarded myself around the left. My brother was very active in the YCL [Young Communist League]. He was the leader of the YCL. But I had not joined any other party, because no other party attracted me from the point of view of its program and its principles."

If there ever was a time not to join the Communist Party, it was probably 1943. While the party was enjoying a brief respite from government persecution, the Cold War was just around the corner. An ideological conflict that was waged worldwide, it would serve to marginalize the Communist Party in Canadian life. Joe Zuken was one of the few Communist politicians in North America who survived that war in office. The significance of that achievement can only be grasped by examining the way the Cold War affected political culture in Canada and, more specfically, in Manitoba.

The federal election of 1945 marked the high-water mark of the Communist Party's support nationally. The Cold War had yet to break out, the Soviet Union was still an ally, and the Red Army was full of conquering heroes. The party targeted a number of key ridings across the country for special attention. One of them was Winnipeg North. The Communists thought they had a chance to take the seat away from the Liberals and at first nominated Jacob Penner. But in January 1945 Penner stepped aside in favour of Zuken.

Even the normally cautious Zuken was caught up in the feeling of postwar hopefulness: "There was a feeling of optimism, of advance, that things were on the move. Mackenzie King, during the election campaign of '45 was compelled to make noises about reforms. I heard him speak in Winnipeg during the '45 election. There was a feeling that things had to be different, working people were making great advances, and the party would be on the move.

"I remember being present in the house of Dr. Ben Victor. This was just before the end of the Second World War. And there was a whole spirit of euphoria then that was sweeping the left. Mao Tse Tung and the Communists were going to win in China. Hitler was kaput, was finished, and the world was going to be different then. There was a euphoric feeling that this was it. And Canada would be part of that great change."

Zuken's main opponent in the election was the CCF candidate Alistair Stewart, and according to David Orlikow, many CCFers were afraid Zuken might be able to pull off an upset victory. After all, in a Montreal by-election in 1943, Labor Progressive candidate Fred Rose defeated David Lewis to win election to Parliament.

Zuken's campaign speeches reflected the spirit of the postwar period and the moderate political line the CP was then espousing:

> History has jumped and landed us in a new era, with Canada both an economic and political power, capable of taking the lead in building understanding between the United Nations. We must rid ourselves of a destructive inferiority complex and learn to use our latent talents. We must unite to form a national and international policy befitting the new role we have to play.

In another speech Zuken attacked those who were calling for a "get tough policy with the Soviet Union," claiming they were "building the fires for another war." Zuken's main piece of campaign literature urged voters to "Make Labor a Partner in Government" and vote Labor Progressive "For a United, Prosperous and Peaceful Canada." Clara Zuken remembered the campaign as a time of tremendous excitement: "Many people thought Joe was going to win. And on election night they were heartbroken, they were all in tears. They thought I would be in tears too; but I wasn't. I didn't think he would win."

That election was the most successful in the party's history. Fred Rose was re-elected, receiving over 10,000 votes; Tim Buck received 7,488 in Toronto-Trinity, just 1,400 less than the winner; and in Toronto-Spadina Sam Carr polled 10,050, though this was not enough to defeat Liberal David Croll. In Winnipeg North Joe Zuken received 9,116 votes, but CCFer Alistair Stewart garnered over 13,000. Not since that time has the Communist Party elected a member of Parliament or received as many votes nationally. The Cold War was about to begin.

The Second World War had been over for less than a year when in March 1946 Winston Churchill made his Iron Curtain speech in the small university town of Fulton, Missouri. It was the unofficial declaration of the start of the Cold War, and a signal that the Grand Alliance was now in pieces. The new world would not be ruled by the "four policemen" that Roosevelt had envisioned; instead East and West would be pitted against each other in a bitter ideological — and at times bloody — war.

At the heart of the Cold War, particularly in its early days, lay a dualistic world view — either the military adventures of imperialist America were leading the world to war or the Soviets, through a mixture of subversion and invasion, were out to conquer the world. In this war, rhetoric and reality were often at odds with one another. While Stalin was quite willing to make the Cold War sound like an international class struggle when using it as an excuse to repress internal dissent, he was equally prepared to countenance the crushing of a left-wing revolt in Greece as the price he had to pay to keep the Americans from meddling in Eastern Europe. For their part, Americans have carried out the war in the name of freedom and democracy, while propping up scores of vicious dictators throughout the Third World. The interests of American corporations were to fare much better than the values of liberal democracy in those countries where the United States chose to wage the Cold War.

Internationally, for its first two decades the Cold War was an era of confrontation and containment — all conducted in the shadow of the atomic bomb. It was the bomb that gave the Cold War its truly horrifying aspect and fed the hysteria that characterized the domestic Cold War waged in Canada and the United States. That war has come to be identified with its most famous campaigner, American senator Joseph McCarthy, and the witchhunt he conducted against leftists in American public life. But while McCarthy represented the extreme end of anti-communism in North American politics, he was only carrying official policies to their logical conclusion.

Canadian Communists were still flushed with their success in the 1945 federal election when an obscure Soviet cipher clerk walked out of the Soviet embassy in Ottawa and into Cold War history. When he defected, Igor Gouzenko brought with him documents pointing to a Soviet spy ring operating in Canada. After some initial confusion over what to do about Gouzenko's allegations, the King government, in keeping with the spirit of the Defence of Canada Regulations, passed a secret order-in-council empowering the RCMP to detain persons suspected of passing information to foreign governments. The Royal Commission on Espionage held in camera hearings at which people were denied the right to counsel or bail. In February 1946, sixteen Canadians were arrested. Accusations of espionage were soon flying, and at the top of the suspect list was the Communist Party's Montreal MP, Fred Rose. The conviction of Rose and eleven others marked the beginning of Canada's domestic Cold War.

The Cold War In Manitoba

On July 9, 1947, Ralph Baker, the president of the Winnipeg Board of Trade, called a hurried meeting of local business leaders to discuss communism. With him at the meeting was John Hladun, a former CP member who was offering his expert services to the board to combat communism. In a letter written after the meeting, E. B. Frost, a senior executive with the Ogilvie Flour Mills in Winnipeg, said that Hladun "gave us a lot of details, mentioned people's names and really we — and I say 'we' meaning a number of businessmen — were distinctly disturbed." These other businessmen included W. H. Carter, the president of the Winnipeg Electric Company (a private company); E. B. Claydon, owner of a large construction firm; A. H. Fisher, a chartered accountant and CEC city councillor; school trustee Joseph Harris; and Dr. Wesley McCurdy, the publisher of the *Winnipeg Tribune.*

These men were so alarmed by what Hladun told them that they agreed to pay his way to Montreal where he could present the Canadian Chamber of Commerce with the details of a proposed anti-Communist campaign. In a letter urging the Canadian chamber to give serious consideration to Hladun's proposal, Frost wrote:

I go back to the year 1919 — the year of the Winnipeg strike — when I was on a committee of one hundred; at that time we knew from information obtained that as long ago as that the money to foment the strike came from Moscow. Here we are twenty-eight years later still sitting in a complaisant way, letting the Communists carry on their vicious campaign.

Hladun's proposed campaign was designed to "wreck the Communist movement in Canada and reduce it to a state of impotency." The plan, which Hladun felt had to be overseen by him directly, involved obtaining the party membership list and exposing it, and carrying on "clandestine work within the Party" as well as "missionary work in the totalitarian countries." While he recognized that legislative repression of the CP was not likely to be effective, Hladun did envision that "certain legislative measures may be needed at the appropriate time." It appears the Canadian chamber was not as taken with Hladun as were his Winnipeg backers. By late 1947 he was still trying to find a backer for his national campaign.

The depth of anti-Communist sentiment and the fierce passions it engendered can be sensed in some of the city council debates in the fall of 1949. Eleven American CP leaders had just been convicted of the strange charge of conspiracy to advocate the overthrow of the government. In response, the five Manitoba Communists holding elected office — William Kardash, Jacob Penner, Joe Forkin, Joe Zuken and Margaret Chun — had sent a letter of protest to American president Harry Truman, listing their official positions when signing the letter. The other city councillors were apoplectic with rage. At the end of a stormy debate, council passed a resolution stating that by "ascribing their names as aldermen of Winnipeg," they (Penner and Forkin) brought "the city, its citizens and elected representatives into shame and disrepute." The resolution also authorized the mayor to write an apology to President Truman, explaining that the council viewed the action as "mischievous, frivolous and typically Communistic." It was Alderman Charles Simonite who touched the tenor of the times when he described the two Communists:

I, personally, feel disgusted. Here are two men who allow themselves to become stooges for subversive propaganda. They lie morning, noon and night. Their souls are warped. They are almost beyond being human beings. I don't know of any men so shrewd who are so mentally weak. I don't know of any men who have sunk to so low a depth.

In November of 1949 the Winnipeg Police Commission released a report that blamed CP members for starting a street brawl the previous month. The battle, which had erupted in the recently reclaimed Ukrainian Labour-Farmer Temple, pitted left-wing Ukrainians against nationalists. According to a newspaper report, the troubles started when a nationalist got on a chair and started singing the Ukrainian anthem during a meeting on life in the Ukraine under Soviet administration. In the same story, the police admitted, apparently for the first time, to the existence of a "subversive squad." Set up along the lines of a morality or traffic squad, the subversive unit had been operating for a year. According to Mayor Garnet Coulter, the officers "worked in conjunction with the R.C.M.P. in tracking down subversive activities within the city limits."

The right-wing anti-labour editorial positions of both the *Free Press* and *Tribune*, coupled with a lengthy lockout of the printing staff of both newspapers, led to the creation of the *Winnipeg Citizen*, the world's first cooperatively owned daily newspaper. With financial backing from the labour unions, the cooperative movement and a left-wing printer named David Simkin, the *Citizen* started printing on March 1, 1948. The people associated with the paper soon found themselves targets for red-baiting. Harry Ferns, the paper's president and a history professor at United College, was warned by the college president that his involvement with the paper could hurt the school's fund-raising campaign. *Tribune* publisher Wesley McCurdy, who was also the chairman of the United College fund-raising committee, was not pleased that a university employee was in competition with him. Eventually Ferns was fired from the college because he refused to resign from the *Citizen*'s board of directors.

The paper survived for little more than thirteen months. Although its coverage of labour issues and the CCF was more even-handed than that of the other daily papers, it certainly was not a Communist paper. However, one of the reasons the paper failed financially was the fact that it could not gain membership in the Canadian Press news service. It is clear from the minutes of the meeting where its candidacy for membership was discussed that one of the reasons for rejection was the belief held by a number of directors that the paper "was permeated with Communists."

Ferns, who had been a CP member while at university in England, rejected this accusation in his memoirs. According to Ferns, there was only one Communist on the paper's board of directors, a machinist named Chester King. He recalled the party's attitude towards the paper as being one of "indifference tinged with hostility." Shortly after the paper was incorporated, Ferns and Simkin were invited to a meeting with leading party figures, including Joe Zuken and Leslie Morris. Ferns wrote:

> Zuken and Morris took a very high tone with us. Did we not know that the Labour-Progressive party was launching its own daily newspaper and that we had no business encroaching on their territory? This did not particularly endear them to me. Dave was practical. He asked them how many copies of a paper published in Toronto they expected to sell in Winnipeg. They ignored this aspect of the matter as if dialectical materialism might enable them to overcome the fact that Toronto is eight hundred miles from Winnipeg and was then 24 to 30 hours away.

Zuken's law career was almost cut short by the Cold War. Ironically it was R. B. Graham, the magistrate Zuken had tangled with on a daily basis during the Defence of Canada trials, who came to his rescue. Although no formal complaint was ever made, Graham revealed to Zuken that a number of "stuffy members of the law society" had become alarmed that a Communist was practising law and wanted to see if some sort of inquiry could be held. Zuken recalled, "Well, Magistrate Graham, to his credit, said he was very incensed about this and said he put a stop to that sort of thing. He said he thought it was absolutely wrong and that there was no justification for such action to be taken against me in any way."

The threat to Zuken's legal practice was not an idle one. In 1948 Gordon Martin, a member of the LPP and a graduate of the University of British Columbia Law School, was refused admission to the Law Society of British Columbia. All persons called to the bar had to swear to "oppose all traitorous conspiracies" and the law society claimed the LPP was exactly such a conspiracy. Martin took his case to the provincial court of appeal, where he lost. One of the judges wrote, "It has become universally accepted in the Western nations that it is dangerous to our way of life to allow a known Communist or Communist sympathizer to remain in a position of trust or influence."

The Peace Movement

In 1949 the Canadian Peace Congress was formed under the leadership of the Reverend James G. Endicott, a left-wing United Church missionary who had resigned his church position in the face of criticism of his support for the Communists in the Chinese civil war. The congress's second convention in 1949 attracted over 1,700 delegates. The congress conducted a number of extremely successful petition campaigns, collecting over 300,000 names in support of the Stockholm Appeal, which was co-authored by Endicott and argued that the first country to use atomic weapons in the future would be guilty of committing a war crime. While Endicott was not an official member of the Communist Party, he most certainly was an energetic fellow traveller, and throughout his career he was a far more vigilant critic of Western warmongering than of the arms race carried out by Eastern Bloc countries. This flowed from his belief that because of the non-competitive nature of Soviet societies, they were less likely to precipitate a nuclear war.

Communists did play a major behind-the-scenes role in the congress. When Endicott sided with the Chinese in the Sino-Soviet split, he was visited by party leader William Kashtan and asked to resign. Endicott did so, but he refused to cite health reasons, as Kashtan had suggested, as the reason for his resignation.

It was as a member of the Canadian Peace Congress that Zuken came into conflict with the federal government in 1950. In November of that year the World Council of Peace was holding an international meeting in Sheffield, England. Zuken, representing the United Jewish People's Organization, was one of the Canadian Peace Congress's twenty-two delegates scheduled to attend. But in early November he was complaining to the press that the government had deliberately delayed his application for a passport. He released a copy of a telegram he had sent to External Affairs Minister Lester Pearson:

> On October 6, I applied for Canadian passport and have received no passport despite letters and telegrams to the passport officer. Only information my Ottawa solicitor has received is that my application has been referred to you for decision.
>
> Long unusual delay would indicate attempt being made to delay passport until too late to attend Sheffield Peace Congress and visit Israel. Such unwarranted delay and obstruction will be regarded as discrimination against me and serious change in government policy....

It was only on November 8, five days before the conference was set to open, that he received a telegram from Pearson saying that a passport would be issued. Ironically, the British Labour government declined to allow some of the delegates from Eastern Europe into the country, so at the last moment the conference was moved from Sheffield to Warsaw.

One might be tempted to suggest Zuken was merely chasing headlines, trying to make an issue out of what may well have been the regular operation of a slow and creaky bureaucracy. But the evidence is now clear — the federal government viewed the control of passports as another Cold War weapon. Leopold Infeld, a University of Toronto physics professor, also attended the Warsaw peace conference, and as a result, the RCMP concluded that his "disloyalty" to Canada was "of long standing" and the Canadian attaché in Poland demanded he return his passport.

In 1950 the federal cabinet debated whether or not, as a matter of policy, Communists should be denied passports, and the following year the minister of external affairs recommended to cabinet that the passports of fifteen "known Communists" be invalidated and that another 101 Communists have their applications turned down if they were to apply for one. These proposals were rejected, in part because the government recognized the hypocrisy involved in creating its own iron curtain while attacking the one the Soviets were erecting. But equal weight was given to the argument that since the list of people who were to be refused passports was the same as the list of people who were slated for internment in the event of war, "the names of the people on the list for internment would by degrees become known to the Communist organization."

The message that Zuken brought back from Warsaw was a predictable, if slightly ingenuous, defence of the independence of the congress. In an address to a meeting of the United Jewish People's Organization, Zuken steadfastly denied that the World Council of Peace was a front organization. "The only politics that we discussed at the Congress — if you call it politics — was how to get the powerful forces of the world to work together." And he also credited the council with helping to block the use of the bomb in the Korean War, which at that point had been raging for half a year. "If the Atom Bomb hasn't been dropped in Korea, it is because those who would pull the trigger for global conflict know the will for peace is stronger than the will for war."

In November 1951, at the height of the Korean conflict, Zuken outlined the basics of his world view in a speech to a meeting of the Student Christian Movement. Reflecting on the anxieties created by the Cold War, Zuken claimed that "misery, and not communism, was the basic fault in the world today and it has inspired hundreds of thousands who are building a new society." The world was being swept by a "liberation movement and a surging forward, not dominated by private ownership or lust for wealth. The dropping of an A-bomb on either Washington or Moscow will not decide the superiority of either Communism or capitalism." And in a conciliatory, if contradictory, vein he added that he believed it is possible for the two social systems to peacefully co-exist.

Zuken and the Free Press

When Joe Zuken died in the spring of 1986, the media was full of tribute. The headline above the *Winnipeg Free Press* editorial read, "A Strong Voice Silenced," and the editorial noted how, even in retirement, "Joe Zuken could still fill a hall for a protest meeting and still deliver a stinging, eloquent, moving, entertaining political speech, a model of its kind." It concluded that "Winnipeg will be a poorer place without him." These tributes reflected the high public esteem in which Zuken was held during the latter years of his public career. But they make even more interesting reading when examined in the context of the treatment Zuken received at the hands of the *Tribune* and more particularly the *Free Press* during the Cold War.

The *Free Press* had of course never been sympathetic to the aspirations of organized labour or the social democratic movement, let alone the Communist Party. But in the postwar years the paper's editorial policy fell to particularly low levels. In his memoirs Tom Kent writes that when he became the paper's editor in 1954, the paper was "not greatly zealous about the quality of its news coverage and, retaining the traditions of strongly partisan journalism, had no inhibitions about using the news columns to support its editorial opinions." These opinions he characterized as representing an "out-dated, right wing liberalism." When Kent left the paper in 1959, he felt it soon quickly fell into its old ways.

From the late Forties on, as Zuken emerged as a particularly effective public representative for the Communist Party, the *Free Press* subjected him to regular editorial attacks. One of the earliest came in 1949 when Zuken, running as an LPP candidate in the upcoming federal election, took out advertisements in the daily newspapers calling for an abolition of the sales tax and an increase in personal income tax exemptions. The *Free Press* characterized this as

> a typical Communist performance. Mr. Zuken, like the rest of the Moscow breed, works on the familiar Communist system. The system, simply put, is to weaken and destroy our system of government. Freedom, in the sense that we know it, and, indeed, extend it to such people as the Zukens, Penners, and Kardashes, is hateful to Communists. They believe in the kind of dictatorship ... which exists in Russia.

While Zuken was supportive of the Soviet government, this sort of attack completely ignored the possibility that his proposed tax reforms might have merited examination.

Zuken was always proud of his abilities as a news maker. Long before the age of media consultants and thirty-second sound bites, he knew how to hone an issue and present it effectively. But as the Cold War dragged on, he began to suspect he was not getting the coverage his actions deserved, and he complained about it. On June 15, 1949, the *Free Press* replied:

He is offering nothing new, nothing that would make him particularly newsworthy. He is merely repeating the much-publicized Soviet propaganda with respect to the Atlantic Pact and the Marshall Plan. On the basis of their value as news Mr. Zuken's speeches are receiving generous coverage. If he is not satisfied with the publicity he is getting he has only himself to blame. If his speeches had less of the redundant effect of a cracked gramophone from Moscow, he might do better. There is yet time.

Despite the paper's campaign against him, Zuken won re-election to the school board in 1949, prompting one of the most bizarre attacks the paper had levelled against him to date. As a part of the 1949 municipal election, there was a general referendum on a school spending by-law. Throughout the campaign both Zuken and the *Free Press* supported the by-law, which was defeated. The *Free Press* pointed out that in those polls where Zuken did well, the by-law did poorly; while in the polls that Zuken lost, the by-law fared much better. From this the paper concluded:

Communists are not concerned about the welfare of this country or its people. They are concerned about electing Communists to office and if they think they can capitalize on issues involving the public weal in order to elect their men, they will quickly do so. Their main ambition is to elect Communists so that they may be able to employ the forum offered by a public body to advance their propaganda.

Since the majority of civic voters also rejected the by-law, the paper might have concluded that they were either not interested in the welfare of the country or that they were Communists; but the editors shrank from the obvious conclusions of their logic. In a withering reply Zuken noted that blaming him for the defeat of the by-law made as much sense as blaming him for the "poor showing of the Winnipeg Blue Bombers." And he went on to attack the paper's editorial writers directly:

> There was a time when the *Free Press* under J. W. Dafoe and G. V. F [Ferguson] could argue with its political opponents with dignity and fairness. Your hysterical insinuation in blaming me in connection with the School By-law is an indication that you are refusing to face the facts, that despite your frenzied efforts I headed the poll in first choices. Isn't it about time that the *Free Press* stopped its convulsions at the sound of my name and ended its silly political tantrums.

The following year the paper ran an editorial with the headline "Source, Please?" questioning where the funds for Zuken's federal election campaign had come from. The paper pointed out that the $4,649.48 reportedly spent on Zuken's campaign rivalled the amounts spent by the leaders of the three major parties. The editors wondered: "Since the Communists, relatively speaking, receive few votes, and, in reality, have little popular support or following in this country, and presumably have no access to normal sources of campaign funds, it would be interesting to know where these Communists' campaign funds came from."

In his response Zuken referred to the various political scandals that had dogged the Liberal Party through its fund-raising history and asked, "Is that what your editorial means when it states that I 'presumably have not access to normal sources of campaign funds?' "

Zuken claimed that his campaigns were funded by small private donations, while "not one dollar was contributed by the big corporations who finance the Liberal and Tory parties and who call their tune. My campaign funds do not include any foreign currency — either Yankee Marshall funds or roubles. What is the source, please, of the pitiful decline of the *Free Press* to the journalistic level of the Hearst Press?"

On the eve of the 1951 municipal election, the paper ran an editorial that made its position explicit. After taking Zuken to task for advocating an increase in provincial government spending on education, the paper called for his defeat:

> What is astonishing is that Mr. Zuken, an avowed Communist, should have the nerve to address the electors of this city at all on the subject of education. To any stranger coming to Winnipeg from a democratic country the one fact about us which would be unbelievable is that the electors of this city, in times like the present, would allow a Communist to hold a seat — of all places on the School Board....
>
> By every test that can be applied, Mr. Zuken is utterly unfitted to have the slightest authority over education in this city.
>
> The only reason that he is a member of the School Board is the indifference of the electors. Communists are elected in ward three because half of the voters fail to vote.
>
> This year, with the world situation as it is, the electors should do their duty and clear the Communists out of the School Board, and to the extent possible, the city council.

The electors did not pay heed to this advice. Instead of defeating him they re-elected Zuken to the board at the top of the poll.

The *Free Press*'s insistence on raising the issue of communism at every opportunity can be seen in the debate over the municipal takeover of the electrical and transportation system in 1952. The paper's publisher, Victor Sifton, was deeply opposed to a government-run hydro-electric monopoly, and the paper campaigned vigorously against the proposal, which was known as Plan C. When Zuken and other members of the Manitoba Communist Party came out in favour of the proposal, the *Free Press* editorialists could barely constrain their glee. Along with a front-page story on the endorsement, the paper ran this short editorial in the spring of 1952: "News item: Our local Communists have approved of Plan C. This is in no way surprising. Plan C has all the characteristics that appeal to the Communist philosophy."

In the fall of 1952 Zuken was once more nominated to run for the LPP in the upcoming federal election in Winnipeg North. The *Free Press* responded with a brief editorial, headlined "Moscow's Man," which concluded:

In short this so-called Labor Progressive Party is the Communist party. The words Labor and Progressive are merely the green glasses and whiskers used by the Communists to hide their identity.

Likewise Mr. Joe Zuken, the nominated candidate, is neither a labor man nor a progressive. He is a straight run-of-the-mill Communist complete with diploma and all the usual credentials from Moscow.

Zuken responded with a letter to the editor, and borrowing from Norman Bethune, he made a suggestion: "Why a Moscow hireling? Why not a British hireling? The theory of socialism was proclaimed in London 60 years before the Russian revolution." He ended by asking the paper to debate "the issues rather than doing a crude imitation of Senator Mc-Carthy." To make sure Zuken did not succeed in getting the last word, the *Free Press* gave a same-day response to this letter with an editorial headlined "Red Star Zuken." This editorialist seemed to feel he had refuted Zuken's argument by pointing out that the British Labour Party regularly expelled Communists. The editorial concluded by reminding readers that the last Communist elected to Parliament, Fred Rose, went into "involuntary" retirement when he was convicted on espionage charges.

The *Free Press* was not alone in making these attacks. In the winter of 1953 the *Tribune* spent a week "exposing" the night school programs run by left-wing Ukrainian and Russian organizations. The series started with an article that had three separate headlines: "Communism for Grade 1," "City Reds Want Children's Minds" and "Night Classes Using Soviet Books." In the breathless prose of the period, the article warned that "an insidious encroachment is being made today by Communist agencies through a program of 'education' aimed at young Canadians, down to the Grade 1 level." The first article revealed that two of the Slavic evening schools in the city used "some of the same books which are used in

Russia." The article is fascinating for the way it attributed
Communists with near mystical abilities to successfully propa-
gandize for their cause.

In dramatic language, the article spoke of how

> during the day most children attend public school, learn-
> ing the Canadian way of life. But for an unfortunate few,
> an opposite course of education is taught at night classes.
> It is here that youngsters are subjected to indoctrination
> of Communist Russia. These rival teachings present chil-
> dren with a conflict of ideas which, through skillful Com-
> munist persuasion, place pre-eminence on the Soviet way
> of life while Canada takes a back seat.

No representatives of either school were interviewed for this
article, nor was there any indication that they had been
contacted.

In the spring of 1955 the *Free Press* topped this series of
articles with a classic work of McCarthy-style red-baiting. The
front page of the Saturday, May 21, 1955, paper bore a brief
story headlined "Boring from Within," with a subtitle, "Winnipeg Scene of Communist Triumph." The story revealed that
three "key Manitoba Communists" had won election to the
executive of the Inkster Home and School Association. Included in this subversive troika were the newly elected association president Anne Ross, the wife of provincial party
leader Bill Ross, W. G. Gilbey, a union organizer who had run
for the LPP in a number of elections, and his wife Anne Gilbey.
Readers were told that to the best of the Home and School
Federation's knowledge, no other local federation had been
infiltrated — and "for a report on how the Communists invaded the Inkster association and what has happened since
they got there, see today's Free Press feature section on Page
27."

There, under a banner headline that screamed "How the
Reds Invaded the Inkster Home and School" and filling three-
quarters of the front page of the weekend supplement, was an
article written by Ted Byfield (who has gone on to become the
publisher of the right-wing *Western Report* and *Alberta Report*)
which detailed the perfidious events. The article was illustrated

with three sets of photos; over pictures of former alderman
Peter Taraska and the school principal ran the headline "They
Bucked Red Invasion...," while over photographs of Gilbey,
Ross and Zuken ran the words "...But Skilled Performers Took
the Day." Under Zuken's picture the caption read, "On A
Fateful Night, A Visitor." The caption for a picture of the
school itself read, "In Peaceful Inkster School, Communism
Won A Battle."

The story started with a description of Anne Ross's recent
brief to the Winnipeg School Board in support of the music
and swimming program. (She had told the board she thought
the instrumental music program helped parents battle "a great
many influences that parents are not very happy about —
comics, TV and the movies.") "Mrs. Ross," Byfield wrote,
"presented her case with a competence not usually acquired
in home and school clubs," suggesting that public speaking
was a sinister art. The trustees had no questions for Ross at the
time, but according to the article, they were all wondering how
she had managed to become a home and school leader.

They got their answer from the former president of the
Inskter Home and School Association, Albert Gable. According to him, the trouble started at a meeting in February 1952
when the association debated a Manitoba Peace Council
proposal to oppose civil defence exercises. Present at the meeting were Anne Ross, William and Anne Gilbey and local
school trustee Joseph Zuken. "Suddenly," Mr. Gable recalled:

> these people began to take over the meeting. They were
> on their feet one after the other. They hammered away
> about war-mongering in the schools. They said our
> children were going to be war-minded.
>
> What could we do about it? We can't make speeches
> like those people. They're trained for things like this.
> We're just ordinary people. And they're convincing. Even
> my wife was taken in and was going to vote for a protest.
> Practically nobody voted against the idea.

The meeting approved the protest, but at a second meeting,
held at the behest of Taraska, the decision was reversed. Ross,
Gilbey and others continued to attend association meetings,

where, according to Gable, they would heckle and interrupt him. In the end he resigned. According to the paper, "since then, new officers have been added to the association executive. The position of 'film convenor' has been added at the suggestion of Mrs. Ross. She herself agreed to take over the position and arrange to have films." Once it was discovered that Ross was a Communist, a Home and School Federation "official quickly checked the films shown to parents, and found that Mrs. Ross's program had included only children's classics and mental health films."

Opposition to the direction the association was taking also came from the school's new principal, Lewis Walker: "I found the association sending feelers into all sorts of irrelevant endeavours" — including "a tot lot, a playground area, and the reopening of an Inkster school rink. Delegations were being planned to that board and this."

Under the so-called red leadership, the association opposed the reduction of the number of school trustees from fifteen to nine; according to Byfield, the proposed reduction was "a clear threat to the seat held by Trustee Zuken." It was in fact a somewhat less than clear threat, since Zuken regularly topped North End polls during this period.

In sum the exposé had exposed very little — Anne Ross had been elected by an open meeting of the Inkster Home and School Association, and the policies she had proposed were hardly subversive, unless music lessons and tot lots were to be seen as the cutting edge of the world Communist conspiracy. She had not told other parents she was involved in the Communist Party, and while the *Free Press* made this out to be deception, it is doubtful that non-Communists were expected to announce their political affiliations upon becoming involved in the association. According to Byfield, Ross was known as "an enthusiastic parent with a passionate interest in home and school." Nowhere was there any suggestion in the article that as a parent with a child attending Inkster School she had a perfectly legitimate right to play a role in the Inster Home and School Association. Judging by the intensely one-sided article, there appear to have been no efforts made to interview Ross, the Gilbeys or Zuken. Of course, the paper felt that all it had to do was prove they were Communists, not that they had actually done anything other than try and improve the quality of education local children were receiving. Given the level of discipline and planning within the Communist Party, it is not unlikely that the party was aware of, and probably approved of, the efforts of some of its leading members to play leadership roles in the home and school association, but it is doubtful the Liberal or Conservative parties discouraged their members from doing the same.

The press's revelations, scanty as they were, had an impact. One fellow executive member, Josephine Johnson, told Byfield: "We had no idea Mrs. Ross was connected with communism. When we read the paper, we began making inquiries. We considered resigning, but we felt it would be best to stay in the association and fight it out."

By the end of May more than 150 parents of students attending Inkster School had signed a petition calling for the disbanding of the home and school association. In the wake of these protests, the provincial home and school association investigated the Inkster branch, but came to the conclusion that it was "legally and democratically" elected.

Citizenship and the Cold War

In its wake the Second World War left millions of uprooted people strewn across Europe. Men and women who had collaborated with the Axis powers, heroes of the resistance, prisoners of war and survivors of the Nazi concentration camps, all of them wandered the face of a devastated continent and filled the bulging refugee camps. Not surprisingly many of these storm-tossed souls looked to the New World for escape. The Canadian government attempted to skim off the most economically promising of these refugees. But efforts also were made to screen out those who for security reasons were undesirable. Despite the fact that the recently completed war had been fought against Nazi Germany, the RCMP officials in charge of security showed far more zeal in excluding left-wing immigrants than ex-Nazis.

In the postwar period the East Bloc countries demanded the repatriation of any of its citizens who were in Western Europe. In 1945 two million such "displaced persons" were returned to the Soviet Union. Many Ukrainian and Polish refugees, having already had a taste of Stalinism, had no desire to return. Ironically, the RCMP and the Canadian Communist Party adopted similar attitudes to these refugees; they did not want them admitted to Canada. The RCMP suspected them because they were fleeing Communist states; it feared that the Soviets had infiltrated this wave of refugees with spies. The Communists believed that the only people who had reason to fear returning to the Soviet Union were Nazis and their collaborators; consequently, they were often fierce critics of postwar immigration policy. When he ran for Parliament in 1953, Zuken argued that Winnipeg North needed a "representative who will effectively fight against the flooding of our country by Fascist D.P.s."

Since Canadian security officials have often viewed both socialism and communism as an alien virus, carried by the foreign-born, it is not surprising that during the Cold War efforts were made to strip leftists of their citizenship or deny it to long-time residents suspected of left-wing sympathies. As with other elements of the Cold War, this was not a new tactic; deportation of radicals had been a visceral response to the Winnipeg General Strike and was extensively practised by the federal government during the early 1930s.

Although senior cabinet ministers and civil servants like Gordon Robertson believed there was a need for "more active use of revocation [of citizenship] against persons who are active Communists and who can properly be regarded as 'disloyal,' " it was in fact a seldom-used tactic. The legal proceedings could be protracted and embarrassing, and there would still be the question of what was to be done with people whose citizenship had been revoked but whom no country was willing to take in.

Denial of citizenship, however, was another matter. In 1948 a county court judge refused to support an application for naturalization because the applicant belonged to the Workers' Benevolent Association, a left-wing insurance organization. Even when applicants navigated their way through the citizenship courts, the immigration minister had the authority to deny citizenship. These cases were usually decided on the basis of RCMP security reports. In 1950 the RCMP submitted negative recommendations in eighty-four cases; some applicants were CP members, while others were married to

Communists, subscribed to left-wing publications or kept "framed portraits of Communist heroes in [their] home." The chairman of the security panel dealing with these cases concluded that "any person identified with the Communist Party, whether by affiliation with a Communist-dominated group or as an active party member, has proved himself unworthy of enjoying the fruits of Canadian citizenship."

It was not until the early Sixties that any organized effort was made to lobby on behalf of those people who had been denied citizenship for political reasons. In 1962 Zuken acted as the counsel for the newly formed Canadian Council of National Groups, a coalition of largely left-wing ethnic organizations that was determined to have the discretionary provisions of the immigration act eliminated. Speaking at a Dominion Day celebration organized by the CCNG in 1962, Zuken outlined the case against the immigration act. Calling it a "disgrace to a civilized country and a crime against democracy," he charged that the RCMP was operating as a political police force, denying citizenship to people who were engaged in perfectly legal political behaviour. He drew laughter with this case: "One woman, for example, was denied citizenship because the RCMP had a record in their files that she once helped to make 'pyrohy' (dumplings) for a social or banquet in a Ukrainian hall. Perry Mason could make something of that. It might well be called 'The Case of the Subversive Pyrohy.' "

He pointed out that the discretionary power accorded the immigration minister under the act allowed violation of provisions of the Bill of Rights. "Citizenship," he argued, "must be considered a constitutional right," a right for all, including the "immigrant and native-born," and not be used as a "piece of candy or a carrot to be dangled before the people as if before a donkey." Zuken and the CCNG took the position that citizenship should be granted to those of eighteen years and older who had resided in Canada for the past five years and not been convicted of treason.

In the fall of 1962 Zuken presented the CCNG's case to the then minister of citizenship and immigration Richard Bell. As in the days of the Defence of Canada Regulations, Zuken found himself at odds with a system that made no provisions for due process. The government was not compelled to give reasons for rejecting citizenship applications; applicants were not allowed the opportunity to refute the evidence the RCMP might enter against them. "It is cold comfort and an exceedingly poor substitute for proper, and democratic appeal procedures, to notify an applicant that in two years' time he has the 'privilege' of being subjected to the same arbitrary cycle of trial by file."

In marshalling its arguments, the CCNG was able to provide numerous cases of people who not only had been denied citizenship, but who had been led to believe that if they would inform on their left-wing friends, the citizenship ruling would likely be reversed in their favour. The campaign to change the immigration act failed, and the continued harassment of foreign-born radicals continued. Zuken's personal papers contain references to the RCMP's questioning of a Dauphin man over his membership in the Association of United Ukrainian Canadians in 1964. That same year two Mounties visited a woman in The Pas to question her on whether she belonged to the Ukrainian Labour- Farmer Temple, who the other members were and what sort of meetings were held there. The following year, the police asked a Swan River, Manitoba, man for his passport and began to question him about local members of the Ukrainian Canadian community.

The Cold War in the Jewish Community

The Cold War also rent asunder the country's Jewish organizations. These battles touched Zuken deeply, for while he was not religiously observant, he most certainly considered himself a Jew. In 1950 he participated in a public debate with a number of leading members of the Jewish community on the topic "Who is a Jew?" In the discussion Zuken argued for a pluralism in Jewish life.

I said we could probably learn from the quotation "In my father's house there are many mansions." In other words there are many roads to being a Jew. And ... while I understand those who follow the religious path, to claim that it is only through the synagogue that one is a Jew; well my mother would never accept that definition. They would face the wrath of my mother if they ever suggested that I was not a Jew.

There is the secular approach. The richness of Jewish literature and culture, the humanism of the Jewish classical writers and their teachings of respect for the Jewish people. The fact that the classical writers attacked those who robbed the widows and the fact that they did not raise material matters to the highest rank. Our literature is full of a cry for social justice and humane treatment.

Zuken was a member of the United Jewish People's Organization, a direct descendant of the Arbeiter Ring or Workers Circle organizations that working-class Jews had established when they first came to North America. Not all of its members belonged to the Communist Party, but the organization generally followed the party line. Its leaders were Communists, it regularly invited Communist politicians to address its functions, and it supported the public campaigns launched by the party. The organization sponsored camps, publications and schools, carrying on the tradition of the Jewish radical and cultural organizations of the turn of the century. The Jewish Communists also took a hard line against Zionism, which they characterized as a "reactionary, bourgeois-nationalist movement." During the Second World War, when support for the CP was at its height, UJPO managed to win admittance into the Canadian Jewish Congress.

On his return from Europe in 1950, Zuken took part in a UJPO-sponsored speaking tour, opposing the proposed rearmament of West Germany. According to Zuken, this campaign was used as a reason for expelling UJPO from the Canadian Jewish Congress. "The pretext was that the left was undertaking campaigns which had not been sanctioned, and that campaigns had to be sanctioned by the national executive and by the congress as a whole. If that campaign had not taken place, another pretext would have been found.... I think the leadership of the Canadian Jewish Congress got the message from the government of Canada, and they acted in the Jewish community as the government of Canada began to react with respect to the left." While the CJC established internal quotas limiting the number of Communists who could be appointed to its committees as early as 1947, it waited until 1951 to expel

UJPO. Zuken remained an active member of UJPO throughout his life, helping the organization develop an increasingly independent position towards the Soviet Union, particularly in regard to its treatment of Soviet Jews.

Life in the Party

The Communist Party of Canada was not an organization a person joined lightly. Not only was a party member likely to be subjected to social ostracism and, at times, state repression, but a Communist also had to submit to the discipline of party life. Members were expected to "implement the decisions of the party, observe party discipline, and oppose everything detrimental to the working class and the party." The key to party decision making was the principle of democratic centralism, a concept involving far more centralism than democracy. Members were obliged to "unconditionally carry out" party decisions, even if they were in disagreement with them.

During the 1950s one of the CP's leading figures in Manitoba was Jacob Penner's son Roland. After serving in the Canadian Army during the Second World War, Roland sat on both the provincial executive and council of the Manitoba branch of the CPC and was also the head of the National Federation of Labour Youth. According to Penner, Zuken did not play a major role in the organizational life of the party during this period. "Joe was very much the individualist, not an organizational type. He was not considered to be one of the leaders of the party like Bill Kardash, my father or Mitch Sago; they were the activists and the organizers. Joe was very much left to do his own thing. I think in a way almost — although I could not document this — this was a matter of decision. [They felt] that Joe's value to the left was as a public official and spokesperson and that part of his activity would be prejudiced by being too actively involved in organization."

Zuken himself recognized that he did not play a leadership role in the party. In part he attributed this to the fact that he was consumed by his legal and political careers. But he also harboured the belief that many in the party were just as glad he was not involved in the inner life of the party. "I am not making a flat-out statement, but there was this suspicion of the intellectuals." In later years Zuken wondered what would have happened if he had taken a greater responsibility for what went on in the party.

Despite this, Zuken was by no means completely divorced from party life, or the party line. The Forties were a period of continual shift for the Communist Party. As noted earlier, following the invasion of the Soviet Union in 1941, the party committed itself all out to the war effort. This commitment led to increased party support for the Liberal Party — CP leaders often criticized CCFers of this period for being too left wing in their policy positions. Later on, when the Labor Progressive Party was formed in 1943, William Kardash wrote to the Manitoba CCF, proposing that the LPP be allowed to affiliate with the CCF. However, when the federal CCF came out in favour of the Marshall Plan, one of the key instruments of President Truman's Cold War policy, the party reverted to form and began attacking the social democrats as sell-outs to capitalism. Zuken was once more enlisted as a candidate in the upcoming federal election, and he took to the attack with apparent vigour. In an campaign broadcast in 1949, he denounced Alistair Stewart for supporting "the war program of the St. Laurent government":

He has joined the Liberals and Tories in endorsing the Marshall Plan over the protest of the Manitoba CCF provincial convention.

He's joined the Liberals and Tories behind the North Atlantic Pact, a war pact which would place Canada and her people at the mercy of American brass hats and war mongers.

Alistair Stewart joins the Chamber of Commerce and the un-American activities committee in developing a spirit of hysteria around the false issue of the menace of Communism which was Hitler's battle cry.

Following the right-wing victory in that year's provincial election in British Columbia, Zuken once more attacked the CCF. "The fact is that the top leadership of the CCF in B.C. was too busy splitting the labor movement and red-baiting to join in an all-out fight against the reactionary coalition."

Stanley Ryerson was for many years one of the Canadian Communist Party's leading theoreticians and intellectuals. He left the party in 1968 following the Soviet invasion of Czechoslovakia. Despite this he maintained a close personal friendship with Zuken until the latter's death in 1986. Ryerson painted a complex picture of the relationship between Zuken and the party. According to Ryerson: "In a certain sense the axis of his life was an identification with what he perceived as the party's reason for being; that is, the problem of creating an alternative society, other than corporate private enterprise society, was absolutely basic in relation to social justice and people's rights. And there was no other political organization, or political current, that embodied the idea of a revolutionary transformation.... This is important to the fact that I believe he remained a member of the Communist Party to the end."

Ryerson recalled that when they encountered each other at national party meetings, they "tended to be on the same wavelength from the point of view of a critical reassessment of orientations and policies, relations of the party to the Soviet party and so forth. I would see him sometimes at central committee meetings where we would be critical of what we saw as either dogmatism or sectarianism or bureaucratic habits." Despite occasional criticism, Zuken was held in high regard by the party's national leadership, and his opinions were always given a hearing.

Ryerson also credited Zuken with bringing to the party a deeper understanding and commitment to democracy. "If you have a lawyer who is on the one hand an excellent embodiment of the profession ... [and on the other hand has] a passionate social conscience, then the question of democracy will stand in a particular way." Ryerson felt Zuken provided an important antidote to the stream of left-wing thought which argues that in light of the undemocratic distribution of economic power in capitalist society, parliamentary democracy is little more than a sham. While holding with much of this critique, Ryerson felt it led the party to "underestimate the democratic ingredient, the democratic content that there is in bourgeois democracy. And that has deep-going political implications in terms of your attitudes towards the electorate, towards neighbourhood, towards people, community groups;

the fact there really is a democratic dimension that is not just formal."

In one very intimate way Zuken was connected with the leadership of the CP in Manitoba. In December 1948 the party selected Bill Ross as its provincial leader. In his first speech as leader, Ross warned that "Manitoba has become a link in the chain of war bases being built by U.S. imperialism to encircle the Soviet Union. Air bases and army camps at Rivers, Mac-Donald, Gimli and Shilo, and in the northern part of the province are being continually enlarged and expanded." Ross also made sure he got in his shots at the CCF, which he accused of "peddling anti-Communism."

The basic organizing unit for the party was the club. These could be established according to workplace, community or any other activity. They were to meet regularly, elect an executive and work to "bring about the closest relationship between the Party and the working people in the area in which it works." According to Penner, Zuken was probably not an active member of any club — "That was one of the dispensations he received."

Clara Zuken's experiences provide an interesting glimpse into the life of a rank-and-file member of the Communist Party. "I found the ideas of the party very interesting; they still are, but there are some things I disagree on. I am more mature, now I can judge things better, but in those days we were so idealistic. In a way, when I told you that when I joined the left-wing movement I felt my mind opening up, I could almost feel the wheels turning physically; after many, many years, and after Khrushchev's speech and all that, I began to feel that my mind had closed. I never doubted that everything that was brought up was just 100 per cent correct."

In the late Thirties, Clara contemplated leaving the party. She was coming under pressure from party members to help organize a union in the garment factory where she worked. "I could not stand it, I didn't want it. I said, 'I am not even a good worker, how can I be a good organizer?' " One day in the midst of this period she was walking with Zuken, talking about the pressure she was feeling. She burst into tears, exclaiming, "I want to leave the party, I can't stand it." And Zuken, who was not even a party member himself at the time, talked her out of her decision, advising her, "This is a very important step to take. Think about it."

Clara found the expectations of party life oppressive: "I did not like the weekly chores — I used to hate going to sell the paper, I used to hate collecting money, I used to hate selling tickets. I don't like to impose my will — to organize people. I will be very happy if you sell me a ticket, and I will give you all the credit. You are doing me a favour because of the fact that I am not selling the ticket, all I have to do is give you money."

Even before the revelations of 1956, Clara was once more thinking of leaving the party. Once she discussed it over coffee with Tim Buck. She recalled telling the party leader, "I am bored, I am not interested, I don't want to attend meetings, I don't like the set-up." Buck dissuaded her, saying it would not be good for Joe, given his emerging political career. "And me being a good kid, I don't want to rock the boat. I was not that active; I just continued, I did not want to create any problems."

The Crisis of 1956

"When Stalin died," recalled Clara Zuken, "do you know what? I cried. We were somewhere — the Ukrainian Labour Temple — someone said he died and I stood up there and I cried as if I had lost my father. And Joe is standing beside me and he says very quietly, 'It should have happened a few years ago.' I will never forget that."

On February 14, 1956, leaders of Communist parties from around the world gathered in Moscow to attend the Twentieth Congress of the Communist Party of the Soviet Union. It was the first party congress since the death of Joseph Stalin in 1953, and it would rock the Communist movement to its core. At the end of the congress, Nikita Khrushchev delivered what may be the world's most publicized "secret" speech. All the foreign delegates were excluded from the session where Khrushchev catalogued the crimes of Stalinism, detailing how one man's tyrannical rule had led to decades of repression.

Zuken had little trouble accepting the Khrushchev speech as valid. As far back as the Moscow show trials, he had experienced misgivings about the events in the Soviet Union. At that time he had been able to put these worries out of his mind when leading members of the British Communist Party had travelled to Moscow and pronounced the trials to be legitimate.

Following the release of the speech in 1956, Buck and other party leaders went to Moscow for a special audience with Khrushchev. On their return, they gave conflicting reports on what they had been told. As the divided leadership toured the country, many long-time party members began to leave. A special meeting of the party national executive adopted a resolution, moved by Jacob Penner's older son Norman, that Tim Buck be removed from his position of leadership in the party. However, before the resolution could be debated by the party's National Committee, Penner withdrew the motion.

Plans were drawn up for a full-scale debate to take place at the party convention in the fall of 1956. The party's establishment put forward a resolution calling for a return to business as usual; Norman Penner proposed a break with the Soviet Union and a new, less divisive approach to the CCF; and a third group of party activists proposed a break with Marxism-Leninism and the development of a "socialist realignment."

In Manitoba, a provincial convention was held in the fall of 1956 in preparation for the national convention. Roland Penner remembered those days: "In anticipation of the provincial convention a number of us sought to formulate a resolution which basically was not particularly condemnatory — just saying something has gone wrong here, let us look into this, let us do something — it was almost as mild as that. Joe and I were the movers of that resolution. And in the end about its sole supporters.

"I will never forget the meeting in the Point Douglas Labour Temple. Person after person got up and denounced us — not Joe particularly, because Joe in a way was always sacrosanct — but I was certainly denounced — 'See what happens when we send them to university; they get tainted with this bourgeois ideology, they think they are better than us.' There was that kind of populist rejection of anything that smacked of intellectualism or skepticism. I know that Joe was very upset at the attitudes which were displayed at that time."

According to Penner, Zuken's speech at the convention emphasized that "clearly there had been grave errors and we have to find out why — the leadership must have known — we have to change our ways."

Party leaders were not interested in changing their ways. The old guard rallied the troops to its defence. Buck and his supporters made sure each provincial convention selected full slates of "pro-party" delegates to be sent to the annual convention in Toronto. The convention's outcome was thus a foregone conclusion. Those calling for a rethinking of the party's direction and its relationship to the Soviet Union were defeated. Within the year, most of them had left the party. Norman Penner waited until after his father was safely re-elected to Winnipeg City Council before severing his party membership. His brother Roland's membership simply "withered on the vine." Roland was also concerned not to do anything that would hurt his parents or could be used by his father's political opponents. "I began doing less and less. I came off the provincial executive. Towards the end I was simply a member of a club and then began simply not attending." Like many former Communists, he is unable to remember the exact year he left the party.

As it became apparent that internal party reform was not possible, Clara Zuken let her membership lapse. She recalled: "One day I said to my friends, 'Look I am leaving the party at the end of December. I am paying my dues to the end of December. I am not making any speeches. You can tell the executive whatever you want, I just don't want to belong to the party anymore.' I paid up my dues — and I stopped going to meetings."

Although Zuken considered leaving the party, in the end he chose to remain. And while he rarely voiced public criticism of the party, he likened the Soviet invasion of Hungary to the actions of the British and French armies during the Suez crisis, telling a *Tribune* reporter that "foreign troops should be withdrawn from Hungary and Egypt." William Kardash told the same reporter the two incidents were not comparable, since the Soviet troops had "acted in response to the request of the Hungarian government."

Between the Khrushchev revelations and the Hungarian invasion, many long-time party members, particularly among the Jewish community, decided it was time to leave. Zuken recalled: "Some people, people that I had known for a number of years, told me they were quitting. They had already made up their minds, they were not kindergarten kids. I said the only question that is really bothering me is, 'Where will you be politically, where will you go? ... Where will you end up, that is, five years after, ten years?' They said they did not know. I said that is the big question you have to face as well. Sure it bothered me. The reason why I didn't [leave] was because the party ... had the best program of any party. And I could not see any other alternative, any other party on the Canadian scene, including the CCF, that was committed to the socialist perspective, and the socialist road ahead, for Canada. So despite my own political reservations, that was it."

While Zuken may have understood why so many people left the party, thirty years later he had harsh words for some ex-members who went public with their criticism of the party. "I cannot accept the position of those who have made a complete flip-flop, who formerly were 180 per cent as a cheering section for the Soviet Union and now that they have left are equally vocal in denouncing the Soviet Union. What I am trying to say is one can as a Communist recognize the role of the Soviet Union.

"I make a distinction between those who left who left honestly, and those who used the events of the Khrushchev disclosures as an excuse for getting out and attacking the party. I can understand those who felt a sense of betrayal and disillusionment.

"But I also looked at the faces of the old-timers who had been working for the party, many of them perhaps not holding a party card. Around the labour halls in Winnipeg, and it is true of every city in Canada, you see the old-timers who for thirty, forty years and more have given their hopes, their dreams, their activities, their Jimmy Higgins work for the party.

"I think that those who left should have also thought of them. Because you don't spit in the face of the people who helped to do the work. And a lot of the work that was done was good work, damn it all, a lot of the work that was done was good work. When Annie Buller and Joe Forkin went up to help to organize some workers in Manitoba, when my brother put his freedom on the line, and went to Flin Flon and went to jail for it, and they are only examples. They were fighting for a cause.

"There were some terrible things that were done in the Soviet Union, under the Stalin regime. I said it before and I repeat it. Stalin died too late. He did some terrible things with his purges, his cult of personality and so on. He became paranoiac, so many enemies of the people, as he called them. OK. But you don't condemn the work of your comrades because of some very terrible things that were done by Stalin during a period of his life. Policies that Stalin put into force — it is a terrible pun, 'in force' — should never happen again, in any socialist country. There are those who left the party and then started to attack the party. For them I have only contempt. Because — I am not asking that their silence be bought or anything like that, but I think they should look at their own role in the party: did they ask questions, what is their estimation of the work that was done by their colleagues or comrades over a period of years, and what is their responsibility to the working people? Are they still socialists?? If so, how are they proving it?"

For any Communist the questions of Stalinism raise complex and often emotional questions. Those, like Zuken, who stayed in the party rarely have addressed those questions publicly, leaving people to guess at how they came to view that period. Often it is smaller things people say and do, not the carefully worded speeches or resolutions, that speak most clearly through the years. One of the books that held pride of place on Joe Zuken's living room bookcase was renegade Marxist Roy Medvedev's monumental history of the crimes of Stalinism, *Let History Judge*.

Just as eloquent perhaps is a small, undated cartoon tucked in Zuken's files on deposit in the Manitoba archives. The cartoon, which was originally run in a Yugoslavian paper, is set in heaven. There, an exasperated-looking God, with a fistful of newspapers in his hand, is admonishing a crest-fallen Stalin. "Joseph, Joseph," says the Lord, "when will you finally understand that you are really dead?"

The three brothers, *(left to right)*
Samuel, Joe and Cecil.

Zuken in Peretz School class picture. Zuken is in the front row,
his brother Cecil (Bill Ross) is the third from the right in second row.

Joe and Clara in 1933.

Clara Goldenberg at age 19 years.

Joe Zuken as a law school graduate, May 1936.

Joe in the New Theatre in 1940.

1964; new Winnipeg aldermen being sworn in by City Clerk, James Kinnear, *(left to right)*, William M. Garva, Mark Danzker, Lloyd Stinson, Terry Hind, Edith Tennant, Slaw Rebchuk, Donovan Swailes, Joseph Zuken and David Mulligan. *Photo credit Gerry Cairns.*

1961; Winnipeg Aldermen Forkin, W. Ross, (Mrs. Penner), J. Penner, J. Zuken.
Photo credit Gerry Cairns

1979; Joe Zuken, city councillor, and mayoralty candidate at his election offices after losing to Bill Norrie.
Photo credit Gerry Cairns.

March 1979; Joe Zuken and supporters defy city council and cross Portage and Main.

1983; Joe Zuken, retiring city councillor, and wife voting in the Winnipeg civic election. This marked the first time in 42 years Zuken could not vote for himself. *Photo credit J. Haggarty.*

SEVEN

A Shield for the Poor
1940-1986

We are living in a ruthless age. You have to see the human being behind the file.

Joseph Zuken graduated from the University of Manitoba Law School in 1936. An award-winning student, he did not go into full-time practice for another four and a half years. The Thirties were tough years for lawyers as well as for working-class Manitobans. During those years Zuken did a smattering of court work, taking on cases for the Canadian Labor Defense League and left-wing unions. Clara was working in garment factories during this period, and she found herself making more than her husband, who was teaching Yiddish history and literature. It was not until 1941, when the federal government used the War Measures Act to swamp Zuken with clients, that he set up his law office in the Confederation Building.

While those early cases were the most dramatic he was to handle, Zuken continued an active practice until his death in 1986. He created a legal firm that became known for its high ethical standards, its commitment to the interests of low-income people and the exceptional talent of its members. Unlike many professed radicals, Zuken was able to successfully incorporate his ideals into his professional life. Those people who worked with Zuken, whether as a client, a partner, an articling student or a secretary, all paint the same picture of him — that of a reserved, generous man who was fully committed to the task at hand and did not take his co-workers for granted.

In the spring of 1941 Mary Harrison was fresh out of Success Commercial College. She had been active for a number of years in various left-wing cultural organizations and was well aware of who Joseph Zuken was. When she heard that he was opening a law office and needed a secretary, she applied. Harrison worked with Zuken until 1948, when she left the firm to raise her family. She returned in 1961 as secretary to Roland Penner, who worked in the same law firm. In 1982 she went to work for the government of Manitoba as the personal secretary to the new attorney general, Roland Penner.

From the beginning, Harrison was struck with Joe Zuken's attitude towards his clients. "He always took a working person's situation into account." According to Harrison, not only did Zuken charge less than the prescribed tariff, he often gave advice away for free. "People would go in and talk to him about things and very often there would be no bill issued. The person walked in and walked out." And the consideration that was shown to clients was also extended to the support staff. Harrison believes the firm was better to work for than any of the bigger and more prestigious firms in the city. "You were allowed to be responsible for something and it was a learning process each time. You were given responsibility for work you had never done before. They let you grow. I think it a good office to work for; after all, I came back." Harrison recalled that when Zuken permitted himself a few moments' rest he could be charming and delightful: "He was a very warm person. If he was able to sit down with you and be relaxed, there would be a marvellous warm rapport going back and forth. That would be the most poignant memory I have of him. Deep down he was a very warm person, you could have a conversation with him about anything. He would not talk politics unless you raised the subject and then he would give you his version. He liked joking with that dry wit that would send us all roaring."

Going to court was not an easy thing for Zuken according to Harrison. "There were times when he had cases he was really unsure of and he would really suffer over them. Whether it was just a traffic ticket or someone charged with taking something from a store or whatever, he put his all into it. He would suffer before he went to court, he would get very tense. And when he came back, we knew right away whether it was a good decision or not by the way that he walked in."

In 1952 Joe and Clara were living in an apartment on Mountain Avenue. One evening they had friends over for dinner. While they were washing the dishes, Clara mentioned to her friend that Joe was a little concerned because his current secretary was getting married. "So my friend said, 'Why don't you work in the office?' I should work in the office! First of all I am not a secretary. I had gone to business college for six weeks and got the theory of shorthand, which I loved, got the theory of the typing, but I was never a good typist. I said, 'How could I work?? I am not experienced.'

"So when they were gone, I said that our friend suggested I should work in the office. I started laughing and Joe said, 'Maybe we should try it.' So we did and I learned on the job. I did the books — I knew nothing about the dual entry book-keeping system. I worked there for nineteen years from '53 to '72.

"I was never an expert typist. When I worked on a brief, it was very hard, it would make Joe nervous. I said, 'I am holding back your work. Why don't you try somebody else.' He said he liked to have me around, that I was very good with the clients. You know, I loved it, I managed to get it done. I was his private secretary for all those years. I am telling you I worked hard, but I loved it."

Roland Penner came to join Zuken's law firm by the most indirect of routes. After finishing university he worked for a year as the secretary of the National Federation of Labour Youth — the Communist Party's youth wing — but the party could not afford his slim salary. A family friend found him work at the Western Furniture shop in downtown Winnipeg. In 1954 he helped establish and manage the Co-op Bookstore, a left-wing bookshop which is still in operation. "But in 1957 I decided that with a salary of forty bucks a week and two children and a third on the way I had to look for another line of work." The first thing he did was obtain a letter from the dean of the University of Manitoba Law School assuring him that he would not be subjected to the sort of treatment Gordon

Martin had received from the British Columbia Law Society a decade earlier.

Then he had to find a firm he could article with, since in those days students studied in the morning and articled in the afternoon. "For some reason or other I did not go to Joe at that stage. I went to Harry Walsh, I went to Roy Stubbs, but either because I left it too late, or my illusions about small-l liberals were just that, illusions, I could not get an articling position. So finally I went to Joe, and Joe said, 'I thought you would never ask.' So I happily accepted an articling position with Joe and that was the beginning of many years of a very happy professional life together.

"Joe was thought of as one of the most ethical of practitioners. There would be no cutting of corners. That attitude to the law was also paralleled by an attitude to fees. If you had a problem and wanted Joe to act, he'd act, there was no question of discussing fees. Much to the chagrin of Clara, who had to keep the books. Clara was not a money grubber, far from it. She was just as modest in her tastes and ways as Joe, but you have to pay the rent every month.

"Joe did not want to deal with the issue of fees, and that continued right to the end of his active practice. From time to time I would be delegated to go in and say, 'Look, Joe, here is what it costs to run this office, here is what we all should be earning (which was the low end of the professional scale), but if we are going to do that, there has to be so much per billable hour — you're charging about a third of that.' 'Oh yes, you are right, you are right. I'll reform.' For a while he would move up to about half an acceptable tariff of fees. He just loathed the idea of charging. On occasion he insisted that the fee be cut down."

Shortly after becoming an articling student, Penner became in effect an informal partner, and on his call to the bar he became a formal partner. "Joe was more than happy to let me take over the reins of management. I became the manager — I would always take the proposal to Joe — 'Look, it is too small on the ninth floor. We have to move to the fifth floor' or 'We need an additional secretary and so on and so forth.'

"He was very much respected by the judges. When Joe came and said something — that this was the law — they knew he was not trying to pull the wool over their eyes. If Joe made a statement as to facts, they knew he would not be misrepresenting the facts. Even though there were some judges who were quite openly anti-Communist, Joe was something special in the courts. He had a commanding presence, with his voice and his preparedness. He set a high standard and he insisted we all live up to it."

Joe's was always a general practice firm involving civil and criminal litigation, labour law, family law, wills and estates and small partnership agreements. Zuken was at times the victim of a very subtle form of political discrimination. In the Seventies, after the passions and apprehensions of the Cold War had subsided, friends of Zuken confessed to him that they had refrained from retaining him for legal work because they did not want to appear politically tainted. "They were afraid to come to me when they wanted to purchase a house or sell a house because my name might be endorsed on documents at the Land Titles Office."

Clara Zuken has particularly fond memories of office life during the late Sixties and early Seventies when the firm was joined by Norman Larsen and David Deutscher. "It was a wonderful time. It was the highlight of the office when the four of them got together." Larsen felt the office presented the perfect social setting for Zuken. "My wife and I would invite the Zukens over to our house on several occasions, but they came only a couple of times because I think it was difficult for Joe to socialize. The office for him was an easy form of socialization, where he was not the centre of attention, but he was the centre. I think that for Joe too, those years [of partnership with Penner, Larsen and Deutscher] would have been the peak years."

Labour Cleans House

In one area Zuken did not enjoy the type of success he would have wished for. He often described himself as a labour lawyer, and while the firm did represent a number of trade unions, the Cold War cut deep into the number of unions willing to hire a Communist to represent them.

The Canadian labour movement made tremendous strides during the Second World War. The war production effort ended the Depression and brought about a period of full employment. Thousands of people were unionized and won improved benefits. And from 1941 onwards Communists played an important role in many of these unions, applying the organizing skills they developed with the Workers Unity League. Their dedication won them leadership positions in a number of unions. These included the Canadian Seamen's Union, the International Woodworkers of America, the United Electrical Workers and the International Union of Mine, Mill and Smelter Workers.

One of the major battles of the Cold War was fought over the leadership of the union movement. In Canada and the United States, Communist-led unions were expelled from most trade union federations, and new unions were created to raid the membership of the so-called Communist unions. The battles — and the language that accompanied them — were bitter and vitriolic. And they contributed little to the well-being of unions. When political parties — and this includes the CCF as well as the CPC — fought for control of unions, they ignored the interests of the union membership. Unionists should well have questioned the wisdom of purges that won the praise of Mackenzie King, who said, "Canada owes a great measure of thanks to the leaders of labour organizations in our country for the part they are actively taking in seeking to suppress any development of Communism." The media continued to serve as a handmaiden to the cold warriors of the day. Typical stories of the period bore headlines like "How Red-Led Unions Gnaw at Heart of Industry" (this particular story was accompanied by a drawing of a huge octopus threatening to crush the country's strategic industry on the orders of Moscow).

Zuken's aspirations as a labour lawyer were largely crushed by this internal Cold War. While he did work for Communist-led unions like the Fur Workers and the Mine, Mill and Smelter Workers, these unions were being rapidly destroyed by their right-wing opponents, few of whom would think of employing a Communist. Consequently, he ended up taking on a variety of smaller organizations, at one point acting on behalf of the Teamsters when they tried, unsuccessfully, to unionize the city's cab drivers.

In 1960 the Mine, Mill and Smelter Workers union gained a toehold in Manitoba when it won the right to represent workers at the new Inco mines in Thompson. The certification was a major break for the union, which had been expelled from the Canadian Congress of Labour in 1949 and had been fending off the United Steelworkers ever since. Mine-Mill in Sudbury came under withering attack from 1958 onwards following an unsuccessful strike. In 1961 two American cabinet members, Robert Kennedy and Arthur Goldberg, attacked it for having a Communist leadership, and Canadian justice minister Davie Fulton echoed the charges in the House of Commons.

In 1962 the Steelworkers succeeded in winning certification at Sudbury. In its weakened condition Mine-Mill had a difficult time fighting off a similar raid in Manitoba. Zuken represented the union at the labour board hearings in February 1962. There he came up against the very incarnation of the social democratic Cold Warrior and the future leader of the federal New Democratic Party, David Lewis. Zuken recalled that "David Lewis was a brilliant lawyer, but during the early stages of the case he sort of took the attitude that he was the authority on labour law who had come down from Toronto to tell the Manitoba Labour Board, and all and sundry, what labour law is and what it should be. He was rather arrogant. But he soon got the message."

In particular, Lewis managed to raise the ire of the grand old man of the Manitoba labour movement, R. B. Russell. A leader of the General Strike and a founder of the One Big Union, Russell was one of the labour appointees to the board. He was put out when Lewis accused Zuken of "putting on an act" and "giving an exhibition of histrionics." Russell rebuked Lewis and suggested that the Steelworkers' lawyer was engaging in exactly the same tactics he was accusing Zuken of employing. For this Lewis apologized to the board.

At the hearings Zuken attacked the impartiality of the labour board, eventually forcing the secretary-treasurer of the Manitoba Federation of Labour, Joseph (Jimmy) James, to disqualify himself from hearing the case. Mine-Mill was accusing the Steelworkers of "misrepresentation of facts bordering on fraud" during their campaign to convince the 2,000 Thompson miners to switch unions. Zuken also produced a parade of witnesses who claimed they had been threatened by Steelworker representatives. Ken Woods, the business agent for Mine-Mill, said he had been told by the Steelworkers' organizer that he had "two weeks to get out of town." In turn, a Steelworker member said he had been followed by Woods and other Mine-Mill employees who called him a "turncoat" and appeared to be trying to start a fight.

Mine-Mill also produced witnesses who claimed Steel was signing up members without requiring them to pay the one-dollar initiation fee. One miner said he was promised a twenty-six-ounce bottle of whiskey and a mickey if he joined the Steelworkers. "I thought it was a bargain, so I paid and signed." He subsequently went to a lawyer and had his membership revoked. A welder said he was recruited by a Steelworker who explained it was best to join the union early — "Later we will have guys here who will be beating people up."

Lewis dismissed the reported threats as falsehoods and suggested that in its beleaguered position Mine-Mill was now a company union, no longer capable of representing the interests of the Inco employees. He backed this up by pointing to the fact that both Zuken and the lawyer representing Inco were opposed to holding a vote to allow miners to choose between the two unions. In his concluding argument, Lewis said that never in his years as a labour lawyer had he seen a case "in which more dust was thrown into the eyes of everybody concerned." He pointed out that the Steelworkers had submitted membership cards for 1,400 workers at Thompson, a quantity that clearly warranted a new certification vote.

For his part, Zuken maintained that the case was "a tragic example of union raiding. This practice is the bleeding paw of the labour movement, a violation of the basic principles and tradition of labour." He argued that because of the evidence of threats and indications that in at least six cases Steel was not collecting initiation fees, the union "went far beyond electioneering" and its application for a vote should be denied.

In the end, the board sided with Lewis and the Steelworkers, as did the miners. Fighting from a weakened position, Mine-

Mill was badly defeated in the certification vote, losing by over 900 votes. The real winner in the battle, however, was Inco, which was able to go an extra nineteen months without giving its workers a pay raise.

A Public Defender

Zuken felt lawyers could improve the public image of their profession by working to eliminate those conditions that gave rise to a law for the rich and a law for the poor. And in fact members of the Manitoba Bar had over the years been in the forefront of providing free legal services.

As far back as 1937 the Law Society of Manitoba created the Indigent Suitors Committee to allow for court proceedings *in forma pauperis*. It was the first time in Canada there had been a formal system established to begin to meet the needs of low-income people. The bulk of the work it handled was family law. In was not until 1947 that the Manitoba Law Society began to address the issue of legal aid in criminal cases. In that year a society committee examining the treatment of low-income people charged with criminal offences concluded that

> poor persons in Manitoba who are charged with crime do not receive the same degree of justice as do persons of means.... Members of the Committee who have had occasion to attend in Magistrate's Courts, felt that very often an accused person who could not employ Counsel, sometimes pleaded guilty when he or she was not guilty and more prevalent was the feeling that the person who did not have the aid of Counsel received much more severe sentences than those who could have had proper representation made on their behalf.

In the wake of this report, the society established the country's first criminal legal aid system. By 1962 the provincial government was providing some financial support to the criminal program.

To Zuken the problem with the law society's legal aid program was its charitable element — proper legal protection should, he felt, be a right. In April 1963 Zuken pushed a motion through Winnipeg City Council calling on the attorney general to provide a public defender system. Speaking at council, Zuken pointed out that the Manitoba Law Society's legal aid program did not cover charges where the sentence was less than six months or where the accused was being charged under the Highway Traffic Act. The public defender, he proposed, would be a full-time experienced lawyer at the disposal of persons appearing in magistrate's court. According to Zuken, "The defender would be more apt to do justice for the accused than someone appearing on a pot-luck basis." In an interview in 1970 he reiterated his position: "I am not impressed by the argument that a public defender paid out of public funds would be too chummy with the crown prosecutor and make deals and all that sort of thing. If you pick the individual with integrity and ability, that could be a reinforcement in shoring up the rights of an accused."

During this period Zuken also demonstrated his personal commitment to reforming legal aid through his work with Olga Foltz and Norman Larsen.

Joe Zuken and Olga Foltz were brought together when Pierre Trudeau liberalized the country's divorce laws in 1968. Foltz, a welfare mother with six children, had been separated for six years and had not seen her husband for the past three years. She wanted to take advantage of the new divorce laws. In her efforts to secure a divorce, she applied for help from the law society's legal aid system. She discovered that legal aid lawyers did not handle divorces except in extraordinary situations. The reason for this rule was simple: the law society feared its legal aid service would be swamped with business if it handled divorces.

Foltz went to a lawyer in private practice and was told the cost of an uncontested divorce would be $1,200. Although the lawyer offered to accept her payment in installments, the price was far beyond her means. "I kept on searching. I did not know where the Law Courts Building was, I knew nothing about law, and I knew nothing beyond the little circle where I lived."

Foltz did in fact know a few things. During the late Sixties, the age of the Just Society, the federal government was engaged in a variety experiments in citizen participation. Foltz was a member of a welfare rights group that held regular meetings at 600 Main Street. And she remembered that a quiet intense lawyer had spoken at one of their meetings. The women at the meeting had outlined their fear of contacting lawyers; they suspected they would be billed for every phone call and every question they asked. According to Foltz, this lawyer had suggested that the women pick one or two leaders to collect all the legal questions the women had and then funnel the questions through the leaders to him. "I remember that so distinctly. We thought, my God, this is such a wonderful person to do that."

But Olga Foltz could not remember this lawyer's name. After a thorough search of the scribblers she had filled to the brim at these meetings, she came across the name Joseph Zuken. By this time Foltz was trying to process her own divorce, but she kept on meeting with rejection from court clerks when she tried to file her documents. "When I found his name, I phoned him and said, 'Mr. Zuken, I am separated six years, I am on welfare. Would you be interested in showing me how to do my divorce step-by-step?' He says, 'No problem. Just make an appointment with my secretary that you are going to be here for half an hour and we will discuss it.' I took one of the outreach workers from the Neighbourhood Services Centre with me. What I wanted was for him to give me the information and I would type it out myself. Of course I was no great typist, I had only six lessons. Everything at that time had to be carbon copies, you could not have Xerox copies.

"He showed me what to do. I would type it out and I would have sloppy papers. He would say, 'The judge will not appreciate sloppy papers in court. You must know how to type out your affidavit by now, Olga; let my secretary type it out.' Those are the kinds of things he would do for us."

There were five other women connected with the Neighbourhood Services Centre who, along with Foltz, were being helped by Zuken to process their own divorces. In an interview published in the *Winnipeg Tribune* in December 1969, just before the cases went to court, Zuken explained why he was handling the cases for free. "My position is that the law society's legal aid committee should extend its services to all indigent cases seeking help for divorces. This is a matter of right for these women, not an act of charity on the part of the legal profession." He suggested other lawyers should also volunteer their time because "it is shameful that deserving cases are deprived of their rights because of economic difficulties."

For Olga Foltz, getting a divorce was the first step towards getting off welfare. In the wake of the publicity that surrounded her divorce, she was contacted by many low-income women seeking divorces. With Zuken's encouragement Foltz applied for a grant to set up a self-help divorce clinic. In the first six months of its operation the clinic processed 600 divorces and 2,000 income tax forms. Foltz found herself supervising an office and counselling others on how to get their divorces. "Once a person learned from our group, they would come back and volunteer." According to Foltz, Zuken was never more than a phone call away, always willing to guide her. "He told me the rules and the regulations, where to get the book. 'Just stick to that and you will be okay. Just don't try and be a lawyer.' I was very careful not to take the place of a lawyer. He showed me how to write to different registries. He showed me a lot of legal things; for me who did not know where the Law Courts Building was it was quite something."

Foltz eventually went on to serve on the board of Legal Aid Manitoba and subsequently worked for Legal Aid Manitoba as a paralegal. In the 1980s she became the executive director of the Manitoba Anti-Poverty Organization. She always credited Zuken for recognizing abilities she did not know she possessed. "I am just amazed at what I learnt. What is good is people seeing it in you and you don't see it in yourself."

In 1968, after graduating from law school, Norman Larsen was looking for a firm to article with. A mature student and former school teacher, Larsen knew that he wanted to work with low-income people. He eventually made arrangements to article with a lawyer in Selkirk, Manitoba, an industrial community a half hour's drive north of Winnipeg. But before he went to work for future Manitoba premier Howard Pawley, he ran into Roland Penner, whom he had known in the late 1950s. Penner convinced him to join Zuken & Penner. He quickly realized it was going to be an unusual experience.

"When I made known the name of the firm with which I would article, I took an immense amount of ribbing from my classmates. I remember, for example, I had a pink shirt, and they kidded me about that shirt: 'Do Zuken & Penner issue these shirts to all their employees?'

"I was a bit concerned about what it would mean to join a 'Communist firm.' I had never been politically active. My left-wing sympathies had always been there — I am still known for that — you don't join Zuken & Penner if you are right wing, at least not for long. So before I joined the firm, I was a little worried about it and started to think about whether I should do it. I went to see Harold Stubbs, who was the secretary of the law society. I knew Joe only by reputation. I told Stubbs I was thinking of joining the firm and I asked if this was going to mark me in some way. And he said, 'Yes, of course, to an extent it will, but I would not worry about it. You'll get terrific experience. He is an excellent man.' I went to another senior lawyer, I can't remember who it was, and he said, 'Do it.' That was enough for me."

It was a decision that he has never regretted. "As an articling student I was told, 'Do Legal Aid.' " The legal aid system was still being operated by the Law Society of Manitoba. Applicants would go to the Law Courts Building on Monday night where they would be interviewed by a volunteer lawyer. The lawyer would take the applications and submit them to a committee that would determine whether or not the applicants were eligible for representation. It was a system fraught with problems. People would often have to wait for several hours to be interviewed, there was no appeal from the committee's decision, there was no choice of lawyer, and — if a lawyer was appointed — there was no change of lawyers. The eligibility rules were very tight: people who owned real estate or cars or who in 1970 had a gross income of over $3,000 were not eligible for the program. Despite this, demand was very high. The society minutes from 1969 noted that the society "makes no bones about the fact that it has shrank [*sic*] from publicizing its services — a reluctance born out of a simple fear that, if the facilities of the Committee become too well-known, the resultant flood of applicants would wash away the entire structure."

Zuken and Penner encouraged Larsen to help break down that structure by establishing a second clinic on Thursday nights at 600 Main Street, the same building Olga Foltz was now working out of. Zuken was one of the sixteen or so lawyers Larsen arranged to have volunteer one night a month at the new clinic. By 1970 Ron Meyers, the director of the law society's legal aid program, was trying to quit his job, claiming the system was governed by "out-dated, inadequate, simply ridiculous rules." In March of 1970 the NDP attorney general, Al Mackling, appointed an eleven-person committee to investigate the question of legal aid. It recommended the creation of "a comprehensive and fully funded legal aid plan, administered by a non-profit, self-governing corporation." Thus, Legal Aid Manitoba came into existence in 1972. Norman Larsen left the firm to become its first lawyer, while Roland Penner was the first chairman of its board of directors.

Larsen is still grateful to Zuken & Penner for letting him spend his articling year doing work that brought in so little income. But it was not until he graduated that he became fully aware of the firm's unusual financial procedures. "I got my call to the bar one morning in June 1969. I went back to the office in the afternoon, and Penner and Zuken said, 'We would like to offer you a partnership.' I accepted — and my salary fell. I made more as an articling student than I did as a full partner!

"Allan Chisvin was our accountant. He did the books every year, and one day he said to me, 'I have never seen so many files and so many entries for such small amounts.' We did a tremendous volume of work for low-income people. We did hundreds of accounts for fifty dollars, twenty-five dollars, and we frequently did not charge anything because our clients did not have anything.

"Penner used to give me hell for the way I billed. Roland was pretty good at billing; he had to be because Joe wasn't so good at it. And I remember Roland saying to me, 'Why did you have to learn to bill from Joe?' Joe's bills were very modest, even when he was doing estate work and the estate could afford it. I remember Roland saying, 'He bills as if the Depression is still on.' "

Like Penner, Larsen recalled how Zuken insisted that the firm do everything (except for, of course, billing) by the book. City councillors are prohibited by a section of the City of Winnipeg Act from doing legal work for the city, and it was a rule that Zuken applied strictly. "There were a couple of cases that I consulted him about — perhaps someone charged under a by-law where I thought it was pretty clear that this was not what that section was intended to cover — but Joe would say, 'Absolutely not.' We had to abide by the strictest possible interpretation of that section."

While working with the firm, Larsen was involved in a number of interesting civil and criminal cases, one of which exposed him to the extremes of left-wing sectarianism that followed the break between China and the Soviet Union. The Sino-Soviet split was mirrored in Canada in the creation of the pro-Chinese Communist Party of Canada (Marxist-Leninist). The CPC-ML, whose members were usually referred to as Maoists, managed to attract a number of very bright, very committed young students at the University of Manitoba. Seven of these students ran afoul of the law when they picketed the CBC to protest a documentary on life in the People's Republic of China. What Larsen later described as a "police riot" ensued and the students ended up being charged under the Criminal Code with causing a disturbance and obstructing a police officer.

"When they came to me to defend them, I tried to talk them out of it. I said, 'I have not got that much experience. Besides, there are two other lawyers in the firm who are experienced in the courtroom and are sympathetic to your point of view. I'm not a Communist.' And they would not accept that. I said, 'Wouldn't you be happier with Joe Zuken?' and they replied, 'No. He ought to know better.' That was their response: Joe should have been a Maoist. They would have nothing to do with him.

"So I defended them — and lost every case. Those were difficult days for radicals. People were generally so scared to death of them and their ideas, judges included."

While most Winnipeggers knew Zuken as a forceful dramatic politician, a casual visitor to the offices of Zuken, Penner and Larsen might never have known there was an important political figure working there. Penner recalled that while Zuken always had the radio on, keeping on top of local news, he would seldom initiate a discussion on political theory. And Larsen noted that he got more of a sense of Zuken's politics from the way people reacted to the name of the firm he belonged to than he ever got from Zuken himself. "It regularly happened that I would wake up in the morning to the dulcet tones of Joe on the radio. The media loved Joe, he was always good for a quotable quote. He was on the radio so often that I got more of a sense from the radio than I did from being in the office of what his views were on political issues."

Larsen had the office next to Zuken's for four and a half years. During those years he would often look in on his partner to see him sitting in rapt concentration, puffing on his pipe, thinking. "That is my main recollection of him. I think he contemplated a good deal. When he was in his office doing work, he took no calls except those dealing with city business. If anybody called him about a barking dog or whatever, that had top priority. And he would get on the phone to the inspectors or whomever and he would get the problem rectified. I think he gave his constituents wonderful service. I must have heard at least ten lawyers say that even though they were Conservatives, they lived in Joe's constituency and they would always vote for Joe, 'even if he was a Communist,' because he was such a good man and a good councillor."

Taking the Silk

At the end of 1970 Manitoba attorney general Al Mackling announced the annual appointment of Queen's Counsels. There was one surprise on the list: Joe Zuken. As soon as the news was made public, Zuken received a phone call from his niece, Janice Dietch, inquiring if he had copped out. "I told her, 'No, I haven't. I'm a Communist and I'm proud to be one. And if I've had to suffer a bit to be one, well, it's been worth it.' " Norm Larsen was bemused by his partner's decision to accept the honour. "I used to kid him that I joined this firm on the distinct understanding that it was an anti-establishment firm. 'What happens, I join and you become respectable.' "

But there were historical reasons for his decision, relating to the fate of Saul Greenberg. Greenberg had handled many of the controversial left-wing cases of the 1930s. His career was, in Zuken's opinion, in keeping with "the best traditions of the bar." Legal historian Dale Gibson noted that "because he dared from an early date to defend left-wing clients and causes, Greenberg was never permitted to wear the Q.C.'s silk gown during his lifetime. This slight was eventually remedied a few years ago with the awarding of what appears to be the first posthumous Q.C. patent ever awarded." So while Zuken believed that the award had been debased over the years to the point where it was a reward for political loyalty rather than legal ability, he nevertheless accepted the appointment. "One of the reasons I accepted the Q.C. when it was offered was because of Saul Greenberg, in order to prove that one has a right not to be discriminated against politically." Following his retirement from city council, Zuken was elected as a bencher of the Law Society of Manitoba — attaining a degree of respectability he himself found almost unbelievable.

In 1979 Vic Savino, a former lawyer with Legal Aid Manitoba, became a partner in the firm. Like so many other lawyers, he had been attracted by Zuken's reputation for integrity and his political commitment. He was surprised to discover that despite his advanced age Zuken was still carrying on an active legal career. "He did the standard run-of-the-mill stuff that most senior lawyers would refer to junior lawyers.... He had been at the bar for over thirty years, and unlike virtually all of his colleagues with that level of experience, he continued to do legal aid work. I remember you could walk into the family court building at the Fort Osborne Barracks and there would be all these wet-behind-the-ears young lawyers — and then Joe would walk in with his client — there was no one else there like him."

Savino maintained that judges also held Zuken in high regard. In the early 1980s the firm was representing a tenant who was fighting an eviction. Savino recalled that in the lower court hearings of the case the judges appeared to be disinterested in the client's argument. "We decided these people need representation from somebody the judges are going to have respect for. Joe agreed to act as counsel. I remember sitting in court marvelling at how he had the judges eating out of his hand with his eloquence and his simplicity."

Zuken was still active in the firm up until his death in March 1986 — it had been his intention to retire from the firm that spring. After Zuken's death, Savino met with the other lawyers in the firm. "It was quite an emotional meeting because all the lawyers let their feelings spill out — talking about how they had been touched by Joe. How their ethics had been touched by Joe, how the way they practised law had been touched by Joe. And that was a very significant contribution that Joe made to the legal profession, the way he affected people's ethics. I don't think many people realize that."

But while Zuken remained a practising lawyer during the Sixties, Seventies and early Eighties, his energies and passion were largely devoted to his work on Winnipeg City Council, to which he was first elected in the fall of 1961.

EIGHT

A Communist at City Hall
1962-1971

Norm Larsen once made a very shrewd remark.... He said
I am quiet, but when I get on the floor of council and have
to deal with a cause in which I believe, then I take off like
the Incredible Hulk. I laughed when I read it, but I felt
that Norman had come very close to something.

In the fall of 1961, Jacob Penner, after serving twenty-eight years on city council, announced his decision to retire from public life. While Penner was still alert and intellectually active, he was now eighty-one years old and the job was taking a physical toll on him. When it came to looking for a candidate to replace him, the Labour Election Committee, the Communist Party's civic wing, did not have many options. Among local Communist politicians only Joe Zuken could hope to match Penner in terms of public reputation and ability. Some party members worried that by running Zuken for council, the LEC risked losing his spot on the school board. But in the end it was Penner himself who nominated Zuken at the LEC's annual meeting.

During the Sixties municipal elections were an annual event, with a portion of the council coming up for election each year. The 1961 civic election was bitterly contested. Three aldermen were to be elected from Ward Three, and Zuken, Alex Turk (a former Liberal MLA and local wrestling promoter endorsed by the Civic Election Committee) and Dr. Isadore Wolch (an NDP member of the school board) were in a three-way battle for the third spot.

As election day neared, Zuken and Wolch engaged in some heated exchanges over Zuken's affiliation to the Communist Party. Wolch accused the Communists of hiding their true colours behind the Labour Election Committee label. Zuken countered by accusing Wolch of employing "McCarthyism and John Birch Society tactics." He said the New Democratic Party must be "running scared," since they were introducing an "obvious red herring into the civic arena." He noted that "the people of Ward 3 have elected me for the past 20 years well knowing my political beliefs."

Because the city used a system of transferable ballots, election results were sometimes not completely tabulated until several days after polling day. In 1961 the election took place on a Wednesday but it was not until late Friday afternoon that the final calculations were made for Ward Three. A *Winnipeg Tribune* headline told the story: "Zuken Outlasts Alex Turk in 6 Round Ward Three Battle." And in a similar cliff-hanger Andrew Bilecki was elected to Zuken's seat on the school board.

Joe Zuken's first ten years on Winnipeg City Council were to prove to be stormy ones. He regularly fought pitched battles with the conservative majority on the council and did not hestitate to attack the NDP when he thought it was deserving of criticism. He had made the shift from the school board to municipal politics at a time when the provincial government had established a second level of municipal government to try to coordinate the common concerns of the city of Winnipeg and the communities surrounding it. This new metropolitan government was to have a tempestuous existence. Zuken, like many other municipal politicians, spent much of the decade wrestling with the problem of how to effectively govern a large urban community without reducing the degree of public participation in that government. For civic politicians this issue dominated the decade — which ended with the creation of a single, amalgamated city. While Zuken made sure his voice was heard throughout that debate, he also honed his skills as a political gadfly, making sure that the questions of racism, housing, fair taxation and open government were not ignored. That he was going to be a force to contend with was apparent from his very first council meeting.

Mayor Stephen Juba had just delivered his 1962 keynote address to council when newly elected alderman Joe Zuken leapt to his feet and, in the words of a *Winnipeg Tribune* reporter, "tore open Winnipeg city council's inaugural meeting with a blistering attack on what he called the Civic Election Committee's 'shameful, machine control' of committee memberships." Zuken, with the support of fellow Communist Joe Forkin and the NDP caucus, managed to "fling an outsized spanner into the usually well-oiled CEC caucus machine, and for half an hour city council was in an uproar."

Zuken had created the stir by charging that the "rights and privileges of council to freely appoint committees are being jeopardized." With his supporters, Zuken called for secret ballot selection of the members of the council's various committees. "This city hall is not the property of the CEC or any other political group. Put an end to this shameful procedure. It's a farce!" The bid failed, and as a consequence Zuken and Forkin left their seats and refused to take part in the election, which predictably saw the CEC capture every committee chairmanship.

It was a dramatic debut for Zuken. Not only did he succeed in capturing centre stage, he also scored a palpable hit in what was to be a twenty-year campaign against the Civic Election Committee. Like Communist and socialist aldermen before him, Zuken was intent on disproving the CEC's claim that it was a non-partisan grouping of individuals dedicated to providing good government on sound business principles. To Zuken, it was a "right-wing coalition of Liberals and Conservatives."

This first meeting was also the only council meeting in Zuken's twenty-two-year career at which he was not the sole representative of the Communist Party. Shortly after the meeting, Forkin, a First World War veteran who been suffering lung problems for many years, was hospitalized.

"I remember Clara and I visiting him in the hospital. But Joe Forkin never got back to city council and within a few weeks he died. It was a very sad occasion when I had to, together with Jake Penner, speak at Joe Forkin's funeral. It was a tremendous outpouring. People came, church people included, because people who were not of the left kept voting for Penner and Forkin.... People voted for them because they recognized that they were good public servants. And people were crying as they walked by the coffin.

"So I only had an ally on city council for one meeting.... I had to rely on independents and sometimes members of the NDP, although from time to time I must say that the word had gone out that the NDP had a general policy that they would not second any motion that I presented unless it was a last resort and they could not help themselves."

The Citizens and the Socialists

The inaugural meeting of council, held each year in early January, had for decades been the scene of bitter debates over the role the Civic Election Committee played on council. It was at this meeting that council committees and committee chairmen were appointed. Left-wing aldermen believed that the CEC put the lie to its claim not be a political party by the way it used its majority position on council to control the appointments. The first wrangle over the selection of the committee chairmanships took place in 1929. According to the *Free Press*, C. F. Green, the managing secretary of the Civic Progress Association, the CEC's direct forerunner, expressed regret that "due to information other than official being given to the press, it was reported that this organization had discussed and prepared plans for the allocation of the various civic chairmanships. 'This is quite erroneous,' the statement says, 'it has repeatedly been pointed out that this association has no intention of dominating affairs at city hall.' "

The CEC would issue many similar denials over the years, just as each year it would pack the committees with its own supporters. *Tribune* reporter Gary Lahoda gave this description of the 1963 meeting: "According to plan, members of the Civic Election Committee stood up and read off a pre-arranged list of nominations. Aldermen voted on the composition of three of the four standing committees but when the voting on the committee on Utilities and Personnel was to take place, the fire works began."

Again it was Zuken who set the fireworks off, claiming the CEC had "rigged and predetermined" the chairmanships and memberships of the standing committees. "In doing so the CEC exposes itself once again as a crude political machine devoid of independence and concerned only with controlling city hall. Merit and fairness are tossed aside by this CEC machine of Liberals and Tories, which operates on the 'principle' of rewarding its members with political plums and punishing its political opponents." The speeches Zuken delivered at the inaugural meetings gave notice of his intent to play political hardball. Not surprisingly, CEC councillors responded with strong language of their own. Terry Hind told Zuken, "I am sure the people who elected me do not want me to sit here and take this nonsense from a Communist." Not only was Zuken unable to get the remarks withdrawn, Hind went on to call the Communist Party "one big world caucus," adding that it was Winnipeg's shame to have a Communist on council.

From these debates it should be clear that Joe Zuken had been elected to one of the country's most ideologically charged city councils. It was in many ways a role he had been in training for all his life. For over forty years Citizens and Socialists, WASPS and aliens, the North End and the South End, had been battling for control of Winnipeg city hall. For the next two decades Zuken would be the pre-eminent socialist on council. During those battles he would be sustained by a sense of continuity, by his identification with the city's long-standing radical community going back as far as the 1919 General Strike. And it was to the same period of heightened class conflict and polarization that his opponents on council, the CEC, would trace their political roots.

The Citizens' Committee of One Thousand had been established by the city's business community to help crush the 1919 General Strike. The end of the strike did not spell the end of the Citizens' Committee, however. On August 20, 1919, three thousand people attended a meeting in the city's Board of Trade Building where it was decided to create the Citizens' League of Winnipeg "to permanently carry on the work of the Citizens' Committee of One Thousand." Isaac Pitblado, Q.C., who was soon to be hired as the crown prosecutor in the General Strike cases, was the league president, while A. K. Godfrey, the president of Monarch Lumber, was one of the key executive members. Of the fifty-six original executive members of the league, ten were professionals, sixteen were involved in the insurance, real estate or grain trade, while ten more were either retail or wholesale merchants. Only nine of them lived north of Portage Avenue.

At a league meeting on September 22, 1919, where prominent city lawyer R. A. C. Manning warned that during the strike there had been "a definite plan of the Reds to seize control all over the country," it was decided to field a slate of candidates in that fall's municipal election. This decision was followed with a full-fledged anti-red campaign. The league's newspaper advertisements told voters, "You'll be casting your vote to decide whether the Radical-Labor ticket or the Citizens shall control Winnipeg." The league won a close victory and quickly began to lobby the province for a redrawing of the municipal boundaries. Provincial politicians were only too happy to oblige the Citizens. As a result, a new city charter was created, designed largely to blunt the political strength of the city's working class. North Winnipeg, with nearly half of the city's population, was to be represented by only a third of the councillors.

The Citizens bloc on council, like the socialist grouping, underwent a series of name changes over the years, at various times being referred to as the Citizens Research League, the Winnipeg Civic Association, the Civic Progress Association and the Civic Election Committee. The Citizens always argued that because they did not have a platform and did not hold caucus meetings, they were not a political party. Rather they were an educational organization, designed to let voters know who the best-qualified candidates were. This mantle of non-partisanship does not stand up to serious examination, particularly when one considers the violent anti-socialist rhetoric the citizens would employ at election time.

University of Manitoba historian Ed Rea conducted a detailed study of city council roll-call votes from 1947 to 1971 that revealed a striking degree of cohesion among CEC councillors. During the course of each year they voted with each other between 71 and 89 per cent of time. The CCF-NDP, which claimed to be a unified political party, was only slightly more cohesive in its voting patterns during this period.

In concluding his study of Winnipeg civic politics, Rea was scathing in his criticism of the Citizens' group. Rea noted the Citizens had successfully controlled council since 1919:

> But control implies responsibility and it seems to have been evaded. The result has been not effective leadership, but as the roll-call votes make clear, interest protection. There is nothing wrong with this situation per se, if the electorate had been able to assign group authority and judge accordingly. The clearest charge against the Citizens has been their failure to acknowledge the political responsibility which their position of power surely entails.

While the CEC and its successor organizations, the Greater Winnipeg Election Committee and the Independent Citizens' Election Committee, were the dominant groups at city hall during the years Joe Zuken was on council, they did not enjoy the type of absolute control they might have expected. For throughout the Fifties, Sixties and Seventies the CEC had to come to terms with the city's perennial mayor, Steve Juba.

The Merchandising Mayor

In the early 1950s Joe Zuken encountered an aspiring civic politician in the studios of a Winnipeg radio station. Both men were there to record speeches for the upcoming election. By then Zuken had a number of election victories under his belt and was on his way to yet another success in Ward Three. Zuken recalled that Steve Juba introduced himself and asked, "How do you get elected? Tell me, what does one have to do to get elected?" In recounting the story, Zuken noted, "He never asked me that again."

Nor was there much need to. Juba was to become one of the most successful politicians in Manitoba history, winning nine elections and serving as mayor from 1956 to 1977. Journalist Paul Grescoe encapsulated Juba's formula for political success: "Be jealously protective of the city's reputation, pick an easily identifiable issue, attack a single recognizable enemy, use an outlandish gimmick that will attract the attention of photographers, and raise an outrageous ruckus that will attract headlines." Juba's enemies list included suburban governments, the provincial government, most of the city council and the Metropolitan Corporation — the second level of city government established in the early 1960s.

His surprise victory in the 1956 mayoral election, when he defeated George Sharpe, a scion of the local establishment and the son of a former mayor, was hailed by many as a coming of age for Winnipeg and for the North End. By becoming the first non-Anglo-Saxon to serve as mayor, Juba carried with him to city hall many of the aspirations of generations of Winnipeggers who had been long denied a voice in the running of their city.

Juba's roots in that community were deep. Born in 1914 in the North End to parents who had immigrated from the Ukraine, Juba grew up a short distance from the CPR yards. Like Zuken he wanted to become a lawyer, but his family could not afford to pay for his education beyond grade ten. Instead he went in and out of a bewildering number of businesses — contracting, inventing, sales — until he established Keystone Supply, a plumbing and electrical distribution company that made him a millionaire. With his financial future secured, Juba turned to politics. In 1953 he won election to the Manitoba legislature as an independent, campaigning for reform of the province's restrictive liquor laws and for the introduction of coloured margarine.

In the legislature Juba had been a whacky, colourful maverick. Few would have expected him to become mayor in 1956; even fewer would have had any idea what he would be like in office. Juba promised a surprised press corps, "I'll give you plenty of things to write about." A *Tribune* reporter summed up Juba's first year in office: "The mayor appears as a screwball gladiator, a brewer of the Boston tea party, a martyr searching for a stake, the conscience of man or the voice in the wilderness." Juba often found himself at odds with the CEC councillors who controlled council. In the weeks before he took office, they barred him from attending a special meeting of the finance committee. All this only fed Juba's public image as defender of the little guy and allowed him to distance himself from any unpopular decisions taken at city hall. Early in his tenure he told a reporter, "When I came down here I realized I had 18 men against me. Nothing has happened to change that opinion very much." According to Zuken, the CEC underestimated Juba. "Steve Juba came into council without any previous experience as an alderman. And they were looking upon him as an aberration ... and that they would beat him down to size. Were they in for a surprise."

In fact, the differences between Juba and the CEC were more differences of style than substance. Councillors were irritated by his avoidance of consultation and his publicity chasing — like New York City mayor Fiorello La Guardia he rode firetrucks and once he joined a group of women who were protesting the city's decision to chop down a large elm tree. But when it came to the major issues confronting the city, urban development, transportation, housing and taxation, the CEC did not find it that difficult to make its peace with Juba.

For the most part Zuken and Juba kept their distance from one another: "He did not attack me personally on the floor of council. But he did use his hearing aid against me. He had a very politicized hearing aid, and he heard what he wanted to hear. But I did not underestimate him, and as time went by I don't think he underestimated me. So it was a relationship at arm's length."

While Zuken respected Juba's political skills, he felt the mayor failed to make use of his influence: "He was very shrewd in the way he did things. He campaigned for a new city hall; he got his new city hall and so on. When you add up what he actually accomplished in his long term of office, you are left with the feeling that he was a very colourful person. But insofar as being able to push basic questions dealing with housing, tax reform — no, these were not glamorous items for Steve Juba.... Juba did not make any contribution insofar as social policy for our city.... He was a powerful mayor, but I don't think his policy was equal to his powers."

Zuken was of course not the only leftist on the council. But the CCF had gone into a decline on council in the postwar years, never winning more than six or less than four seats on the council. In the early Sixties a number of the younger CCF-NDP councillors had gone on to larger political arenas such as the Manitoba legislature and the House of Commons, while the other councillors were in some cases near the end of very long and honourable careers. The issues that the CCF had pushed on the municipal level — the protection of municipally owned civic services such as Winnipeg Hydro and the extension of the public sector into housing and public transit — were losing some of their public allure.

Juba helped this process along by combining the ideological orientation of the CEC with an electoral base in North Winnipeg. He regularly painted himself as the defender of the "little guy," but never presented a threat, or ever wished to present a threat, to the city's business community. He papered over, but did not heal, the wounds in a divided city.

Zuken's relationship with the NDP caucus varied from year to year and councillor to councillor. In the early Sixties many of the NDP aldermen were veterans of the left's internal Cold War. The ill feelings generated by decades of left-wing infighting did not dissipate quickly, nor was Zuken particularly conciliatory. He staked out his position and stood his ground. But he had considerable respect for Lloyd Stinson, the leader of the NDP caucus at city hall. Zuken noted that "Lloyd was quite capable, but he was not too keen on making any formal steps of showing cooperation with me. But on certain social policy issues it was inevitable that we end up on the same side." In his memoirs Stinson described Zuken as an "able lawyer, strong speaker and ruthless politician. Friendly, even humble in private, Joe was a holy terror on the floor of council, always ready to challenge the CEC, sometimes turning his wrath on the NDP. Fearless, vindictive, logical and eloquent, Zuken possessed a wry sense of humor." It was not until the 1970s, when members of a younger generation began to show up in the NDP caucus, that relations between Zuken and the civic NDP enjoyed a mild improvement.

By the early 1960s it was clear that while Winnipeg was going to dominate the provincial economy, the city was entering a period of decline relative to other Canadian cities its size. As the Alberta economy began to prosper, Winnipeg could no longer count on being the premier city of Western Canada. One of the problems facing the city was the way political responsibility had become diffused. There were sixteen separate municipalities surrounding the city of Winnipeg proper. This divided authority meant urban planning was virtually non-existent. The simple matter of building new bridges across the two rivers that passed through the various cities and municipalities would often mean drawn-out negotiations between several governments. The inner city was being forced to provide a variety of downtown services suburban residents took advantage of on a daily basis without having to support through their property taxes. At the same time many suburban politicians were fearful that their local communities would lose their identities if they were drawn into one amalgamated city.

The search for a solution to these problems would engage provincial and municipal governments for over a decade. The Conservative government of Duff Roblin chose to create a second, metropolitan, level of government. Metro was given responsibility for main streets and roadways, parks, bridges and planning, while the existing local governments retained control over education, police and fire services. For the purpose of eliminating regional tensions, there were only ten Metro councillors, each of whom represented a wedge-shaped ward that included parts of inner-city and suburban Winnipeg. Metro fulfilled some of its initial functions quite well, and a number of long-needed improvements in the city's infrastructure were carried out. But from the outset Metro had a very dangerous enemy in the person of Steve Juba.

An amalgamationist at heart, Juba viewed Metro as an unwanted intrusion on his turf. The Metro Corporation was particularly vulnerable to Juba's attacks because its first chairman, Richard Bonnycastle, had been appointed by the Roblin government, rather than elected to office. In addition, Metro had no direct taxing powers of its own; the various municipalities ended up turning considerable portions of their revenues over to a level of government over which they had no direct influence. Juba brought his considerable political skills to bear in his battles with Metro, going to great lengths to frustrate the corporation. At one point he even held a civic referendum on whether Metro should be abolished.

Like Juba, Zuken was an early critic of Metro. In a 1964 letter to the papers he criticized "the lack of adequate financial support by the provincial government so that the extra costs of this new level of government are imposed on the tax bills of the homeowner." He was also irritated by the fact that the chairman of Metro had been appointed by the provincial premier, rather than elected by the Metro council itself (from its own members), or better still, elected through a direct vote of the people of Winnipeg.

While Zuken agreed that a unified city government was needed to properly address the various problems facing the city, unlike Juba he never tried to use Metro as an excuse for not addressing the city's pressing social problems — particularly its deteriorating housing stock.

The Bulldozer Effect

It was during the 1960s that the City of Winnipeg began to take the first, halting steps towards urban redevelopment. These included the construction of a 165-unit Burrows-Keewatin housing project in northwest Winnipeg and the Lord Selkirk project just north of the CPR yards. From his first year on council Zuken was a strong proponent of the development of public housing. In the fall of 1962 he put forward a three-point plan designed to "solve the misery of the people living in the Jarvis Avenue slums": a rent-control program, more low-cost public housing and the relocation of what he termed "hard-core" cases.

Jarvis Street was located in the heart of a particularly run-down neighbourhood. In a report to the city's welfare committee on the growing social problems in the area, a Winnipeg police officer concluded that while the area had been in decline for a number of years, the problem was being exacerbated by the arrival of "more and more persons of Indian racial ancestry." According to police inspector Robert Young, "The district now appears to have become an Indian and Metis community." Young noted that twenty-seven single- and multiple-dwelling units were occupied by persons of native origin. There had also been over one hundred arrests in the area in the first nine months of the year. "These people are content to lead a drunken and immoral life.... It is not expected these figures will show a decrease because they accept arrest ... and jail ... not as a deterrent but as a way of life." Inspector Young said there would be little improvement in the area until the residents were cut off welfare and forced to look for work.

Zuken was outraged by the report. "The police are throwing around racial tags. Indians get a raw deal — there isn't a people more exploited in the world." He said the city should stop subsidizing slum landlords and "crack down on the racketeers, send them to jail like they do in New York."

The public-housing projects undertaken by the city during this period were characterized by what Zuken called the "bulldozer effect." Neighbourhoods were flattened and barracks-like buildings tossed up in their place. Zuken thus found himself simultaneously supporting the concept of a public-housing program and criticizing the specific projects being developed in the city. In keeping with the city's history of short-changing the North End, little attention was paid to the provision of recreational space. This was a particularly sore point with the Lord Selkirk development: "The proposed four acres for playground is not adequate. This area is a showpiece [and] it should have more than a minimum program. There will be howls and screams from these people when they find out how little they have. This has been a deprived area. These people need assistance."

Zuken was also an early proponent of improved tenants' rights. In the late Sixties he described the existing landlord and tenant act as "bad, oppressive, and unconscionable ... class legislation" drawing on "feudalistic concepts ... of the lord of the manor and the serf." In his critique of the act, he noted it had no reference to the landlord's responsibility to repair, while tenants have three basic rights — to pay rent, repair damage and keep quiet.

He proposed numerous changes to the act, and on at least one occasion managed to get council's support for substantial changes. These included the creation of a landlord and tenant review board to mediate disputes and investigate complaints; three months' notice of rent increases; an obligation on the landlord's part to maintain the premises in a state fit for habitation and to carry out ordinary repairs; and a prohibition of eviction without just cause. Many of these proposals were incorporated in the Landlord and Tenant Act brought in by Ed Schreyer's NDP government in the early 1970s.

The proposals for changes to the Landlord and Tenant Act had come out of a special urban renewal committee of council, of which Zuken was a key member. Its work had been deemed as so successful that in 1969 it was transformed into what became known as the grievance committee. This committee, comprised of Zuken, Stinson and Robert Taft, played the role of civic ombudsman. The committee met every second Monday night at city hall, and according to Zuken, "anyone with a beef or complaint could come before the committee." It handled a bewildering variety of cases and enjoyed an enviable track record in solving the problems brought before it. When twenty-eight senior citizens were evicted from a Main Street apartment building in the middle of winter, the committee was able to arrange winter lodgings for them. The Winnipeg Tenants Association, an organization Zuken was highly supportive of, used the committee as a platform to air numerous such grievances with landlords.

In the fall of 1970 a delegation of pensioners appeared before the committee complaining that politicians had not kept their promise to provide housing for the elderly. John Masyk of the Senior Citizens Day Centres said that many of them "live in housing conditions that are unsanitary, unsafe and even dangerous. This is degrading to human dignity." Zuken drew a round of applause when he suggested they go down and occupy the Royal Alexandra Hotel, the luxurious CPR hotel that then stood vacant, awaiting the wrecker's ball. "If a bunch of elderly citizens moved into the Royal Alex and invited Mr. Richardson [a Manitoba member of the Trudeau cabinet] it might bring things to a head." The grievance committee was eventually abolished, largely because CEC councillors felt Zuken was getting too much publicity from its operations.

Things Done in Secret

When Zuken walked out of a school board committee meeting to protest its decision to go in camera, he said, "I should have done this a long time ago." During his time on Winnipeg City Council, Zuken was excluded from most of the key committees and was consequently not given the opportunity to make many dramatic exits. But over the years he was able to transform the high degree of secrecy exercised by the council and its committees into a potent political issue. Those councillors who had served with him on the school board knew what to expect, and from the beginning they suggested Zuken was simply indiscreet. When Zuken was nominated to the city welfare committee in 1962, Edith Tennant, another committee member and a former school trustee, opposed the appointment. Zuken's well-known opposition to closed meetings would create problems she said, because "in camera sessions are needed to protect welfare recipients."

During his first two years on council Zuken was particularly angered by the way the civic welfare committee dealt with the Civic Charities Endorsement Bureau. In 1963 Zuken had been instrumental in getting a law through council requiring charities endorsed by the Charities Bureau to provide the city with statements of their expenses detailing how they disposed of the funds they collected. Zuken felt the bureau was not taking an active enough role in regulating the competition among various charities in the city. He felt it should restrict charities on the basis of inefficiency or duplication of services. In December 1963 he refused to attend a joint meeting of the welfare committee and the Charities Bureau because it was being held in private. "Closed, hush-hush sessions of council committees are absolutely contrary to democratic practice," he told the press. "I am not going to be blackmailed into a situation where we are told the bureau will come to a meeting if we hold it in camera. The whole point of the meeting is to get a public accounting of the charity situation. Not to conduct a witch hunt against charity members."

As a result of these experiences Zuken proposed that in camera committee meetings be restricted to discussions of legal claims against the city, the acquisition or sale of property, welfare appeals and personnel cases involving discipline. In February 1964 this motion sparked a bitter eighty-minute debate at city council. Zuken kicked it off by saying it was "arrogant and insulting for a committee to resort unnecessarily to holding closed meetings." He angered a number of his opponents by suggesting that at a recent in camera finance committee meeting they had attacked and undermined Juba's opposition to Metro. When they called Zuken a liar, he responded by saying, "Of course you are going to deny it. You're embarrassed." The resolution was defeated by an 11 to 5 vote.

Occasionally Zuken got the support of the local media in his campaign for more openness in civic government. In the spring of 1968 reporters from the *Tribune* and *Free Press* refused to leave the committee room when the finance committee decided to go in camera. According to CCF councillor Gordon Fines, the committee members simply wanted to sit down without the press and "throw out ideas" about taxation, city grants and wages. They held the aldermanic bull session the following day, at a time and location they declined to reveal in advance. The following year Zuken took up the case of reporters who were told to "scram" when the finance committee prepared to discuss upcoming meetings with the school board and the Metro executive.

During the 1969 civic election campaign Zuken got his knuckles rapped for telling a group of senior citizens that a municipal housing project for seniors was in the offing. "Something is definitely being planned. There will be an announcement in the next 30-60 days. We can't divulge the area as we have to keep speculators out." The chair of the urban renewal committee, Lillian Hallonquist, took this as yet another example of why Zuken should not be privy to confidential information. Angrily she told reporters "he has no right to talk about it yet. Joe can't contain himself ... that man should never have been allowed on that committee."

Righting Historical Wrongs

Once on council Zuken undertook to right some of the historical wrongs he felt had been inflicted on the North End. These included lack of recreational space, inadequate health-care facilities and the poor transportation links between the North End and the rest of the city. He also wanted to bring to an end the tremendous tax exemptions the CPR had wrested from the city when it located there in the 1880s.

The North End was in fact a creation of the CPR; it split the city, already divided by two large rivers, into a number of isolated communities. The dirty and noisy CPR yards were a constant reminder to North End residents of the various injustices the community had experienced. During his period on council Zuken worked not only to have the CPR pay its full share of taxes, but to improve the city's urban landscape by having the yards relocated. And in the interim he attempted to lessen the impact the yards had on the surrounding community.

The railway paid nothing to the city for this land until the mid-1950s. In 1954 a deal was arranged where the CPR paid $250,000 a year instead of taxes. In 1958 Mayor Steve Juba admitted this agreement was saving the railway half a million dollars a year. As early as 1963 Zuken was making speeches calling on the province to eliminate the property tax exemption enjoyed by the railway. In 1965 the Roblin government reached an agreement with the CPR whereby the railway would start to pay civic taxes, but would not pay its full assessment until the year 2005. In 1972 Zuken presented the NDP government with a petition containing over 4,000 names calling for a renegotiation of the CPR tax agreement. He wanted the railway to start paying its full share of taxes in 1973. In any settlement regarding the future of the yards, such as their relocation, he wanted the "many millions of dollars received by the CPR since the 1880s taken into account." Noting that the original agreement signed with the CPR had been approved by only 150 ratepayers, Zuken suggested, "We're actually being ruled from the grave, by the dead." Under the arrangement that had been reached with the Roblin government the railway was saving close to $4 million in taxes a year. "If the CPR had to pay full taxes like ordinary citizens in Winnipeg, the city by the year 2005 will have received $13 million additional municipal tax revenue." It was not until the early 1980s, during Eugene Kostyra's term as minister of urban affairs, did the province make arrangements to have the railway pay full freight.

For most of his career Zuken campaigned for improvements in the links between North and South Winnipeg. The improvements could come in either one of two ways: by relocating the yards to property north of the city or by building additional bridges over the yards and replacing the existing one. While Zuken always said he would prefer to see the yards moved out of the city's core area, he was not prepared to allow the promise of future rail relocation to be used as an excuse not to build what he believed were needed transportation links. For much of the time Zuken was on council, this debate focused on whether a new bridge should be built to link Sherbrook Street in the core area with McGregor Street in the city's North End. The controversy over the Sherbrook-McGregor Overpass was to create a number of strange alliances. By supporting the construction of the Sherbrook-McGregor Overpass, Zuken was joining forces with many in the CEC who were committed to developing a freeway system for the city. Such a system could only increase private vehicle use, cut into the number of people using public transit and facilitate suburban sprawl — all things Zuken opposed.

During the early 1970s one of the strongest opponents of the bridge was also one of Zuken's main allies on council. Lawrie Cherniack had been elected in the 1971 election to represent an inner-city ward on the south side of the CPR yards. It was one of the poorest communities in the city, and Cherniack believed the bridge would be destructive to an already fragile community. At times he resented Zuken's attempts to portray the issue as being a question of the South End of the city refusing to provide the North End with proper services. Their differences, however, never marred their relationship: "It was a chess game with him. Every opportunity he had, he would try and push it, and every opportunity I had, I would try and move it away. There were all sorts of procedural wrangles. One of the things I learned from him was how to make speeches on things that were not on the agenda and still make them relevant."

As with many matters before Winnipeg City Council it was a long time before the overpass question was dealt with. Not until February 1981, in the wake of a strong public campaign mounted by the bridge's opponents, did council finally reject the overpass proposal. Although he had long been an overpass supporter, Zuken abstained from this vote. He explained that he could not vote on the issue because he was the lawyer for the People's Co-operative Dairy, which stood beside the route of the overpass and would have been involved in legal action with the city should the bridge have been built.

On another question touching on the needs of the North End for improved services — the provision of health care — Zuken enjoyed considerably more success.

The North End had historically been neglected when it came to the provision of public health services. Water and sewage services were connected in South Winnipeg long before they came to the North End, and as a result children born north of the CPR tracks stood a much greater chance of dying in infancy than those born in the South End. By the 1960s the differences were not as glaring, but one long-standing grievance required addressing: with the closing of the St. Joseph's Hospital in the 1950s, there were no hospitals in North Winnipeg. When Zuken was elected to council, the city had committed itself to the partial funding of such a facility if the province would agree to providing the rest of the money. Zuken became one of the hospital's strongest advocates, fighting a battle that lasted for over fifteen years.

Zuken felt that members of the city's medical establishment were actively trying to scuttle the proposed Seven Oaks Hospital. At one point he claimed that the city's General Hospital discriminated against doctors from the city's North End by restricting hospital beds to staff doctors. He pointed out that many patients were not able to use the doctor of their own choice because of these restrictions. Hospital officials explained that the restrictions were needed if the hospital was to function as a teaching facility, but they did admit that the facility was not used by North End doctors.

From 1965 onward Zuken headed a city committee charged with the task of establishing a new hospital. After he had been in the position for two years, the CEC tried to have him replaced, but he went public with his concerns and was reappointed. The committee met with roadblock after roadblock. By 1968 two sites were under consideration, but the following year the province indicated it would not be willing to fund construction until 1973. In 1971 the Schreyer government was examining the proposal, but was considering the establishment of a community clinic in the North End, rather than a hospital. It was only in 1972 that Zuken felt confident enough to arrange for the hiring of a full-time executive director of the hospital. He told the press: "It has taken us ten years, but now I think we're finally on our way to getting a hospital into the North End area." At that point the city was committed to paying for 20 per cent of the hospital's construction, with the rest coming from the provincial Health Services Commission.

The creation of the Seven Oaks Hospital marked one of the few times in his political career that Zuken was able to operate in a creative capacity rather than as a critic. In his role as the chairman of the civic committee dealing with the establishment of the hospital and later as the chairman of the hospital's board of directors, Zuken had to guide a large and complex organization into existence. As the hospital's executive director, Gudmundur Myrdal worked closely with Zuken throughout this period and gained a unique perspective on him. Myrdal was particularly appreciative of the meticulous approach Zuken took towards the establishment of the hospital: "He had a way of sitting back and taking things in and when he spoke, he really meant what he said. He had digested things before he opened his mouth.

"He was extroverted in another sense though, in that if he was convinced of something he would fight like hell to accomplish it. He was always working for the people who he thought were taking the dirty end of the stick. It took me a long time to fully appreciate him in terms of the depth of his thinking, his fairness, just what a great person he was."

Although in 1973 Zuken optimistically predicted construction on the hospital would begin the following year, it continued to run up against one problem after another. In 1976 the *Winnipeg Tribune* ran the headline "North End Hospital Is Finally Approved" over what would be only one of a long series of stories proclaiming the hospital's "final" approval. In the wake of the Conservative victory in the 1977 provincial election, the hospital underwent yet another re-evaluation as the Sterling Lyon administration implemented its restraint policies. The opening ceremonies at the hospital did not take place until September 1980, and the first patient was not admitted until the beginning of 1981. By 1984 the hospital had over three hundred beds, and in that year it opened a fitness centre. Following Zuken's death, the centre would be renamed the Joseph Zuken Fitness Centre.

A Platoon of Councillors

Just as on the school board, Zuken was discriminated against when it came to the selection of municipal delegations to national conferences. In March 1966 senior CEC councillor Robert Moffat made it clear he would never support a nomination to send Zuken to the annual convention of the Federation of Mayors and Municipalities. "It is important," Moffat said, "[that] we have responsible people representing the city." The following year Zuken was demanding "the right to refuse to go" to the federation's conference, but he was also developing what would be an annual attack on the size of civic delegations. In Canada's centennial year, when the convention was held in Montreal, Zuken suggested the six-person Winnipeg delegation was really taking a "side-trip to Expo."

In 1976 Zuken questioned the wisdom of sending a dozen councillors to the federation's Vancouver conference. "If this thing was in Medicine Hat or Saskatoon you wouldn't see 12 of them going. It is just a junket." That spring, when the police chief and two councillors travelled to Las Vegas in preparation for the opening of a casino at the Winnipeg Convention Centre, Zuken suggested that in the future councillors and administration officials receive prior approval for out-of-province travel. And he was also angered, perhaps unfairly, given his remarks about Medicine Hat and Saskatoon, over a decision to send parks committee members to a recreation conference in Cornerbrook, Newfoundland.

Zuken's reputation for sticking up for the taxpayer was nurtured by these clashes, particularly since the junketing councillors chose to respond in alternately belligerent or shamefaced fashion. In 1977 he branded the city's twelve-person delegation to the Mayors and Municipalities Convention, held this time in Toronto, "a platoon." The following year he was able to add secrecy to the charge of junketeering at the public expense when the finance committee made an in camera decision to send two councillors to Beersheba, Winnipeg's twin city in Israel.

Zuken's critics often suggested that he was taking a narrow view, failing to see the benefits that would accrue to the city and the administration from contact with fellow municipal politicians. In response, Zuken said the travelling councillors should share the fruits of their experiences with the rest of the council. This gave him the opportunity to tear into the three-page report submitted by the seven councillors, another "platoon," who had attended a recreation conference in Miami Beach. To Zuken the study was not worth "one dollar, let alone the $1,750 it cost to send the councillors to Florida." The major benefits cited by the report were the fostering of "good personal relations between parts of our country and the entire U.S.A." and the "opportunity to meet other delegates and discuss their operations."

On the few occasions that Zuken was included in a civic delegation, he was accompanied by Clara, travelling of course at private rather than public expense. At times she became frustrated by Zuken's rigorous efforts to avoid any charges of junketeering — he kept detailed records of his every expense on these trips and once wanted to write the city a cheque for several dollars when he discovered that he had underspent his allowed daily expenses.

Law and Order

On a number of occasions Zuken found himself at odds with the Winnipeg police force. As a general principle he believed there should be an independent agency for the review of complaints levied against the force. He was also alarmed by the arbitrary authority council granted the police. In 1963 council came very close to passing a by-law that would have given the police chief the right to refuse parade permits if he thought the parade would include banners, signs or devices that were "unsafe, indecent or likely to cause a breach of the peace." Zuken pointed out that under the by-law "any policeman would be a censor of placards and signs carried in a parade."

In 1967 Zuken took police chief George Blow to task for publicly supporting a Canadian Police Chiefs' Association position paper that recommended retaining the lash in the prison system and giving police the right to enter homes without a warrant and to demand the name and address of any person. Two years later, when the chief said the courts were giving "active criminals" a "licence to steal" by making bail too accessible, an incensed Zuken reminded Blow that he was not "the chief of the courts."

It is certainly not within the prerogative of the police chief to interfere with the judicial process. The matter of bail should be decided by the courts. I think there has been interference. This is a vital issue. If a man is denied bail it means in effect he's sentenced before his trial has taken place. There may be some extreme cases but that is for the court to decide, not the chief of police.

In the summer of 1969 Zuken participated in a re-enactment of the Winnipeg General Strike. In May of that year Councillor Slaw Rebchuk attended a United Steelworkers of America conference in Montreal. There the union had presented the city with a plaque which bore this inscription:

In honor of the people of Winnipeg whose sacrifice for union recognition helped millions of Canadians win the benefits of collective bargaining. Presented to the city of Winnipeg by the Canadian members of the United Steelworkers on the anniversary of the Winnipeg General Strike — 1919-1969.

Councillors could not decide what to do with the plaque. Councillor Taft said the strike was a near insurrection and its memory should not be perpetuated at all. He suggested the plaque be turned over to the Manitoba Federation of Labour to mount in the Union Centre. Zuken wanted it mounted by the doors of the council chamber. He argued that "it's an historic document ... part of the history of our city and our country.... It was presented to the city and it should be displayed by the city." With the support of the NDP aldermen and a number of independents, Zuken's position carried the day.

Life on Anderson Avenue

For Zuken the Sixties and Seventies were a period of considerable personal satisfaction. On June 1, 1965, he and Clara moved into a one-and-a-half-storey house on Anderson Avenue. This was the first house they had lived in by themselves; prior to that they had occupied a number of apartments on Mountain Avenue in the North End. It was Clara who found the house and initiated the purchase. "One day I was sitting at work, reading the paper, when I saw an ad for 181 Anderson. I thought, 'This is a nice district for us.' " They quickly decided to make the purchase. According to Clara, "The happiest part of life was spent here. Joe was settled and established. Everything in the house reminds me of trips we took — to Montreal, Toronto or Europe. And Joe loved the house. He used to really relax when he came home."

Janice Dietch remained close to the Zukens during this period of their lives. She underlines the important role that Clara Zuken played in her husband's life. "Like any marriage it was not always smooth sailing. But in their own ways they worked on that marriage. And he could not have done the things that he did without her. She made it easy for him. She never demanded time.

"He never bought his own clothes. She went out and bought them and he did her the favour of trying them on — and I mean he did her the favour. Because if he were tired or in a bad mood, he wouldn't try them on until he was good and ready to."

From the early Sixties onward Joe and Clara travelled every year, sometimes to Toronto and Montreal to visit friends like Stanley and Mila Ryerson; at other times they travelled much further afield, to Mexico, the Soviet Union, Romania, Yugoslavia and Czechoslovakia. Occasionally they were accompanied by Janice. She recalled these trips with fondness: "When they were on a trip they loved to go shopping. They would be in and out of stores like a couple of kids. He liked nice things, and he liked her to have nice things — he thought she was cute."

Conflict with the Party

After Zuken's death, Clara noted that throughout his life he had remained loyal to the Communist Party. "He would not do anything in public to besmirch the party because he felt the basic ideas are still wonderful; it is just that they have not been accomplished yet. But there were some things on which he did not see eye to eye with the party — on these he deviated." The deviations came, not on the party's national or civic policies — after all, the party's federal policies were only slightly more radical than the NDP's, and Zuken had what amounted to free rein when it came to civic policy — but on international questions.

The first major issue to be addressed in the 1960s was the Soviet Union's policy towards the State of Israel. The Canadian Communist Party viewed Israel as a reactionary state. In the wake of the Six Day War in 1967 the party condemned Israel as an aggressor nation, while the Soviet ambassador to the United Nations compared Israel to Nazi Germany. Clara and Joe used to frequently discuss these events with their friends. "Joe was very, very upset. He used to take these things very seriously, and feel them very deeply.... On the question of Israel he went public. It just tore him apart sometimes. But he had to do it. He could not keep quiet and have any respect for himself." He sent the following letter to the local papers:

The most urgent necessity in the continuing crisis in the Middle East is to enforce the end of war. Unless the Middle East is to be condemned to wage war every decade, fair and just political settlements must be negotiated. There is no alternative to peaceful co-existence except an uneasy armed truce and turmoil as an interval between wars.

Peace will not prevail unless the just rights of the state of Israel and her Arab neighbors are safeguarded. Fundamental to the achievement of peace is the necessity of the Arab states to recognize for all time Israel's right to survive and live free from continual threats of extermination and her right of access to her economic lifeline of waters such as the Gulf of Aqaba and the Suez Canal. The UN must assist Israel and the Arab states to reach a constructive solution regarding the Arab refugees — already too long neglected and explosive as a human problem and time bomb. Peace cannot long endure in a climate of conqueror and conquered. Israel has proved her military capability. She should now demonstrate with statesmanship at the conference table that her terms of settlement will not sow the seeds of a future war.

Was Israel the "aggressor" when war erupted? Who fired first in this particular conflict is yet to be determined. Certainly the element of surprise was with Israel, but this has to be viewed in the context of the following facts. Threatened by President Nasser and other Arab leaders with proclaimed plans to "exterminate Israel," menaced by the mobilization of the encircling armies and by the imposition of a crucial blockade of access to the Gulf of Aqaba, Israel had the right to defend herself. The remark of Ambassador Fedorenko, comparing the actions of the state of Israel with Hitler, is most unfortunate and historically objectionable. The comparison is particularly inappropriate when applied to a state which has been built by survivors of a people against whom Hitler waged a war with the intended "final solution" of total extermination.

As a matter of principle I feel it necessary to make this statement publicly.

The Communist Party did not take such a challenge lightly. Zuken's deviation from the party line was noted and condemned by the party's central committee. According to Bill Ross, it marked the beginning of a series of battles between Zuken and the party leadership. "The position the party took was that while they did not agree with his statement, we hoped that he would subsequently see the correctness of the position of our party." This never happened, and Zuken also began to speak out on the Soviet Union's restrictions on Jewish emigration. In a 1973 article in *Canadian Jewish Outlook* he drew attention to the fact that Leopold Trepper, the former head of the Red Orchestra, the Soviet Union's spy network during the Second World War, was being refused the right to leave Poland: "Why, why, why?" he wrote. "To be silent in the face of this injustice is a crime."

The Zukens travelled to Eastern Europe in early 1968 and witnessed the Prague Spring. He was back in Winnipeg when in August of that year the Soviet tanks rumbled over the Czech border. Like the Khrushchev speech and the Hungarian invasion of 1956, the ousting of the Dubcek government sparked another crisis in the Communist Party. For people like Stanley Ryerson it was the final straw; he let his long-time membership lapse. But the leadership refused to deviate.

One long-time associate of Zuken's recalled visiting him in his law office shortly after the news broke. "I was very upset.

I went into his office and I said, 'What the hell is going on?' ... And he said it looks like the leaders of the Soviet Party felt they had to step in or capitalism was going to be restored and the Czechs would go over to the Americans. And I asked him if he believed that. And he said, 'No, not for a second.' And I asked, 'And you can still stay a member of the Communist Party?' And he said, 'Yes.' "

Fifteen years after the event, Zuken still had difficulty reconciling himself to the Soviet invasion of Czechoslovakia: "But the question that bothered me then is [still] bothering me: Why were events allowed to accumulate and fester without correction, without corrective steps being taken by the party in the country, so that it does not lead to a situation where there is need for a major military intervention?... But it was too late and the hardliners took the road of military intervention. I can see the argument, it is easy for me from a distance of thousands of miles, as a person who can afford the luxury of intellectualizing about the situation, those are key areas, of vital national and international concerns for the Soviet Union, or the Soviet bloc. And an argument could be made. But I could not see why the party within Czechoslovakia, within Hungary, and within the Soviet Union, why they failed to act in a Marxist way to avert that major surgery."

Zuken's growing unhappiness with party policy, particularly in relation to the Soviet Union, strained his relationship with his brother. Clara Zuken had these recollections of the period: "The boys were really very close. But because of this difference, when we were together we did not discuss politics, so there would not be any tension. But you see when there is a subject between friends — a certain subject [that] is not to be referred to — it does create a different relationship. So that was a barrier.

"Joe used to belong to the committees, and then Joe would state his position as Joe would, and Bill would state his position as he would, and they would have it out there. But it is bound to leave something in their personal relationship. I think we all felt that was sad. There was nothing that could be done about it."

Bill Ross confirmed that this was period of growing differences between himself and his brother: "He was criticized both formally and informally. Formally in the committees, and in personal discussions by myself. The fact that he was my brother I don't think hindered either of us taking up the issues at hand. It didn't change our personal relationship, but the fact of the matter is ... on many questions and on his role as a public representative he and I differed.... So it was known throughout the party that there were differences between himself and the party on some questions and that there were personal differences between himself and myself, who happened at that period of time to be the leader of the party."

The Coming of Unicity

Throughout the Sixties much of the debate on council focused on the need for structural reform. At the end of his second year on council Zuken wrote a letter to the editor of the *Free Press* outlining the changes he would like to see brought into effect. He started by opposing recent suggestions that the number of councillors be reduced. This proposal, he said, was "aimed at reducing labour representation and ... designed to fasten clique control more securely over civic government." He called for regular town hall meetings that councillors and school trustees would be required to attend, a lowering of the voting age to eighteen, an end to the system where only property owners were allowed to vote on money by-laws, and "ending the obnoxious tendency of public bodies discussing public business at in camera sessions." Summing up, he wrote: "The people pay the bills and the price for weak uninspired civic leadership. Is it not high time that they raised their voices in developing a vigorous and free-swinging public debate on the reforms necessary to revitalize our local government?"

In 1970 Zuken drafted the city's brief to a joint Senate-Commons constitutional committee. In it he wrote that "the constitutional status of the municipalities under the existing constitution is one of colonial dependency ... [and] reflects a master-servant relationship [that] is outmoded and archaic." Moving on to an issue that had bothered him since his election to the school board thirty years earlier, he wrote: "There are no existing constitutional guarantees for municipalities and they are at the whim or mercy of the senior governments" while "carrying a staggering load of expenditures for education, health and welfare, the financial responsibility for which should be the responsibility of the senior governments." He concluded the report by noting that municipalities and cities are "excluded from any realistic involvement in matters in which [they] are inevitably concerned and from discussion of basic issues of public policy. This must change and Canadian cities must be given constitutional status and equality of treatment which will enable them better to serve their constituents and Canada."

The election of a New Democratic Party government in the summer of 1969 spelt the end for Metro. The NDP had campaigned on a promise to create a single urban government for Winnipeg. The government's first urban affairs minister was Saul Cherniack, Zuken's colleague from the days of the New Theatre and the school board. Cherniack, who had also served as a member of both Winnipeg and Metro council, devoted tremendous energy to the creation of what came to be known as Unicity. A special task force was established and given a broad mandate: to provide a blueprint for a single unified, but decentralized, government that would have the power to deal with the various problems confronting an urban community of half a million people and that would simultaneously give individual citizens a greater role in determining the affairs of that community. A second and equally important goal was to establish a way to increase the degree of political responsibility at city hall. This would involve the introduction of some form of parliamentary government and force the majority group on council — be it the Citizens or the NDP — to be held accountable for the policies the city was pursuing.

With the task force's recommendations concerning these admittedly ambitious goals in hand, the NDP proposed an act that would abolish most of the previously existing boards and commissions and create of a fifty-member council in their stead. A series of standing committees were to be created that would report to council through the executive policy committee, which was intended to serve the council as a surrogate cabinet. To balance all this centralization, a second set of committees, called community committees, would come into being. These committees were to be based on the boundaries of the old municipalities and the wards of the city of Winnipeg and were to be charged with dealing with local issues. Coupled with them was a proposal for a series of residents advisory groups, or RAGs as they became known. These groups were intended to allow interested citizens to play a more direct role in the city's decision making and were one of the act's most daring innovations.

The Unicity proposals generated considerable controversy. The leaders of the various suburban governments being legislated out of existence were quick to go on the defensive. However, the NDP's proposals won the overall support of both Metro and Winnipeg City Council. The press described Zuken as one of the "most avid supporters of the plan," recognizing that it incorporated many of his proposals for change in urban government. But there had to be one serious change to the proposed act before it was acceptable to Steve Juba. In keeping with the decision to introduce some measure of parliamentary democracy to city hall, the NDP had recommended that the mayor be selected, not by the voters at large, but by a majority vote of council. Juba recognized that a council dominated by former municipal politicians whose noses he had been tweaking for the better part of a decade was hardly likely to select him as leader. On the other hand, he correctly judged that no other civic politician could beat him in an at-large election. Therefore, Juba lobbied long and hard to have the mayor continue to be chosen by a general election. In his brief to the legislative committee dealing with the act, Juba claimed that "if the mayor was elected by council he would be a little puppy dog to the majority of the council." In his campaign he had considerable support both from within the NDP cabinet, where some members believed the new city would be too decentralized without a mayor who could claim to speak for all the people, and from Joe Zuken, who argued for the maintenance of an independent voice that could counter the majority on council. In the end Juba won out. In one of the few major amendments to the Unicity proposals, the NDP agreed to continue city-wide mayoral elections. The new City of Winnipeg Act was adopted in 1971.

In the fall of 1971 the new city's first council was elected. While many had feared that the NDP, which enjoyed considerable support in North Winnipeg at the federal and provincial levels, would dominate the new council, the results told a different story. A reorganized CEC, now called the Independent Citizens' Election Committee, won a sweeping victory. One of the few voices of opposition on the new council would belong to Joe Zuken.

NINE

The Unicity Years
1972-1983

I remember an image of him: standing slightly bent over, straight from the waist, shaking slightly and his fist clenched with his arms down and swaying while he spoke and looking down. I remember the tremendous eloquence of his speeches.

— Lawrie Cherniack

On January 1, 1972, a new City of Winnipeg came into being. Conceived as a bold experiment in democracy and urban government, the new council had broader powers and a larger field of play than virtually any other city government in Canada. The council faced numerous problems: a decaying core, an unfair tax assessment system and a declining industrial sector. However, unlike past city governments it had the power and the opportunity to deal with these problems in a comprehensive manner. Suburban sprawl could have been capped; a proper start on urban redevelopment — with a focus on meeting social needs rather than those of multinational development corporations — could have been made; and there existed the machinery to allow local residents a greater say in the development of their communities.

None of this has transpired. Instead Winnipeg has become a playground for developers. Tremendous amounts of public money have gone into subsidizing a series of downtown high-rise projects, while the suburbs have grown to suit the interests of a clutch of development companies. Inner-city social problems that were first identified in the early Sixties are now reaching crisis proportions.

Some have argued that the Unicity concept was flawed from the beginning, saying that amalgamation left the city core at the mercy of the growing suburban community. Joe Zuken did not subscribe to this view. Instead he felt the City of Winnipeg Act was foiled by politicians who had no sympathy with its goals. Looking back on Unicity on the occasion of his retirement from city council, Zuken had these thoughts:

> The idea is still a fine and creative idea. I think it is the driver and the direction that it has taken that is wrong. The main purpose of Unicity was to bring the people closer to local government, local government closer to the people.
>
> There is a great deal of dissatisfaction now, because it has not reached its potential.... But that is not because of the idea of Unicity.

Zuken laid the blame for the policy vacuum at city hall at the door of the political coalition that controlled the new council — the Independent Citizens' Election Committee.

The creation of Unicity contributed to the further restructuring of the Citizens' bloc on council. Many of the suburban councillors who had opposed amalgamation, such as Fort Garry mayor Richard Wankling and West Kildonan mayor Abe Yanofsky, and Metro politicians like Steve Juba's long-time enemy Bernie Wolfe, were to play leading roles in this new political entity — the Independent Citizens' Election Committee. In two advertisements for the 1971 election the ICEC stressed its non-partisan nature:

> We need councillors who will put public interest ahead of old party loyalties ... Independent Citizens' Election Committee candidates answer to no political party: they answer to YOU.
>
> I.C.E.C. candidates are concerned, dedicated people whose objective would be to strive for the City's best

interests and your best interests without partisan political
commitments.

This strategy, as it had in the past, paid off in spades for the
Citizens. They won thirty-seven seats on council, while the
NDP, suffering from the Schreyer government's mid-term un-
popularity, took only seven seats. At the new council's first
meeting, the ICEC re-enacted the historical division of the
spoils with a vengeance. Of the twenty-nine committee positions to be appointed, twenty-eight went to members of the
ICEC. ICEC councillor June Westbury underlined the rather
dubious significance of the word "independent" when she
explained, "We don't want the NDP on the committees when
it means our own independents may not be named."

The NDP caucus was far from unified. As Lawrie Cherniack
noted, "There were many issues on which the best we could
do was agree to disagree." At the same time, in keeping with
the spirit of Unicity, the NDP strove to play the role of official
opposition, developing positions on every issue that arose.
"Joe didn't do that. He spoke on the issues that were important
to him. It was incredible how he could find an issue in a
resolution that did not look like an issue."

Cherniack also recalled that there was considerable distrust
of Zuken within his caucus. "I was certainly the only one in
my caucus that spoke to him regularly. Occasionally, he would
ask me to second a motion. I had no trouble doing that, although I sometimes took some flak from my colleagues."
Cherniack only served on council for one term, but in later
years Zuken established working relationships with Cyril
Keeper and Harvey Smith. But there was never a time when
he and the NDP caucus were truly working together.

While the NDP enjoyed less than complete success playing
the role of official opposition, the ICEC successfully eluded the
burden of political responsibility that governing parties must
normally shoulder. This was in no small measure due to the
Schreyer government's decision to allow for the continued
at-large election of the mayor. Juba easily won two terms as
Unicity mayor, and he spent those years undermining those
members of the ICEC who attempted to provide city-wide
leadership. It was common for Juba to wait and see which way
the wind was blowing before taking a public position on issues

— and in some cases he would switch his views to match shifting public opinion. What emerged in place of some form of government based on policy was government based on deal making.

The consummate deal maker was Robert Steen. A veteran of the Conservative Party backrooms, Steen enjoyed an on-again, off-again relationship with the ICEC. The deals Steen engineered were neither illegal nor corrupt; rather they were examples of intricate political backscratching. He gave a description of one such deal to a provincial inquiry into the City of Winnipeg Act. Steen's problems had started when the city's board of commissioners deleted a $100,000 street renovation project, slated for Steen's ward, from the budget. As Steen explained:

> This of course would cause me ... acute embarrassment and my political opponents would make sure that everybody in the street knew this. So to put the $100,000 item back into the budget I had to go around the council and make deals. One million, six hundred thousand dollars later and with about 30 different deals around the place, it was back in.

The Unicity council took control of a city that was going into a significant decline. This was due in part to the planning paralysis of the previous decade when the city council, the surrounding municipalities and the Metropolitan Corporation were waging their corrosive battles. The railways were abandoning their yards and rail transportation was losing its significance. A flourishing garment trade located in the old warehouse buildings of downtown Winnipeg was all but gone, leaving the city's core full of empty and abandoned buildings. Working-class families, in many cases following the industries that employed them, were fleeing to the suburbs.

Throughout the Sixties a number of efforts were made to revive the downtown section. A new city hall, concert hall, museum and theatre centre were constructed just north of Portage and Main, and the Richardson family built a thirty-four-storey office tower on the corner of Portage and Main. But other projects seemed designed to frustrate these developments; suburban sprawl, and the opening of large regional shopping centres, continued unabated. By the end of the Sixties civic officials had come to the conclusion that downtown redevelopment was a necessity and that such renewal could only be financed by outside investment. Just as the city councillors of the 1880s had gone wooing the CPR, the councillors of the 1970s began to examine ways to attract international development companies to Winnipeg.

At a time when the council, on the evidence of one of its leading members, was barely prepared to make coherent decisions as to which streets to pave, the city plunged into a series of multimillion-dollar deals involving the privatization of civic services, suburban expansion and downtown renewal. It is small wonder the council was transformed into a rubber stamp for development projects.

Sell-out at Portage and Main

On a cold and blustering day in early March 1979 over a hundred onlookers crowded the street corners at Portage and Main, an intersection Winnipeggers have proudly claimed to be the coldest in the world. A stiff breeze was blowing and the temperature hovered just below the freezing point. From the crush of people, a dozen parka-clad figures, including three people in wheelchairs, began to do a very ordinary thing — they crossed the intersection. When they reached one corner, they turned and headed for the next one. When they completed a circuit, the crowd let go a big cheer and one onlooker rushed out to shake the hand of the slight man who was at the centre of this strange expedition. "Mr. Zuken," he said, "you are a very good man."

This little parade, which won Zuken national attention, was in fact an act of civil disobedience. The day before, a city by-law had come into effect prohibiting pedestrians from making surface-level crossings at Portage and Main. If they wanted to get from one side of the street to the other, they would have to use an underground concourse that funnelled people through a commercial mall. That mall was controlled by one of the world's most powerful real estate developers, the Trizec Corporation. Zuken and his supporters were protesting not only the way the city was converting public space into private property, but the decade-long relationship between city council and Trizec. At the heart of the conflict was Winnipeg City Council's century-old willingness, in the name of development, to play handmaiden to private industry.

The Trizec development started as a proposal for an underground parking garage south of Portage and Main. The parkade was expected to cost the city a total of $5 million. But it soon grew into a massive redevelopment plan involving three of the country's major banks (Montreal, Nova Scotia and Toronto-Dominion), Marathon Reality (a subsidiary of Canadian Pacific), the city's largest grain company, James Richardson and Sons, and the Trizec Corporation. These corporate high rollers were able to extract a seemingly endless series of commitments from a development-hungry council. In order to get Trizec, the second-largest development company in Canada, to undertake this development at one of the most-used intersections in Winnipeg, city council had to agree to expropriate an entire city block on behalf of Trizec, base the rent on the cost rather than the value of the land (and then agree not to raise the rent for forty years), build a parking garage, give Trizec two years of land use rent free, and pay the bulk of the costs for the construction of the underground concourses connecting the four corners of the intersection. After winning these concessions Trizec proceeded with a scaled-down version of the development model it had been waving under the council's nose for eight years.

Even before the creation of Unicity, the groundwork for the Trizec project was being done. In September 1968 Juba appeared at a meeting of the Winnipeg Parking Authority, a city-appointed board that dealt with downtown parking issues, and indicated that a major investor was interested in coming to the city if the amount of downtown parking were increased. That same year the Bank of Nova Scotia made the decision to build its new regional headquarters in Winnipeg at the corner of Portage and Main, kitty-corner to the Richardson Building. The Richardsons were interested in seeing further development of the intersection, and particularly the construction of an underground concourse, since a retail mall in the basement of their office building was turning out to be unprofitable. An underground pedestrian corridor might improve the retail trade.

It was at this point that the Trizec Corporation entered onto the scene. Trizec was formed in 1960 to complete the construction of Place Ville Marie in Montreal. Urban development critic Donald Gutstein, in words which sound only too familiar to anyone who has spent time around the Trizec Building, described Place Ville Marie as "the prototype for all that is happening in downtown Canada — huge skyscrapers, vast bleak plazas, underground parking lots and underground shopping malls." Trizec itself was owned by the English Property Corporation of London, England, which in turn was controlled by the Eagle Star Insurance Company. During the course of the Seventies, in a move to elude the authority of the Foreign Investment Review Agency, voting control of Trizec was sold to a branch of the Bronfman family. At that time British shareholders of English Property were given assurances that they retained control of the company.

In Canada, Trizec enjoyed close relations with the Bank of Nova Scotia; leading Canadian businessmen served on the board of both corporations. When the bank decided to build at the corner of Portage and Main, it entered into a development agreement with Trizec. The first news the public received of this potential development was in February 1971, when Trizec held a press conference to announce its intention to construct a 300,000-square-foot regional bank headquarters. Other potential pieces of the development plan were a major retail outlet, a hotel and a high-rise apartment building. Juba was in attendance at the press conference and spoke of the possibility of a joint venture between the city and Trizec. A few days later council authorized the mayor to "continue negotiations with the Trizec Corporation, the Bank of Nova Scotia and any other interested developers."

Zuken was one of the five councillors to oppose the deal at a June 1972 council meeting. He pointed out that there was no detailed breakdown of the costs of the project, nor had the councillors had any time to study its implications. Finally he said it was difficult to see what obligations Trizec was undertaking under the agreement. One of the agreement's most controversial clauses explained that Trizec "confirmed its desire to achieve the implementation of such plan on the understanding that circumstances could well frustrate such implementation and therefore it could not obligate itself in any way to give effect to such plan notwithstanding the grant of the lease of the air rights." In other words, the city would assemble the land and construct the foundation and parking garage and then Trizec might not build anything. As it turned out, stalling on Trizec's part meant the building was not completed for nearly a decade.

In 1974 Trizec was back before council. Corporation executives came equipped with a series of drawings and models all depicting two thirty-four-storey buildings, a mall and a hotel. But Trizec officials explained that while they wanted the city to go ahead and start work on the parking garage, the corporation was only willing to commit itself to developing a 300,000-square-foot project — not the 1.5-million-square-foot development shown in the models and the slide show presentation. Council opposition to the plan was growing; at this meeting Zuken once more led the attack, noting, "You look at the model, and it's a beautiful concept. But as you look at the agreement, this view changes ... just as if you were descending in a parachute. We are making too many concessions."

As the opponents of Trizec grew in number, Juba became more defensive. At an August 22, 1974, meeting of council when the deal came up for reconsideration, Juba told those councillors who were having second thoughts, "If you want to admit now that you have made a bad decision, you should resign your elected office immediately because you are not capable of handling public funds."

The strength of the growing public opposition to the project was reflected at the first council meeting after the 1975 civic election. A motion to halt any more expenditures on the project was defeated by three votes. By this time most of the buildings on the block had been expropriated and demolished. Zuken and others were angry that even though the city had bought and cleared the land on Trizec's behalf, the corporation had still not given any indication as to what the final project would encompass.

Meanwhile corporate pressure for the construction of an underground concourse was mounting. Trizec and the Richardsons were particularly interested in the development of the shopping corridor. However, by this point, even ICEC members of council were beginning to balk at the cost of the concourse. In April of 1976 Trizec responded to this threat by announcing that it would not commence construction until a concourse agreement was signed.

The corporate campaign did its job. In December 1976 council was presented with the concourse proposal. It was at this meeting that a motion allowing for the blocking of pedestrian traffic at Portage and Main was adopted. Zuken and others made three different attempts to have the ban on pedestrian crossing dropped from the agreement. In the end, the vote was so close that Juba was required to use his right to cast a double vote, winning final approval for the project.

The city had hoped the concourse costs would be split three ways, with the province, the city and the companies on the four street corners each picking up a third of the cost. But the province declined to pay for any of it, while the four corporations limited their contribution to $1.45 million, leaving the city with the bill for the remaining 80 per cent of the project. The city had to promise the banks not to lease space in the concourse to "another bank, a trust company, a credit union or a deposit-taking financial institution." The city also assumed full operating and maintenance costs for the concourse. Not only was the city spending millions of dollars to enhance the value of the property controlled by a series of banks and multinational corporations, it also agreed to exempt them from any tax increases resulting from the increases in their property values.

As the city continued to make investment after investment and commitment after commitment, it was still not apparent what Trizec intended to do. It was not until January of 1978 that the Bank of Nova Scotia unveiled its final plans — a very small building right on the corner of Portage and Main. If there was going to be a high rise, Trizec would have to build it by itself. It was in February of that year that the city signed an agreement with Canpark to operate the parking garage. Under the agreement, motorists would be charged thirty-five dollars a month. The city had spent $5 million on a garage, the purpose of which would be to encourage motorists to ignore public transit and bring their cars to the busiest intersection in the city.

In October 1978 Trizec let the public in on the scope of the development that would be taking place at Portage and Main. Gone was the hotel, gone was the high-rise apartment building, and the shopping centre had been considerably scaled down. Trizec president Harold Milavsky said the company would be constructing a thirty-one-storey office tower that would serve as the new home of the Winnipeg Commodity Exchange. By this point in the development the city had committed itself to close to $20 million of expenses on behalf of the Trizec development; Milavsky estimated the cost of the new building as $40 million. At the time Zuken noted that once borrowing costs were figured into the city's expenses, the price tag for this redevelopment would be close to $35 million.

The Trizec controversy was the major fight on council in the 1970s, and Zuken had these thoughts on it in retrospect: "It was an historic loss to our city. But as I sometimes remark, the dominant group at city hall would even sell the city hall if they thought they could make a profit on it."

Zuken's defiant act of jaywalking did not win him a day in court. He had said he did not want his case to receive any special treatment. But provincial attorney general Gerry Mercier, a former supporter of the Trizec project when he was a member of city council, was not interested in giving Zuken the opportunity to cause the city any further embarrassment. He announced that charges would not be laid against Zuken or the eleven other people who accompanied him because the city had been informed of the crossing in advance. "From now on," he warned, "the traffic bylaw of the City of Winnipeg will be enforced."

"Let them find it"

The early 1970s saw the emergence of a national urban reform movement. In Toronto, Vancouver and Montreal, a new generation of politicians and social critics was taking aim at the deeply entrenched political organizations that had ruled those cities for many years. They began to put into political perspective many issues that had long been seen as apolitical, particularly housing and transportation. One of these critics was Winnipeg-born-and-bred James Lorimer, author of a number of books and articles on city politics in Canada. He helped develop the argument that most civic governments saw their real business as servicing what he called the "property industry." This involved the direct provision of city services, such as roads, sidewalks and plumbing, and the zoning and regulation of land. These two activities were crucial in determining the value of a piece of property. The property industry was defined as a complex of companies and professionals involved in the building, selling and financing of new and existing buildings. As such, it included not only construction companies and real estate agents, but property insurance companies, lawyers and mortgage lenders. The interests of this industry were served, Lorimer argued, by policies that kept property taxes low, protected and maximized property values, and encouraged new growth on land controlled by the property industry. These policies, with a few exceptions, run counter to the interests of most Canadians, whose first requirement from the property industry is affordable shelter.

Lorimer concluded his argument by suggesting that the property industry had succeeded in capturing control of civic governments across the country. He never suggested there was any illegality or personal corruption involved in these relationships, but he was indicating that in all likelihood city councils controlled by members of the property industry would enact policies that would benefit that industry.

Zuken largely concurred with Lorimer's analysis, which in fact was a refinement of many of the charges he had been making for years.

There are two voting blocs in city council. There is no doubt that the first Unicity council is under the control of the Right, and can achieve in municipal politics what they are still groping for in provincial politics. I call them a political mafia. There is no doubt that the voting record on key development issues proves they're catering to the big developers. When the big developers sneeze, the ICEC caucus says "bless you" and rushes to give them assistance. This is true with the Kenaston [a development project which despite numerous city concessions never did get off the ground] and the Trizec deals. When the people get the full information about these development deals, they will throw them out.

I think the ICEC is property-oriented and motivated. I think it is completely obsessed with catering to big business. I'm not making any charge that they are being bribed, but it would be interesting to examine the source of the campaign funds that are given to them. It is interesting to note how they are resisting my proposals for city councillors to reveal their real-estate holdings.

Growing concern over the influence the development industry could exercise over city council had led Zuken to launch a campaign for improved conflict-of-interest legislation governing city politicians. In 1972 he proposed that all councillors be required to make a full disclosure of their real estate holdings; this way, he said, Winnipeg would be able to retain its reputation as "the incorruptible city." He also wanted councillors to list any share certificates they held in corporations doing business with the city. These ideas were voted down in committee; their opponents said that while they had nothing against conflict-of-interest laws per se, they worried that Zuken was being too rigid. ICEC councillor Roy Parkill, possibly missing the point, said Zuken's suggested rules would inhibit the day-to-day business dealings of lawyers and real estate agents who were also members of council.

The 1974 civic election saw a number of ICEC councillors become embroiled in the type of conflict-of-interest scenarios Zuken had been raising. Lorne Leech was attacked for being the part owner of a parcel of land being appropriated by the city for purposes of land banking; Abe Yanofsky's former law partner was found to be acting for a client who was selling land to a property developer at the same time that the council committee Yanofsky headed was rezoning the land; and Deputy Mayor Bernie Wolfe came under fire for trying, in his capacity as real estate developer, to establish a winter racetrack on the outskirts of the city. While there was no indication that any of these councillors used their influence in improper ways, the events underlined the need for full public knowledge of the business activities of those elected to council.

It was not until the fall of 1976 that council appointed provincial chief justice C. Rhodes Smith, a former city alderman, to conduct a public inquiry into the need for conflict-of-interest legislation at city hall. The commission had been set up with the reluctant support of the ICEC caucus, and one caucus member anonymously told the media that he doubted ICEC members would bother to testify before it. Those who did, this councillor felt, would "be looked upon as a squealer by the other 39." In explaining his lack of interest in the inquiry, ICEC councillor Jim Ernst said, "If they think there is a conflict of interest, let them go find it." Gerry Mercier said conflict of interest is "best determined by individuals, and not commissions."

In the end, only six councillors bothered to appear before Justice Smith, who expressed disappointment that no ICEC councillors had bothered to present a brief. Zuken was angry that the city administration did not bother to put in a formal appearance to explain how the city currently dealt with conflict-of-interest questions. In his submission, Zuken said councillors, commissioners and key civic workers should be required to make full disclosure of their assets, including real estate owned wholly or partially by themselves or their spouses. There should also be details of shares in corporations, directorships and interest in investment funds, mutual funds and investment trusts. Anyone making a false statement should, Zuken felt, forfeit his or her council seat.

When Smith finally submitted his report, with recommendations for a fairly stringent policy, the council simply sidestepped the question by referring the matter to the provincial government, asking it to enact legislation covering all municipalities. Zuken suggested the move was tantamount to "throwing the report in the dustbin."

Zuken was to have the last laugh in the spring of 1980 when three senior ICEC councillors, Jim Ernst, Jim Moore and Michael O'Shaughnessy, became entangled in conflict-of-interest situations. Ernst was forced to apologize to the council for not abstaining on a committee vote dealing with a company in which he had a financial interest. O'Shaughnessy had to apologize for painting an inaccurate picture of the amount of business a city-owned corporation was doing with Moore. O'Shaughnessy had said there was no contract between the Winnipeg Enterprises Corporation and Moore when in fact there was a formal agreement between Moore, a former advertising executive, and the Enterprise's board under which Moore would receive a 15 per cent commission on an $800 Eaton's ad. After the senior councillors wiped the egg off their faces, they once more ducked the issue by asking the province to pass conflict-of-interest laws governing civic politics.

The Developers' City

The creation of Unicity was followed by an explosion in the price of suburban real estate. According to one study, a fifty-five-foot suburban lot was selling for $4,675 in 1972; four years later the price had risen to $14,300. Discounting the increase in the cost of servicing the lot, developers would receive a speculative profit of close to $8,000. During these years four major land development companies, Genstar, Metropolitan, Qualico and Ladco, put together a 13,000-acre land bank. This gave them effective control over the city's development pattern for the next fifteen years. The rapidly rising prices and the concentration of land ownership in the hands of few national and even multinational corporations did not raise many eyebrows at city hall.

As in the case of the Trizec development and the conflict-of-interest legislation, Zuken felt the council confused the needs of the developers with the needs of the public. In the pre-Unicity days, he said, the developers would play one municipality off against another, always going to the highest bidder. In the Unicity period the developers found themselves playing on a larger field at a time when demand for new housing was expanding. The ICEC for its part had no overall housing policy for the city. This lack of policy direction led to charges that the city's planning department was alternately incompetent, demoralized or acquiescent in regard to the demands of large-scale developers.

It was not until the fall of 1976 that concerns over who was benefiting from rapidly rising housing prices spilled over into public debate. Through a series of highly publicized allegations, Zuken and NDP councillor Brian Corrin helped clear the way for a provincial inquiry into land costs. They claimed that during the early 1970s speculators had slipped around the city administration to make huge profits on the sale of land designated for a civic land assembly. In the case Zuken was referring to, two development companies, with the same boards of directors, had bought and sold land in South St. Vital for a quick half-million-dollar profit. The sale, to the Qualico Development company, came just five months before the city's executive policy committee dealt with a recommendation that the city engage in its own land-banking scheme. In October of that year Zuken and Corrin brought forward further cases of what they believed to be profiteering from land speculation. A piece of land in Transcona, for example, valued at $28,815 in 1970, was sold three times in 1973, once for $115,000, once for $223,000 and finally to Qualico for $346,745. Another parcel of land was bought for $74,000 in 1974 and sold to the city the following year for $240,000.

On the urging of a somewhat chagrined city council the provincial government appointed University of Manitoba economist Ruben Bellan to head up a provincial commission of inquiry into land prices in Manitoba.

In his brief to the inquiry, Zuken said the city must become more involved in the housing market. As well as calling for an increase in public housing, Zuken recommended the imposition of a tax on the increase in the value of land when it is rezoned by the city and a new tax on underused land. Such taxes would serve to discourage speculation in land values. "If the land value increases because the government gives approval for its use to change from agriculture to commercial or residential why should the government not receive some of the profit?" The tax on underused land would be aimed at those who are "storing land for speculative reasons, not at farmers who wish to continue farming."

He cautioned the inquiry not to judge public land-banking on the basis of the "bungling on again off again effort at city hall." He said that the substantial speculative profits that had been achieved during the land-banking procedure could have been avoided if the city had known more about the land companies under discussion. To combat this, he called for changes to the Companies Act so that interested parties could get detailed statements of who the directors and beneficiaries of real estate companies were.

While the land prices inquiry and the conflict-of-interest investigation were going on, a *Winnipeg Tribune* reporter asked a very sensitive question: "Should councillors wine and dine on the housing industry?" Tom Shillington was commenting on a host of end-of-the-year parties the property industry laid on for councillors and civic officials. These included a lavish dinner hosted by Castlewood Homes, a supper sponsored by Kensington Homes and a number of big spreads put on by local architectural firms. Zuken was only too happy to play the role of Grinch, telling Shillington that he thought the developers were engaging in social bribery. "I think councillors should watch it.... They aren't just a usual Christmas get-together.... We should be dealing with these people at arms length."

The fact that the relationships were anything but at arm's length was underscored by the revelation that during the 1974 civic election the president of Metropolitan Properties, Vic Krepart, had offered to defray the expenses of candidates who "we as a corporation felt merited our support." When the press learned of this offer, Krepart told the *Tribune*, "I don't feel apologetic nor do I feel I have done anything improper. *It is unfortunate that I put anything in writing*" (emphasis added). While Krepart was publicly regretting putting his mouth where his money was, another of the city's major developers, Ladco, was sending out invitations to a reception it was holding for the newly elected city council.

In his report Bellan concluded the explosion in housing prices, which had led them to double over a four-year period, was the result of the operation of the laws of supply and demand. Baby boomers were growing up, and as they left home they were driving up the cost of housing. But he did note that the four major corporations were developing 80 per cent of the city's new homes, and he recognized that these companies were restricting the number of homes coming onto the market. However, in his opinion there was no "dirty business" — collusion or the use of inside information to drive up property values — and so he saw nothing particularly wrong with the oligopolistic practices of the land developers. On the one point where Bellan and Zuken saw eye to eye — the need for a tax that would allow civic government to reclaim the value that it added to property when it made land eligible for development — the newly elected Conservative government of Sterling Lyon had no interest in acting.

A Committee Man at Last

Zuken made sure that the scrap over committee appointments continued into the Unicity era. In the fall of 1974 he was in high dudgeon, calling a list circulated by the ICEC caucus "a railroad list, achieved as a result of wheeling and dealing, which shed some blood. The list was submitted not only to the ICEC caucus but to Norman Turner [a local businessman and the chairman of the ICEC] and to Sidney Spivak [the leader of the provincial Conservative Party]. To compel councillors to vote for this list is to make them a party to a travesty of justice." Zuken had even more grounds for complaint, since the ICEC refrained from appointing him to any of the city's standing committees.

Lawrie Cherniack, who was himself excluded from most city committees, felt the ICEC's treatment of Zuken was a real loss to the city: "He had no opportunity to show his tremendous ability on simple day-to-day issues. It was a real, rotten shame. Because in committee work there is a lot of stuff you can do. So what could he do? He would come to the meetings. He would have read the agendas, these incredible lengthy agendas, and he would speak to them, he would make eloquent speeches. And that was all he could do. He had the ability to take an issue and make people understand why it hit home to them."

This situation was only remedied in 1977 when the NDP amended the City of Winnipeg Act to stipulate that every councillor serve on a regular committee of council. *Winnipeg Tribune* civic affairs reporter Bill Burdeyny wrote at the time, "I never thought I would live to see the day when Coun. Joe Zuken would be sitting on a regular city hall committee."

Zuken was resentful of the six-year period he spent in isolation: "I always felt the ICEC were damned stupid. They thought they could muzzle me by keeping me off a committee. I understand during the ICEC caucus talks, there were suggestions made in my favour for a committee position but the majority wouldn't go for it. The only committee they allowed me to serve on was the library board. Why?? Because most of them don't read and don't know what it is all about."

The Next Mayor of Winnipeg

On the afternoon of May 25, 1979, Joe Zuken held a news conference in the press room located in the basement of the city hall building. He confirmed the truth of the rumour that had been circulating around city hall for several days: he would be running in the mayoral by-election scheduled for June 20. Winnipeg, which had gone for over twenty years without a truly contested mayoral election, was going to be blessed with two such elections in a two-year period. This sequence of events was set in motion in 1977 when Steve Juba left the mayor's office. His departure was as surprising as his arrival. Ever since his first victory, Juba had hinted that each term would be his last. He continued to make such hints in 1977, but at the same time he went ahead and filed his nomination papers. With Juba in the race, potential opponents like Bernie Wolfe decided not to go ahead with their plans to run for mayor. After the deadline for nominations had passed, Juba withdrew his candidacy.

The race was then between Bob Steen, who by this time had left the ICEC after battling with them over a number of issues, including the Trizec development, and Bill Norrie, a lawyer and prominent ICEC member. Norrie had been one of the strongest supporters of Trizec and suburban development on the council. No clear ideological differences could be discerned between the two men, and when the lack-lustre campaign lurched across the finish line, Steen had won with a slim majority. Steen's tenure as mayor was brief and rocky. Throughout it, he found himself battling with his former ICEC caucus colleagues; at the council's inaugural meeting they elected Bill Norrie, who had retained his council seat, to the position of deputy mayor. Steen's administration was brought to a tragic end in the spring of 1979 when he succumbed to cancer. When Norrie, then acting mayor, set the by-election date, he announced his intention to run for mayor again.

From the beginning, Zuken made it clear he was going to be attempting to link the ICEC to the Lyon government. At his opening press conference he attacked the "clubby cozy atmosphere" between civic and provincial Conservative politicians. Pointing to the fact that at least seventeen councillors were Conservatives, he suggested the ICEC had turned city hall into a branch office of the provincial government. A secondary campaign theme would be to link Bill Norrie to the ICEC, which was not that difficult, since Norrie, who was running as an independent, had been an ICEC member since its inception. "This is not a personal vendetta against Bill Norrie, but Norrie will have to defend his stand on Trizec, on housing, and he will have to defend the actions of the ICEC as its titular and actual head."

He also returned to issues he had been raising throughout his career, criticizing the city's executive policy committee for holding a secret meeting that week at the John Blumberg Golf Course. The ICEC councillors, he suggested, "haven't the courage to say in public what they say in private." Zuken admitted he might have trouble gaining council support for his positions, but if necessary, he said, he would "talk to the people" through public meetings so that by the following year's general election the electorate would know what the majority group had and had not done.

Norrie said he welcomed Zuken's candidacy, but he claimed the ICEC issue was a phony one. In a foretaste of what the rest of the campaign would be like, Norrie said, "It would be just as valid for me to claim that we shouldn't have a Communist mayor." When Zuken was questioned about the issue of his communism at his first press conference, he replied, "I've been so-labeled for the last 40 years and it hasn't hurt me. Let the people judge me on my record as school trustee and councillor."

Winnipeg Free Press columnist Fred Cleverley was quick to pick up on the issue. In a May 31, 1979, column he wrote:

If Zuken wins the mayor's office next month, both his platform and his record will disappear from view outside Winnipeg and people who do not know where Winnipeg is will learn that the city has a Communist mayor, possibly even before they learn his name. This is precisely what is worrying J. Frank Johnston, the provincial cabinet minister responsible for economic development.

Johnston has spent the last two years explaining to the investment communities of the world that Manitoba no longer has a socialist government. If Zuken wins, how will Johnston explain away the fact that Manitoba's largest community, containing half the provincial population, has just elected a communist mayor?

It is small wonder that Johnston's phone has been busy attempting to organize an effective opposition to Zuken in the municipal election.

Cleverley added a new twist to the standard anti-Communist tactics by admitting that Zuken's public record was beyond reproach, noting that "these are the actions of a conscientious councillor, not part of the Communist Party line. In fact, it has become almost unthinkable to throw the word communist up to Joe Zuken." In effect, Cleverley was basing his arguments not on fear of communism, but on fear of fear of communism — Winnipeggers should reject Zuken not because he was the Communist bogeyman, but because the people who ran the international investment banks might not invest in a city with a Communist mayor.

While Zuken may have been looking forward to a two-way battle between himself and Norrie, the waters were soon to get muddied as ten more candidates, including three New Democrats, jumped into the race. The most prominent of these was J. Frank Syms. A good friend of Ed Schreyer, Syms had served as head of the provincial liquor control commission during the NDP's term in office. In the 1979 federal election earlier that year, Syms had come within a whisker of being elected to Parliament in the riding of Winnipeg-St. James. That campaign had generated considerable controversy within NDP ranks, since, in a bid to take votes away from the Conservatives, Syms had come out with a last-minute pamphlet proclaiming his support for capital punishment and opposition to bilingualism.

Alf Skowron, an NDP city councillor on the party's right wing, also entered the fray. He and Syms were more than willing to do the lion's share of red-baiting during the campaign. This allowed Norrie to keep to the high road, although he found it difficult to pass up opportunities to suggest Winnipeg was not ready for a Communist mayor.

Skowron had been hoping to win official endorsement from the NDP, but the NDP's provincial council chose to make no endorsation. Party officials pointed out that the usual process was for candidates to seek the party endorsation first, then to declare their official candidacy. Skowron claimed that the party failed to endorse him because it did not want to discipline the three hundred party members he claimed were involved in the Zuken campaign. Skowron never provided any documentation for this figure, but as the election progressed, no journalists called him to account and the number became accepted as factual.

The campaign came to resemble a three-ring circus rather than the head-to-head class struggle Zuken had envisioned. Aside from the disgruntled New Democrats, the field included several other councillors and a handful of fringe candidates, ranging from a music teacher who said he simply wanted to get involved in civic affairs to an unemployed accountant who claimed the sun had told him to enter the race during the February 1979 solar eclipse.

Zuken had been impressed with the federal NDP's 1979 election campaign, where Ed Broadbent had made use of dramatic backdrops for his news conferences while issuing a series of policy statements. It was decided that Zuken would conduct a similar sort of campaign — though in a smaller way — focusing on a number of key issues: housing, transit, Trizec, deterioration in civic services and the need for replacing the ICEC with a form of open and accountable government.

Zuken's success in getting media attention was reflected in the criticism some of the candidates aimed at the media. Frank Syms in particular thought the *Tribune* was giving Zuken too much attention. In a post-election column the paper's ombudsman, Dave Cross, responded to the criticism: "Even I was getting tired of seeing stories about Joe Zuken. I felt, as a reader, that he was being over-exposed. But then, as a long time newspaperman, I realized that Mr. Zuken is a streetwise politician who knows what he has to do and say to get his name in the paper. He generated much of the publicity through his own actions and words."

Despite Zuken's relatively successful efforts to use the media to raise issues, there was no dodging the question of his

political affiliation. At the campaign's outset Bill Neville, a
University of Manitoba political scientist and a former aide to
provincial Conservative leader Sidney Spivak, spoke on CBC
radio about Zuken's qualities as a politician: "Joe Zuken has
largely gone beyond all the party baggage and party labels.
His hallmarks as a municipal politician are integrity, courage,
a devotion to the people he serves and to no one else. And
above all his intelligence in defining and articulating the issues
facing the city."

Without endorsing him, Neville said he hoped the question
of Zuken's communism would not be allowed to obscure the
important questions his campaign might raise. These hopes
were to be frustrated. A June 15 *Tribune* story reported that
Zuken "is quickly becoming the issue in the mayoral by-election." According to the story, whenever Zuken appeared on
open-line shows or at all-candidates meetings, he was regularly peppered with questions about his political beliefs. These
were standard questions, and he had standard responses,
usually pointing out that he was perhaps the most inde-
pendent-minded member of caucus. At other times he would
say, much to the displeasure of local Communists, that while
he was a party member, "I do not carry my Communist Party
card into civic affairs." When questioned about the impact he
would have on local business, Zuken would often joke, "I
think I'd make a rather good tourist attraction."

The red-baiting reached a crescendo on the Friday before
the election when Peter Warren, the host of the city's top-rated
radio phone-in show, devoted his entire program to the election. Warren started the show with this brief commentary:

It is time for the citizens of Winnipeg to stop for a moment
and consider the consequences of what this city might
face if the people vote a Communist to the position of
mayor. This is not intended to hit out at Joe Zuken the
man or Joe Zuken the councillor. It is a suggestion that all
of us take a long hard look at the general principle of the
election, in a democracy, of a Communist as the
figurehead, as the representative leader of six hundred
thousand people, of a Communist as the mayor of

Canada's fourth-largest city. If it happens it will be front-page news around the world.

The first guest on the program was Alf Skowron, who readily repeated his charges that the NDP had been infiltrated by socialists who were working for the Zuken campaign (the way Skowron explained it, it sounded more like the CP had been infiltrated by the NDP). After a brief interview with NDP leader Howard Pawley, who pointed out that Skowron had not backed up with any significant documentation his allegation that three hundred NDPers supported Zuken, Warren got Zuken on the line. The exchange between the two men is interesting both because it demonstrates the simplistic approach Warren brought to the issue and because of the distance Zuken was prepared to put between himself and the Communist Party.

> ZUKEN: My reaction is that the people have judged me for 38 years. I do not, I do not carry into city hall any direction of any kind from the Communist Party. I am on my own, I take my position on issues and the guarantee that the people have in voting for me for mayor is one that they have seen for 38 years, they have judged my honesty, my integrity and my public service.... Now I am prepared to be judged by the way I function. I function without any direction or influence from the Communist Party.
> WARREN: Do you carry a Communist Party card?
> ZUKEN: I have a card, but I do not carry that card into city hall.... For fifteen years no one has raised any question about this issue. You yourself have referred people to me with city hall problems. I never ask people who come for help how did you vote. I deal with people on a problem basis.
> There are a whole number of people who have come to work on my campaign. Not because of the Communist Party. Despite it.
> WARREN: Would you rip up your Communist Party card if you became mayor?
> ZUKEN: If there is any interference, and I don't expect there will be. If there is any attempt at interference of the

way I arrive at a position on a civic issue I will make it
clear I do not subscribe to that interference.

Growing hysterical, Warren demanded to know if Zuken
was a Communist. Zuken readily acknowledged that he was,
claiming that "that does not mean I carry a Communist program into city hall."

As was his habit, in the pursuit of the sensational, Warren
had failed to ask the really interesting questions. If Joe Zuken
took no direction from the Communist Party when it came to
municipal politics, and if he had so many serious reservations
about the party's international policies, why did he not do
formally what he had very clearly done in an informal manner
— why didn't he sever his connection with the party?

A quick examination of the Zuken campaign organization
would have revealed some interesting facts, the main one
being that if any party had a right to be angered by Joe Zuken's
bid for the mayoralty it was the Communist Party of Canada.
At Zuken's first strategy meeting in late May there were
a number of New Democrats present, the most well known
being Andy Robertson. There were also a number of aca-
demics who were attracted to Zuken because of his position
on a series of civic issues, most specifically urban development
and the Trizec project. Aside from the candidate, however,
there were no Communists at that meeting. It quickly became
apparent to the organizers that Zuken had made no effort
to clear his candidacy with the CPC or to ask for its direct
support.

Although some party members were angered at being left
out, the party did decide to place its resources at the disposal
of the campaign. This did not sit well with some of the members of the campaign planning committee, who did not want
the Communist Party publicly identified with the campaign.
Similarly, the campaign underwent a period of internal conflict before any members of the Communist Party were allowed to sit on the campaign committee. In the end, the party
was represented by the candidate's brother, Bill Ross. In short,
from the CPC's view, a group of NDPers and political independents had, under cover of night, infiltrated the party and
stolen its most successful candidate.

The question of the three hundred New Democrats involved in the campaign remains a gross exaggeration. There never were more than three hundred people in total involved in the Zuken campaign, and to belabour a cliché, they were drawn from all walks of life and largely attracted to Zuken not because he was, or was not, a Communist, but because of the reputation for personal integrity he had established in the city. It is impossible to put a number on the New Democrats involved in the Zuken campaign, but those who were involved at a central level did not exercise significant influence in either the CP or NDP and were certainly not using the mayoral election as a means to infiltrate either organization.

Two days before the election Syms launched his final assault on Zuken and his supporters. Voters, he said, should "not regard as novel or meaningless the organized efforts" to elect Zuken. Speaking of those New Democrats who supported Zuken, Syms wondered "why a group of Marxist/Status of Women/Social Activist militants with the NDP have volunteered to support an independent mayoralty candidate who is a member of the Communist Party." Ominously, Syms said that "what may be less well known is that this group has a majority grip on the provincial executive of the party in Manitoba." On the same day Skowron repeated his claims that three hundred party members were working for the Zuken campaign, insisting that they should be subjected to party discipline.

While Syms and Skowron were slinging mud, Norrie managed to sail through the campaign, never having to deal with his own record on the issues. His literature urged voters to opt for "continued strong leadership" and kept to the traditional "non-partisan" and boosteristic issues long favoured by the ICEC, such as the need to keep taxes low and the Winnipeg Jets in the city.

On the evening of June 20, Winnipeg was hit by a torrential downpour, a heavy rain that led to sewer backups throughout the city. Only one in three eligible Winnipeggers bothered to cast a vote. And the vast majority chose to vote for Bill Norrie. He received 101,299 votes, while Zuken finished in second place with 24,650. Zuken could take some solace from the fact that the third-place finisher, Frank Syms, only received 1,998 votes and Alf Skowron took only 1,421 votes. As Norrie told his supporters, the voters had rejected "the socialist philosophy of Joe Zuken."

The Zuken campaign celebrated the defeat with an election-night party in the National Council of Jewish Women's Golden Age Club, fittingly located at 410 Pritchard, the site of the home of the Jewish left, the Liberty Temple. Neither the rain nor the electoral thumping could dampen the spirits in the hall. In his speech Zuken was unrepentant: "There is no gloom here, there is no despair. We are celebrating a very credible and important campaign. We have no regrets, no despondency. Something was started which was not going to go away." In the future it might be possible, he said, to make "city hall the citadel of the real needs of the people" instead of a "branch plant of a reactionary government." He told reporters:

> Bill Norrie had no answers to the questions we raised in this campaign, so he dredged up the ghost of Joe McCarthy. I am not going to be intimidated by talk-show people like Peter Warren, they did a real hatchet job.
>
> We threw a scare into the Norrie machine. But he rode in on the false issue of my political affiliation which covered up his failure to deal with the real issues. Joe McCarthy was born again here in Winnipeg tonight.
>
> Against us, and this is not an excuse because we have no regrets or reason for despondency, but against us was an alignment of the ICEC councillors and the corporate elite of this city. When my campaign emerged we also had to deal with the intervention of at least one cabinet minister. The ICEC has transformed city hall into a branch office of the Lyon government and that's going to change. There is a broadly-based citizens' committee which has come together, including individual NDPers, Conservatives, Liberals and those with no political affiliation.

For Zuken the final salvoes in the election campaign were fired in mid-June when Peter Warren, angered by Zuken's election-night criticism of this open-line show, used his column in the *Winnipeg Tribune* to attack Zuken. Under the headline "Open Letter to J. Zuken on Red Rules," Warren claimed his actions differed from McCarthyism because he only pointed the finger at one person, and at a bona fide Communist at that. Then in as strange a bit of red-baiting to grace a major daily newspaper as one could find in the 1970s, Warren went on:

May I also remind you, Joe, of the following:

In May, 1919, at Dusseldorf, Germany, the Allied Forces obtained a copy of some of the "Communist Rules for Revolution."
Now sixty years later, the Reds are still following them. After reading the list, stop after each item and think about the present day situation where you live — and all around our nation.

Rules for Revolution

The Red Rules:
A. Corrupt the young, get them away from religion. Get them interested in sex. Make them superficial; destroy their ruggedness.
B. Get control of all means of publicity, thereby:
1. Get people's minds off their government by focusing their attention on athletics, sexy books and plays and other trivialities.
2. Divide the people into hostile groups by constantly harping on controversial matters of no importance.
3. Destroy the people's faith in their natural leaders by holding the latter up to contempt, ridicule and disgrace.
4. Always preach true democracy, but seize power as fast and ruthlessly as possible.
5. By encouraging government extravagance, destroy its credit, produce fear of inflation with rising prices and general discontent.
6. Incite unnecessary strikes in vital industries, encourage civil disorders and foster a lenient and soft attitude on the part of government toward such disorders.
7. By specious argument cause the breakdown of the old moral virtues, honesty, sobriety, self restraint, faith in the pledged word, ruggedness.
8. Cause the registration of all firearms on some pretext,

with a view to confiscating them and leaving the population helpless.

Zuken responded a few days later, noting that he had never heard of the so-called Red Rules and suggesting they were an anti-Communist equivalent of the anti-Semitic forgery *The Protocols of the Elders of Zion*. He pointed out that as recently as April 25, 1979, Warren had written that Zuken was "an excellent politician. Winnipeg would have been poorer if it had not been for him." He then went back to the broadcast Warren had made just before the election. "Here was an opportunity for an experienced and influential Action Line host to contribute to the understanding of these vital civic issues. Instead you concentrated on the 'Red Menace' and used Councillor Skowron to play your McCarthyite game."

In July the NDP's provincial executive held its first meeting in the wake of the federal and mayoral elections. No disciplinary action was taken against those party members who supported Joe Zuken. A complaint against Frank Syms for his conduct in the federal election was also heard. It was also decided that no disciplinary action would be taken in his case, although the executive did term Syms's support for capital punishment and opposition to bilingualism "inappropriate."

There was, however, one politician who, in the fall-out of the 1979 election, was censured by his political party. According to Bill Ross, Communist Party members were angered by Zuken's performance on the Peter Warren radio show, particularly by the distance Zuken had placed between himself and the party. "The program on which Joe was elected, the program on which he campaigned, the issues that he raised, both at the school board and the city council, were determined by the Labour Election Committee. For him to say that he decided what to raise and what not to raise — to be charitable, it did not conform to facts. Joe was very able in the presentation of what he advocated, but he alone did not determine what he raised.

"In that latter period I must say, and I am being as objective as I can, there was a tendency on the part of Joe to dissociate himself from the Labour Election Committee, the body which endorsed him, financed him, and shaped the nature and character of his campaigns. In most of his speeches and interviews he rarely mentioned the Labour Election Committee. There was always a tendency to make it a Joe Zuken campaign, a Joe Zuken issue."

The party's central committee called Zuken up on the carpet and passed a resolution criticizing him for the comments he had made on the Warren show about his relationship to the LEC.

The Odd Couple

During his last four years on council Zuken developed a close friendship with Bill Neville. It was not the sort of relationship a casual observer of council might expect, since Neville represented the Tuxedo Heights Ward, one of the wealthiest in the city. A political science professor, he had served in the past as an assistant to former provincial Conservative Party leader Sidney Spivak. "In the Fifties and early Sixties when I grew up in Winnipeg, Joe Zuken's name was synonymous with all that one had to fear.... There was a perception that in addition to being a Communist and radical and fire-breathing and fire-eating, he was also reputed to be very intelligent and very effective, a good debater and quick on his feet. Probably more fearful for being so intelligent."

Zuken and Neville met in the Seventies when they both served on the library board. Neville was extremely impressed by Zuken. "I was rather deferential to him, not least because he was thirty years older than I, and I was a product of a generation where you treated grey hairs with a certain respect. But I was impressed in our initial contacts with the fact that he was clearly intelligent, well-read, and he struck me ... as someone who observed and operated within the conventions of the system.... He did not come across as someone who was there simply to raise hell.... The other citizen members of the board, some of whom had been around for a fairly long period of time, representing a range of political views, regarded him as a substantial person, who had something to contribute to a library board."

Then in the fall of 1979 Neville decided to run for city council in a by-election held in Mayor Norrie's recently vacated ward. In doing so, he received both the endorsation of the ICEC and a brief note from Zuken extending him best wishes. These two endorsements, one public, one quite private, signal the rather contradictory nature of Bill Neville's own political career on council. At the time, Neville said he expected his relations with Zuken to be "positive and comfortable." "That we were at rather different points on the political spectrum did not present any insuperable barrier to recognizing his qualities or appreciating the contribution he made to local government in the city. I assumed that was reciprocal." And it was. Although they rarely discussed the apparent irony involved in a deepening friendship between a Conservative and a Communist, when Zuken retired from council he made the point of crediting Neville with "civilizing the ICEC."

Although Zuken and Neville were in their own ways effective politicians with considerable oratorical skills, they were also intellectuals stuck in the clubhouse atmosphere of civic politics. And they responded well to each other's bookish nature. Neville recalled: "We would occasionally exchange notes during council meetings, and not infrequently they would contain literary allusions. One or the other of us, during the course of a speech, would use some quotation, and by the time whichever was speaking had sat down, the other would have some different quotation which was either appropriate or argued the opposite. This would be communicated in a note which was passed down the table. So there was fun in our relationship, and wit. It carried us over and carried us through some of the differences."

The closeness of the friendship can be measured by the fact that Neville was a pallbearer at Zuken's funeral, and delivered, along with Bill Ross, a brief speech at the unveiling of the headstone. Neville's comments on the role Zuken played in city council reveal how in his final years on council Zuken, while remaining an anti-establishment figure, emerged as an elder statesman. "He was partly gadfly, partly conscience, and on many issues, a kind of unofficial leader of the opposition.... I think there were many issues, whether development issues, or social policy questions or the question of spending priorities where he saw his role as that of providing an alternative point of view."

Over time Zuken even came to exert some impact on the direction council would take. As he grew in public esteem, politicians found that by supporting his positions they would not necessarily receive the kiss of death. Even when councillors were not willing to follow Zuken's lead, they realized his was a voice which could not be ignored. Neville noticed this shortly after he joined the ICEC caucus: "Very often things would be packaged by the ICEC with at least one eye cocked on the position that Joe Zuken might take to get mileage out of a given issue. I use the word 'packaged' deliberately because I am not sure that on substance the majority necessarily paid that much attention to his views."

In the summer of 1983 Zuken announced that due to failing health he would not be standing for re-election in that year's civic election. He broke the news to a tearful meeting of the Labour Election Committee. He said that while he had no serious health problem, he suffered from hypertension and had received professional advice to retire. Zuken soon found himself saluted from every side — he had become respectable. It was the culmination of a process that had begun in the mid-Sixties.

In the country's centennial year he was given a City of Winnipeg Community Service Award for "outstanding leadership in the administration of the city's affairs and in the field of community service." Four years later the Manitoba Historical Society presented him with a medal in recognition of a "lifetime of concern towards the improvement of the welfare of the underprivileged, particularly in the north end of Winnipeg." And in 1974, on the occasion of Winnipeg's one hundredth anniversary, Zuken received an honorary doctorate of law from the University of Winnipeg. And at its fall 1983 convocation the University of Manitoba presented two distinguished service medals, one to Jack Gallagher, the chairman of the financially beleaguered Dome Petroleum Corporation, and the other to Joe Zuken.

He claimed to wear his honours lightly, but he was pleased that his efforts were being recognized. "At first I was stereotyped.... It was said, and it was true, that Joe was a member of the Communist Party. They expected that you were a stereotyped guy, treading a stereotyped path.

"As the work unfolded, people began to see that maybe this guy isn't that bad. Maybe he isn't the devil that we thought he was. Now that doesn't mean that your political opponents throw in the towel. As I became more effective the contrary was the case. But still the acceptance grew.... After I announced I would no longer be contesting the ward, people began to add up the forty-two years and drew their own conclusions. And then it bust loose."

After Zuken announced his retirement, a decision was made to name a park in his honour. History slyly chose to repeat itself. The president of the Point Douglas Historical Association opposed the move, saying, "The name is not appropriate. It is not in keeping with the era of the heritage park." She pointed out that Ross House, the oldest building in Manitoba, dating back to 1854, was to be moved to the park grounds. Apparently unaware of who Joe Zuken's brother was, she suggested the new park be called William Ross Park (not in honour of Bill Ross, but of the son of an early Red River Valley settler). The park naming did, however, go ahead.

At Joe Zuken's last council meeting on October 19, 1983, there were more than 150 people in attendance. He received a standing ovation and a plaque from council bearing this inscription:

The selfless dedication in which Joe Zuken has served his constituents and all the citizens of Winnipeg has set a standard to which elected officials everywhere should aspire.

Joe Zuken had provided Winnipeg City Council with some of its most dramatic and confrontational moments. And while in his final years he was being treated as some sort of civic treasure, he wanted to make it clear it was council, not he, who had come around in its views. Speaking as a councillor for the last time, he said, "Tonight, when I leave this place — and I've grown very accustomed to this place — for the last time, I will walk out as a confirmed Canadian socialist."

It was no time for conciliatory words. He was, in fact, in the midst of his last battle with council, and it was one that would only increase the public's affection for him.

The Last Hurrah

On a bitterly cold evening in January 1984, over five hundred people jammed into Winnipeg's Playhouse Theatre. Situated across the street from city hall, the venerable theatre had, under the name of The Pantages, been the home of vaudeville in turn-of-the-century Winnipeg. On this night it would be the scene of Joe Zuken's last major public speech. When Zuken came to the podium, the crowd, which contained a large number of senior citizens, gave him a standing ovation. He congratulated the people for showing up on such a frosty evening. "It's a myth that the people don't care, that the people are apathetic. The issue that brought them out is the injustice of the too-rich, too-fat pension scheme." It was an archetypal Zuken speech, full of fight and scorn for many of his former colleagues. At issue was a controversial pension plan the council was on the verge of awarding itself. In full flight, Zuken asked, "Who would have thought this council would have the *chutzpah*, the brazen gall, to enact such a plan? This council has no worry about funding this plan. They merely have to raise property taxes."

The fight against the councillors' pension scheme (and the word "scheme" was to resonate through this debate) was Joe Zuken's last hurrah. And it allowed him to end his political career on a richly satisfying note. It incorporated many of the key issues his political career had revolved around — respect for the public purse, social equity and open government. This battle — against a rich, publicly funded pension scheme conceived behind closed doors and approved by an overanxious council — was ready-made for Joe Zuken, the newly retired councillor.

But Zuken was not opportunistically seizing on a popular issue. As far back as February 1964 Zuken had made clear his opposition to even the idea of a pension plan for city councillors. At that time Zuken was speaking against a resolution calling on the provincial government to establish a pension fund for councillors. Zuken had said, "There is no justification for such a self-serving and self-rewarding action by the aldermen. No one compels an alderman to stand for public office. Why should the tax-payer help to pay for an aldermanic pension." The proposal died at that point, but Zuken gave an almost identical speech in 1969 when a similar resolution was sent to the provincial legislature. He went on to tie the pension claim to the question of councillors' salaries: "The implementation of a pension plan for aldermen is one part of a pincer movement against the tax-payers and will likely be followed by the other part of the pincer movement in the form of a scheme to increase the salaries of aldermen. Both such measures should be resolutely opposed by the people of Winnipeg."

One need not be too familiar with the history of left-wing political movements to know that one long-sought political reform was the proper payment of elected officials, at all levels. Early Winnipeg civic politics had been dominated by wealthy, self-styled "gentlemen" who were able to devote themselves to political questions on a full-time basis because of their financial security. In 1910 there were nineteen millionaires living in Winnipeg; two of them had been mayor, one had served as city controller, and seven others had sat on city council. Thus, in taking a hard line against major improvements in both council salaries and pensions, Zuken was running counter to established socialist orthodoxy. And in doing so he often incurred the wrath of NDP councillors, some of whom attempted to serve as full-time councillors.

The first pension plan was only adopted in 1969 after a stormy debate during which extra police officers were put on duty to control the 150 demonstrators who filled the public galleries at city hall. To qualify for the pension, which had a maximum value of $1,800 a year, a councillor had to be over fifty-five years of age and have served at least eight years on council, including three consecutive two-year terms. Zuken was particularly critical of the decision to hold off dealing with the pension question until after the civic election.

At the heart of the controversies that were to rage in ensuing years about councillors' pensions were questions of process: primarily, who should be allowed to establish the benefits and what role should the public have in reviewing these decisions? And while it may be fair to say that, for the sake of scoring political points, Zuken was overzealous in his protection of the public purse, it should be noted that for the most part council badly handled these important questions of process.

Just as he opted out of the pension plan, Zuken began to decline the pay increases council regularly voted for itself. In 1975 the *Tribune* reported that the city was richer by $1,267 because Zuken refused to accept a recently approved 15 per cent pay increase. Zuken was also not making use of the $912 cost-of-living allowance councillors were eligible for. Although he served on council for another eight years, he refused to accept another increase in the $5,700 base pay he had been receiving in 1975.

In the summer of 1979 council decided to attempt to extricate itself from the political problems Zuken was creating for it by commissioning an independent review of council benefits. This review was carried out by appeal court justice Gordon Hall, who concluded that, when compared with elected officials across the country, Winnipeg city councillors were indeed significantly underpaid. To alleviate the situation he called for a 47.5 per cent increase in councillors' salaries. He also proposed that the pension scheme be remodelled on the basis of the one in effect for civic employees.

Hall's report came out in 1982 when the nation was in the grip of a recession. A council committee reviewed the recommendations and concluded that in a time of restraint such a large increase in pay was unreasonable. Instead, the committee suggest there be a 6 per cent pay increase and the creation of a pension scheme modelled on the one available to provincial politicians. By choosing to create their own pension scheme, council left itself open for the type of criticism Zuken would soon be levelling at it.

At a November 1982 meeting of council the pension plan was given approval in principle. The plan was then referred for technical drafting to an ad hoc committee of the council headed by Jim Ernst. The committee's recommendations came back to council in the summer of 1983. Under the plan, any councillor whose age and years of service totalled fifty-five or more would be eligible for the pension, whose maximum benefit would be $12,000 a year (the maximum benefit from the old plan was $1,800 a year). Zuken was quick to attack the plan as "a fringe benefit, a perk that councillors should not take advantage of." He later wrote this description of the meeting where the pension plan was adopted:

On Aug. 14, 1983 the council members' pension plan
bylaw was rushed through council with all three readings
approved in minutes without any debate or questions by
the councillors present. I became ill at this meeting and
had to leave the council chamber. Upon my return, after
an absence of only 10 minutes, I checked with the city
clerk and was informed by him that council had already
passed all three readings of the bylaw....

Did the councillors understand all the details of the
bylaw? And if they did, which I doubt, why the indecent
hurry to push through all readings in a few minutes?

There the issue might well have died, but during the course
of the 1983 civic election it became apparent that many councillors, as Zuken noted, did not fully understand the
generosity of the pension plan they had approved for themselves. This was due to the fact that the relatively technical by-law
council approved in the summer of 1983 provided significantly richer benefits than those envisioned in the resolution that
council had passed the year before. In particular, the pension
for the mayor and the chairs of council committees was calculated on their total salaries, not their base salaries as councillors. In the case of Mayor Bill Norrie this meant he was eligible
for a fully indexed pension of $25,000. As these details seeped
out in the weeks before the election, the press turned to Zuken,
who obligingly attacked the pension as a "sweetheart deal."
He noted that if he were to invest $6,200 in the pension scheme,
he would receive $12,000 a year. But as he prepared to retire,
he said, "I've turned it down before and I'm not going to sell
out on this question now."

Both the *Free Press* and the CBC television supper-hour
news program "24 Hours" took aim at the pension plan, pointing out that it was twice as rich as the plans other cities
provided for their politicians. The *Free Press* weighed in with
a series of editorials calling for a repeal of the pension scheme:
"It resembles privileged treatment for a privileged few who
have lost touch with the ordinary people to whom councillors
claim to be so close. It also resembles shameless greed. It
should be wound up immediately."

While some of the pension plan opponents were simply
reflecting a generalized dislike of politicians, there were a

series of quite specific complaints raised about the details of the plan. These are best understood by comparing it to the plan proposed by Judge Hall. Unless councillors had more than thirty years of service they would not, under the Hall proposal, receive a pension until they were sixty-five years of age. The adopted plan based eligibility on a combination of a councillor's age and years of service. A councillor who was elected at the age of thirty-seven and served for three consecutive terms would be eligible for a full pension at the age of forty-six.

But it was the size of the pension pay-out that caused the greatest consternation. The revised plan was 150 per cent more generous than Hall's, and 66.33 per cent more generous than the plan available to members of the provincial legislature, the model presumably being followed. Hall had recommended that only the base salaries be considered in determining the pension pay-out. Instead the councillors included the extra pay that committee members and chairs receive. This again was richer than the plan for members of the legislature. On top of these complaints was the fact that because it would be financed, not out of a separate pension fund, but out of the general revenues of the city, no effort had been made to determine how much the plan would cost.

As the political heat mounted, Jim Ernst admitted that the plan was richer than the one authorized by council the year before, but he said this was due to errors made by civic administrators in drafting the by-law. He said the officials had not fully understood how the provincial government's pension scheme had operated and therefore had inadvertently made the council plan more generous. As voting day neared, Norrie said he would be willing to ask Judge Hall to review the plan.

Once the election was over, Judge Hall indicated that he could see no reason why he should review the pension plan — he had already made his views perfectly clear. At first Norrie suggested there might thus be no review of the plan, but in the face of public criticism, a three-person committee, comprised of two retired city councillors, Harold Piercy and Art Coulter, and accountant Mark Fenny, was appointed to review the pension plan. In early December this committee submitted an interim report saying it felt parts of the plan were inappropriate for elected officials and recommending that the plan not go into effect in January 1984 as scheduled, but be delayed until the committee's final report was ready in the new year.

Without making the interim report public, the executive policy committee (EPC) allowed the plan to come into effect. The committee chairman Jim Ernst said the EPC had turned down the review committee's request for funding to hire an actuarial accountant to compute the total cost of the pension plan because the large number of variables in the plan would render such an estimate meaningless.

It was at this point that Zuken announced his intention to launch a public campaign against the pension plan. He participated in the creation of a new group, Citizens Alert, which he hoped would monitor the actions of city hall and bring to public attention those cases where the council was riding roughshod over the public interest. The meeting at the Playhouse was organized by Citizens Alert.

The pension review committee submitted its report in February and called for a number of major changes to the way the plan would be operated. In particular, the Piercy committee called on council to do away with indexing, to create a separate fund to cover the pension and to reduce the value of the pension by two-thirds. Late that month the EPC rejected all three recommendations.

On February 29, 1984, the councillors came close to getting what they wanted. Nearly four hundred very angry people, under the watchful eyes of a special police contingent, jammed into the council chambers for that night's council meeting. After the councillors rejected the Piercy plan, they voted to accept a modified pension plan proposed by Ernst. This plan involved a 45 per cent reduction in the value of the pension pay-out, but it retained many of the plan's other unpopular elements. To a chorus of boos, the council voted down a motion that implementation of the new plan be delayed until there could be an actuarial study into how much it would cost the city. Harvey Smith, one of the NDP councillors who opposed the plan, said, "If we dealt with everything ... in [this] manner, people would think we are crazy." It was left to Ernst to carry the can for the council majority. He accused the opponents of "whipping up a furore amongst the people" and creating the false impression that councillors wanted a "fat, juicy, pension plan."

Citizens Alert launched a petition campaign, calling for a repealing of the pension plan. By the fall of 1984 over 25,000 names had been gathered. While public resentment towards the pension scheme remained high, Citizens Alert was not able to sustain its opposition. Fresh, if brief, life was breathed into the organization when Winnipeg school trustees considered raising their pay by 45 per cent. One of the organization's last meetings was in April 1985, less than a year before Zuken's death. There he reported on his brief to a provincial committee reviewing the City of Winnipeg Act. Zuken explained that he had called for changes that would have given citizens more control over the politicians they elect. "Once councillors are in office they turn their noses up at the people who put them there. A system should be put in place to ensure elected officials will be truly accountable to the public."

A Working-Class Perspective

Joe Zuken never was the sort of politician to thumb his nose at the public. He was a committed public servant, held in high esteem by many Winnipeggers. But his lengthy and successful political career still raises a number of interrelated questions. How, for example, did his political career survive the Cold War?? Many other dedicated left-wing politicians saw their public lives come to a dead end in the 1950s; why not Joe Zuken? Given Zuken's independent turn of mind and unwillingness to take orders, why did he remain a member of a political party that was dogmatic, sectarian and intellectually stagnant? And arising out of these questions comes a third point: what did Joe Zuken see as the role of a Communist on city council?

Zuken entered political life on the coattails of the Communist Party. In 1941, when he replaced his brother on the Winnipeg School Board, he was only one of three Manitoba Communists elected to public office that year. In those years the party enjoyed a measure of public support, not merely because people like Jacob Penner and Joe Forkin were talented and dedicated politicians, but because they articulated a revolutionary ideology that spoke of the need for social transformation. In the postwar years, as the nature of Stalinism became more apparent, that ideology lost much of its attraction. However, by then people had become familiar with Zuken's personal qualities. He had these thoughts on why he had been so successful: "It wasn't only the left vote. The left vote, before suburbia, before many people moved away from Ward Three, was quite strong. But the left vote by itself, could not have led to successive re-election.... But I think that what helped were my ties with people and with groups of people in the North End. So that is the way they saw me and I became accepted by the people.

"We went through the Korean War and later on the Hungarian events, and so many other events both in the school board days and when I was on council.... And I sort of became a kind of habit, whether it was good or bad, I was accepted. Maybe there was a kind of curious pride and some people said, 'We've got our local Communist, you know.' Maybe they felt it reflected well on their democratic spirit. But I have always been too busy to really try and analyze what made them all go to the ballot box and mark my name."

His success was in no small way due to his ability to articulate a type of left-wing populism. He was one of the few politicians of the left who was publicly credible on what has traditionally been *the* issue of the right at city council — the control of the public purse. Throughout his career Zuken successfully painted his opponents as the ones who were financially irresponsible; he was the taxpayers' man at city hall — there to make sure their money was not squandered.

While he noted that Zuken hardly fitted the conventional description of a populist, Bill Neville recognized the populist streak in his political style. "He was predisposed not to believe that the public, particularly if one was talking about the little people, however defined, could be wrong.... There were some kinds of issues for which the litmus test for him would have been, 'What do the little people, what do the average people say about this?' "

In a similar vein Lawrie Cherniack commented that Zuken rarely used the standard language of the left: "He never took

an apparently leftist line. He would never speak about a cooperative society or different visions of the world. I don't remember
ever hearing him speak like that. He stood for tolerance and
progressive things. He stayed away from anything which would
have allowed him to be called a Communist.

"If you had a tape of all of his speeches, you would not find
anything which would identify him as a Communist, or even
as a leftist — a progressive, a humanitarian, but not a leftist."

Zuken's continued electoral success can best be credited to
a fairly even mix of the North End's willingness to support
left-wing candidates and Zuken's own reputation for service
and integrity, coupled with his canny sense as to how to express the concerns of his constituents.

But the question remains, why did he remain a party member? While he regularly distanced himself from the party,
criticizing the Soviet Union and declaring his personal independence, he remained a party member to his death. In the fall
of 1984 he spoke of the positive role he saw for the Communist
Party in the coming years. "I think its weakness still is that its
membership is not big enough to make the impact that a Communist Party should be making on the Canadian scene. Its
strength is that some of the ideas it has been advocating sometimes have come into even sharper focus: the relationship with
the United States, the question of Canadian independence,
peace. It is good that the NDP and other people have taken up
the question of peace, Star Wars, the fight against Star Wars.
But the party made a contribution on that when it was not
good enough to talk about peace. What I am saying is that the
basic program of the party is being proven to be correct and
of more relevance than ever before. What the party needs is
renewal of membership.... I think the ideas of the party are
very significant, I think that what the part has to do is or-
ganizationally begin to match the size of its ideas with more
public activity."

While many members of the public were disturbed by Zuken's
membership in the Communist Party, many Communists were
less than pleased by the behaviour of one of the party's most
prominent members. Trying to put a charitable face on the
question, Bill Ross noted that his brother had a tendency to do
things on his own and was not accustomed by temperament

or profession to being a member of a collective. At times there was pressure from some party members to have Zuken expelled. Certainly a disciplined organization like the CPC was not used to tolerating the degree of independence Zuken exhibited. But, according to Ross, leading party officials could not see what would be served by such a move. The party supported the positions Zuken took in the municipal field and so a *modus vivendi* was reached. Zuken could have his differences with the party but he was not supposed to air them publicly. Ross conceded that this could leave the impression that Zuken had left the party in all but the formal sense, since he rarely spoke on national and international issues and had declared himself an independent operator in the municipal field.

It is very dangerous to speculate as to why Joe Zuken continued to support the Communist Party. Loyalty had a great deal to do with it — loyalty to a brother who had sacrificed his academic career for Joe's sake and his life for the party's sake; loyalty to memories, to the men and women who had been interned, who had been harassed by the police for their efforts to build the union movement; loyalty to people who had elected and maintained him in public life. Though he rarely spoke of it, Zuken also believed in the need for radical change in Canadian society, one that could only be brought into effect through the efforts of a dedicated political organization. By remaining in the party he was remaining true to his vision of the future.

The Communist Party also offered Zuken a political vehicle. And it was as a politician that Zuken bloomed: "Looking back I realize that, as an individual, I would not have been completely fulfilled if I had not had that public aspect to my life. Particularly a person like myself, who is such an introverted and shy person.... Were I not given the opportunity to be sent as a representative to a public arena and to utilize it as a public arena of ideas and of conflict and of opposites — well, I would have remained a Communist who was practising law, but I would not have been able to come forward in a public way on issues on a city-wide basis."

While Joe Zuken was a very popular politician, there is no doubt that in his later years, when his differences with the CP were becoming more pronounced, he would have experienced great difficulty in putting together a political machine to ensure his election without the support of the party. A politician who by his own admission never knocked on more than twenty-five doors in his entire career does not lightly toss aside a political organization that has served him well for forty years. There should be little doubt that the *modus vivendi* worked out between Zuken and the CPC had benefits for Zuken as well as for the Communist Party.

But while Zuken can be criticized for not breaking with Stalinism in a more forthright fashion, his public career is in fact an endless rebuke of the principles of Stalinism, or any other authoritarian, non-democratic regime. On the matters that came before him, his commitment to democracy and social justice, and to the importance of pairing these two values, was clear and outspoken. His references to the "people" were not rhetorical; his respect for them and their views and needs was genuine. When I asked him to tote up his accomplishments on council he spoke first, not of legislation he had helped get through council or the good fights he had lost and won, but of the perspective he had brought to each issue before the council.

"Because I grew up in the North End, because I had an attachment to the labour movement, because I turned left, I brought what I think was a working-class perspective and philosophy to local government. It's a rather strange combination because I had done very little physical labour in my life.

"From that philosophy sprang a rather cohesive, coherent program, one that was being continually refurbished. From when I started I knew where my sympathies were and where I wanted to go.... If I didn't have the attachment to groups of people, citizens' movements, I would have been an individual in the wilderness."

A gadfly, a loner, a dissident, a fighter, an outsider — Joe Zuken was all these things — and at the same time he wove himself deep into the heart of his community.

Epilogue

Although Zuken retired from city council in 1983, he did not cease his involvement in public life. The campaign against the councillors' pension plan consumed much of his energies during the next two years. He continued to go to his law office on a daily basis, making regular courtroom appearances. He also found the time to indulge in his cultural interests as well, preparing a number of lectures on Yiddish literature.

But his health was failing. During his last years on council he had suffered from a nervous condition that led him to shake quite noticeably when he spoke in public — not that this in any way interfered with his public-speaking ability. In 1983 he had had to choose between resigning from council or his law firm, as he could no longer carry the double load. Although he gained tremendous personal satisfaction from his political work, he was also concerned that Clara be left financially secure. While he was not taking a great deal out of the law firm, it was more than his council salary, which he had voluntarily frozen a decade earlier.

In early 1986 his health took a turn for the worse. After a visit to his physician he was hospitalized at Seven Oaks for a week and treated for fluid in his lungs. He was released and appeared to be recovering. But on the evening of March 24, 1986, Clara became disturbed by his shallow irregular breathing. While Zuken lay on a bed in the study, she arranged for Bill and Ann Ross to drop by for a visit. His niece Janice Dietch was also there that evening. Zuken claimed he was not in pain, but he did need Clara's help to go upstairs to bed. Around midnight he asked for a cup of tea. Clara noticed he was not drinking it and asked if he would like her to hold it for him. He said, "No, I am just very tired. You had better go back to bed. You must be exhausted."

That night Janice spent the night on the living room couch, while Clara slept in the den. When Clara went to check on Joe in the morning, he was dead. The family physician told Clara that his heart had simply given up, worn out by the years of work.

The papers were filled with tributes. Steve Juba hailed him as the conscience of city hall, Slaw Rebchuk commented on his commitment to the underprivileged, and Roland Penner spoke of his personal integrity. Ted Byfield in *Western Report* suggested Zuken might go to heaven, even if he did not think it existed. The *Free Press*, once one of his strongest critics, editorialized: "With his passing a mighty voice has been silenced. A part of the North End experience has passed into history. Winnipeg will be a poorer place without him."

Over four hundred mourners turned out to the Chesed Shel Emel synagogue for the funeral. Zuken's long-time friend Ben Chud gave the eulogy. It was an eloquent speech; its rich and striking imagery was reminiscent of speeches Zuken himself had delivered on many occasions. Chud artfully stitched together the many sides of Joe Zuken.

How can we explain the fact that the media in Canada picked up the story of the passing of someone they describe as a communist, a civic politician, a lawyer and a Jew, and treat all of these characteristics of this man with such dignity and respect?

I want to suggest to you that part of the answer is to be found in the fact that Joe Zuken destroyed every stereotype associated with being a communist, a politician, a lawyer and a Jew.

Everyone knew that for Joe communism meant the eradication of exploitation, it meant the brotherhood and the sisterhood of people, it meant a secure life for all, it meant the distribution of the resources of our planet in an equitable fashion and it meant a world without war.

Everyone knew that as a politician Joe Zuken always stood on principle. He never bent with the wind. He was never self-serving and he could not be bought.

As a lawyer Joe knew that the law was not equally applied for the rich and the poor. All of his professional life was spent in an attempt to rectify that wrong.

Joe loved his people and the Yiddish language rang rich and pure on his tongue. He loved the literature of his people. Peretz was for him a guiding light....

How well I remember Joe's reading of Peretz's "Mayn Nit." How Joe Zuken's voice rang out as he came to the last line of the poem: "Mayn nit les di, v'les dien." Don't ever believe there is no trial and no judgement....

Thus does the listing of Joe's characteristics come together in a totally integrated manner. Let no one de-emphasize any part of the man, for by so doing they are demeaning and devaluing Joe....

In the words of the Soviet poet, Itzik Feffer — He was a *mensch!* He served his people well.

Interviews

Ruben Bellan
Andrew Bilecki
Lawrie Cherniack
Saul Cherniack
Sybil Cherniack
Janice Dietch
Olga Foltz
Mary Harrison
William Kardash
David Landy
Norman Larsen
Gordon MacDonnell
Pat McEvoy
Gudmundur Myrdal
Fred Narvey
Bill Neville
David Orlikow
Norman Penner
Roland Penner
Andrew Robertson
Bill Ross
Stanley Ryerson
Vic Savino
Harold Stubbs
Harry Walsh
Clara Zuken
Joseph Zuken

Bibliography

Books

Abella, Irving M. *Nationalism, Communism and Canadian Labour.* Toronto, 1973.

Angus, Ian. *Canadian Bolsheviks: The Early Years of the Communist Party of Canada.* Montreal, 1981.

Artibise, Allan F. J. *Winnipeg: A Social History of Urban Growth 1874-1914.* Montreal, 1975.

———. *Winnipeg: An Illustrated History.* Toronto, 1977.

Aubin, Henry. *City for Sale.* Toronto, 1977.

Austin, Gilbert R. *Early Childhood Education: An International Perspective.* New York, 1976.

Avakumovic, Ivan. *The Communist Party of Canada: A History.* Toronto, 1975.

Avery, Donald. *Dangerous Foreigners: European Immigrant Workers and Labour Radicalism in Canada, 1896-1932.* Toronto, 1976.

Bercuson, David J. *Confrontation at Winnipeg.* Montreal, 1974.

Berger, Thomas. *Fragile Freedoms: Human Rights and Dissent in Canada.* Toronto, 1981.

Betcherman, Lita-Rose. *The Little Band: The Clashes between the Communists and the Political and Legal Establishment in Canada, 1928-1932.* Ottawa, 1980.

———. *The Swastika and the Maple Leaf.* Pickering, 1975.

Brownstone, Meyer, and T. J. Plunkett. *Metropolitan Winnipeg: Politics and Reform in Local Government.* Berkeley, 1983.

Buck, Tim. *Yours in the Struggle: Reminiscences of Tim Buck,* edited by William Beeching and Phyllis Clarke. Toronto, 1977.

Buhle, Paul. *Marxism in the USA: Remapping the History of the American Left.* London, 1987.

Caute, David. *The Great Fear: The Anti-Communist Purge under Truman and Eisenhower.* London, 1978.

Chafe, J. W. *Chalk, Sweat and Cheers: A History of the Manitoba Teachers Society.* Winnipeg, 1969.

Clement, Wallace. *Hardrock Mining: Industrial Relations and Technological Changes at Inco.* Toronto, 1981.

Communist Party of Canada. *Canada's Party of Socialism*. Toronto, 1982.

Crooks, Harold. *Dirty Business: The Inside Story of the New Garbage Agglomerates*. Toronto, 1983.

Deutscher, Isaac. *Stalin: A Political Biography*. London, 1949.

Draper, Theodore. *American Communism and Soviet Russia*. New York, 1960.

Endicott, Stephen. *James G. Endicott: Rebel out of China*. Toronto, 1980.

Ferns, H. S. *Reading from Left to Right: One Man's Political History*. Toronto, 1983.

Fortin, Gerald, and Boyce Richardson. *Life of the Party*. Montreal, 1984.

Gibson, Dale, and Lee Gibson. *Substantial Justice: Law and Lawyers in Manitoba*. Winnipeg, 1972.

Gornick, Vivian. *The Romance of American Communism*. New York, 1977.

Gray, James H. *The Winter Years*. Toronto, 1973.

———. *The Boy from Winnipeg*. Toronto, 1970.

———. *The Roar of the Twenties*. Markham, 1982.

———. *Troublemaker!* Toronto, 1978.

Gregor, Alexander, and Keith Wilson. *The Development of Education in Manitoba*. Dubuque, 1984.

Gutkin, Harry, with Mildred Gutkin. *The Worst of Times, the Best of Times: Growing Up in Winnipeg's North End*. Markham, 1987.

Gutkin, Harry. *Journey into Our Heritage: The Story of the Jewish People in the Canadian West*. Toronto, 1980.

Harbutt, Fraser J. *The Iron Curtain: Churchill, America and the Origins of the Cold War*. New York, 1986.

Harvey, Cameron. *The Law Society of Manitoba 1877-1977*. Winnipeg, 1977.

Howe, Irving, ed. *World of Our Fathers*. New York, 1976.

Hunter, Peter. *Which Side Are You On Boys: Canadian Life on the Left*. Toronto, 1988.

Isserman, Maurice. *Which Side Were You On? The American Communist Party during the Second World War*. Middleton, 1982.

Jewish Historical Society of Western Canada. *Jewish Life and Times: A Collection of Essays*. Winnipeg, 1983.

Kaplan, Harold. *Reform, Planning and City Politics*. Toronto, 1982.

Kaplan, William. *State and Salvation: The Jehovah's Witnesses and Their Fight for Civil Rights*. Toronto, 1989.

Kent, Tom. *A Public Purpose: An Experience of Liberal Opposition and Canadian Government*. Kingston, 1988.

Klehr, Harvey. *The Heyday of American Communism: The Depression Decade*. New York, 1984.

Kolasky, John. *The Shattered Illusion, The History of the Ukrainian Pro-Communist Organizations in Canada.* Toronto, 1979.

LaFeber, Walter. *America, Russia and the Cold War: 1945-1984.* New York, 1985.

Levine, Allan. *Your Worship: The Lives of Eight of Canada's Most Unforgettable Mayors.* Toronto, 1989.

Lewis, Sinclair. *It Can't Happen Here.* New York, 1935.

Littleton, James. *Target Nation: Canada and the Western Intelligence Network.* Toronto, 1986.

Lorimer, James. *A Citizen's Guide to City Politics.* Toronto, 1972.

———. *The Developers.* Toronto, 1978.

Lorimer, James, and Evelyn Ross, eds. *The Second City Book.* Toronto, 1977.

McCormick, A. R. *Reformers, Rebels and Revolutionaries: The Western Radical Movement, 1899-1919.* Toronto, 1977.

McEwen, Tom. *The Forge Glows Red: From Blacksmith to Revolutionary.* Toronto, 1974.

Morton, W. L. *Manitoba: A History.* Toronto, 1957.

Palmer, Bryan. *Working Class Experience.* Toronto, 1983.

Paris, Erna. *Jews: An Account of Their Experience in Canada.* Toronto, 1980.

Penner, Norman. *Canadian Communism: The Stalin Years and Beyond.* Toronto, 1988.

———. *The Canadian Left: A Critical Analysis.* Scarborough, 1977.

Rankin, Harry. *Rankin's Law: Recollections of a Radical.* Vancouver, 1975.

Rea, J. E. *Parties and Power: An Analysis of Winnipeg City Council 1919-1975.* Winnipeg, 1976.

Repka, William, and Kathleen M. Repka. *Dangerous Patriots.* Vancouver, 1982.

Rodney, William. *Soldiers of the International: A History of the Communist Party of Canada, 1919-1929.* Toronto, 1968.

Rosenthal, Henry M., and Catherine Berson, eds. *The* Canadian Jewish Outlook *Anthology.* Vancouver, 1988.

Ryan, Toby Gordon. *Stage Left: Canadian Theatre in the Thirties — A Memoir.* Toronto, 1981.

Samuel, Raphael, Ewan MacColl, and Stuart Cosgrove. *Theatres of the Left: 1880-1935 Workers' Theatre Movements in Britain and America.* London, 1985.

Sangster, Joan. *Dreams of Equality: Women on the Canadian Left, 1920-1950.* Toronto, 1989.

Smith, A. E. *All My Life: An Autobiography.* Toronto, 1949.

Smith, Doug. *Let Us Rise! An Illustrated History of the Manitoba Labour Movement.* Vancouver, 1985.

Socknat, Thomas P. *Witness Against War: Pacifism in Canada 1900-1945*. Toronto, 1987.

Solski, Mike, and John Smaller. *Mine Mill: The History of the International Union of Mine, Mill, and Smelter Workers in Canada Since 1895*. Ottawa, 1984.

Stanton, John. *Never Say Die! The Life and Times of a Pioneer Labour Lawyer*. Ottawa, 1987.

Stinson, Lloyd. *Political Warriors: Recollections of a Social Democrat*. Winnipeg, 1975.

Stubbs, Lewis St. George. *A Majority of One: The Life and Times of Lewis St. George Stubbs*. Winnipeg, 1983.

Stubbs, Roy St. George. *Prairie Portraits*. Toronto, 1954.

Sutherland, Neil. *Children in English-Canadian Society: Framing the Twentieth-Century Consensus*. Toronto, 1976.

Taraska, Peter. *Report and Recommendations of the Committee of Review, City of Winnipeg Act*. Winnipeg, 1976.

Walker, David. *The Great Winnipeg Dream*. Oakville, 1979.

Watson, Louise. *She Was Never Afraid: The Biography of Annie Buller*. Toronto, 1976.

Whitaker, Reg. *Double Standard: The Secret History of Canadian Immigration*. Toronto, 1987.

Wiseman, Nelson. *Social Democracy in Manitoba: A History of the CCF/NDP*. Winnipeg, 1983.

Wright, Richard, and Robin Endres, eds. *Eight Men Speak and Other Plays from the Canadian Workers' Theatre*. Toronto, 1976.

Articles

Allan, Ted. "Once 'a black eye to Winnipeg,' Zuken has become respectable, a local curiosity piece." *Winnipeg Free Press*, March 30, 1976.

Avery, Donald. "Ethnic Loyalties and the Proletarian Revolution: A Case Study of Communist Political Activity in Winnipeg, 1923-1936." In *Ethnicity, Power & Politics in Canada*, edited by Jorgen Dahlie and Tissa Fernando. Toronto, 1981.

Babin, Ronald, Eric Shragge, and Jean-François Beaudet. "Non-Alignment and Detente from Below." In *Roots of Peace*, edited by Ronald Babin, Eric Shragge, and Jean-Guy Vaillancourt. Toronto, 1986.

City Magazine editorial. "Land and city politics in Winnipeg." *City Magazine* 2, no. 8.

———. "Reform Politics in Winnipeg: Opening Things Up." *City Magazine* 1, no 3.

Cook, Ramsay. "Canadian Freedom in Wartime, 1939-1945." In *His Own Man: Essays in Honour of A. R. M. Lower,* edited by W. H. Heick and Roger Graham. Montreal, 1974.

Cramer, Phillip. "Manitoba's Red Bencher: Still an Activist." *Ontario Lawyers' Weekly,* January 24, 1986.

Edwards, Rod. "Zuken looks back on 33 years in office." *Winnipeg Free Press,* December 27, 1973.

Garland, Aileen. "Old, Unhappy Far Off Things and Battles of Long Ago." *Manitoba Teacher,* November-December 1968.

Gibson, Dale. "An Anecdotal Sample." In *The Law Society of Manitoba 1877-1977,* edited by Cameron Harvey. Winnipeg, 1977.

Goldstein, Jay. "Has the popularity of Anglo-Conformity Waned? A study of school naming events in Winnipeg, 1881-1979." *Canadian Ethnic Studies* 13, no. 2: 81.

Gutstein, Donald. "Genstar: Portrait of a conglomerate developer." *City Magazine* 2, no. 1.

Jacobs, Steve. "Wheeling and dealing in Winnipeg land." *City Magazine* 4, no. 1.

Kiernan, Matthew J., and David C. Walker. "Winnipeg." In *City Politics in Canada,* edited by Warren Magnusson and Andrew Sancton. Toronto, 1983.

Larsen, Norman. "Legal Aid in Manitoba." In *The Law Society of Manitoba 1877-1977,* edited by Cameron Harvey. Winnipeg, 1977.

Levine, Allan. "Stephen Juba: The Great City Salesman." In *Your Worship: The Lives of Eight of Canada's Most Unforgettable Mayors,* edited by Allan Levine. Toronto, 1989.

Lorimer, James. "Gerecke comment touches off furor." *City Magazine* 2, no. 5.

———. "Smoking out the liberals." *City Magazine* 1, no. 1.

———. "Suburban Land: an independent view." *City Magazine* 3, no. 2.

Moon, Peter. "Joseph Zuken, Queen's Counsel, Sure Is a Nice Commie." *Canadian Magazine,* August 7, 1971.

Penner, Jacob. "Recollections of the Early Socialist Movement in Winnipeg" (with an introduction by Norman Penner). *Histoire Sociale/Social History* 7, no. 13 (May 1974).

Petryshyn, J. "Class Conflict and Civil Liberties: The Origins and Activities of the Canadian Labour Defense League, 1925-1940." *Labour/Le Travaille* 10 (Autumn 1982).

Phillips, Paul, " 'Power Politics': Municipal Affairs and Seymour James Farmer, 1909-1924." In *Cities in the West: Papers of the Western Canadian History Conference,* edited by A. R. McCormack and Ian MacPherson. Ottawa, 1975.

Posner, Gerald. "In Camera: An Interview with Joe Zuken." *Canadian Lawyer*, April 1980.

Rea, J. E. "My main line is the kiddies ... make them good Christians and good Canadians, which is the same thing." In *Identities: The Impact of Ethnicity Upon Canadian Society*, edited by Wsevolod Isajiw. Toronto, 1977.

Salopek, Marijan. "Western Canadians and Civil Defence: The Korean War Years." *Prairie Forum* 14, no. 1.

Salutin, Rick. "It Happened Here. Earlier. And Worse." In *Marginal Notes: Challenges to the Mainstream*. Toronto, 1984.

Smith, Doug. "Bridge a mixed blessing." *City Magazine* 4, no. 2.

———. "The Big Red Scare of 1979." *Last Post* 7, no. 6 (November 1979).

Thompson, John Herd. "The Political Career of Ralph H. Webb." *Red River Valley Historian*, Spring 1976.

Trachtenberg, Henry. "The Winnipeg Jewish Community and Politics: The Inter-War Period, 1919-1939." *Historical and Scientific Society of Manitoba Transactions*.

Whitaker, Reginald. "Left-wing Dissent and the State: Canada in the Cold War Era." In *Dissent and the State*, edited by C. E. S. Franks. Toronto, 1989.

———. "Fighting the Cold War on the Home Front: America, Britain, Australia and Canada." In *The Socialist Register 1984*, edited by Ralph Miliband, John Saville, and Marcel Liebman. London, 1984.

———. "Origins of the Canadian Government's Internal Security System, 1946-1952." *Canadian Historical Review* 65, no. 2 (June 1984).

———. "What Is the Cold War and Why Is It Still With Us?" *Studies in Political Economy*, Spring 1986.

———. "Official Repression of Communism During World War II." *Labour/Le Travail* 17 (Spring 1986).

Wichern, Phil. "An election unlike — and very much like — the others." *City Magazine* 3, nos. 4, 5.

Zuken, Joseph. "Legacy for the Living." In *The Canadian Jewish Outlook Anthology*, edited by Henry M. Rosenthal and S. Catherine Berson. Vancouver, 1988.

———. "Observations on a Centenary." In *The Canadian Jewish Outlook Anthology*, edited by Henry M. Rosenthal and S. Catherine Berson. Vancouver, 1988.

———. "The Impact of the Depression on the Jewish Community." In *Jewish Life and Times: A Collection of Essays*. Winnipeg, 1983.

———. "Is the Public School the Arena for Religious Education?" In *The Canadian Jewish Outlook Anthology*, edited by Henry M. Rosenthal and S. Catherine Berson. Vancouver, 1988.

Theses and Unpublished Papers

Barber, Paul. "Class Conflict in Winnipeg Civic Politics: The Role of the Citizens' and Civic Election Organizations." 1970.

Barber, Paul. "The Nationalization of the Winnipeg Electric Company: The Dispute over Plan 'C.'" June 1971.

Chisick, Ernie. "The Development of Winnipeg's Socialist Movement, 1900-1915." Unpublished thesis, University of Manitoba, 1972.

Enns, David. "The Knights of Labour in Winnipeg." Unpublished essay, 1980.

Goeres, Michael. "Disorder, Dependency and Fiscal Responsibility: Unemployment Relief in Winnipeg, 1907-1942." Unpublished thesis, University of Manitoba, 1974.

Goldstein, Kenneth J. "The *Winnipeg Citizen:* A history and analysis of the world's first co-operatively-owned newspaper." Ryerson Polytechnical Institute, 1966.

Gonick, Fay. "Social Values in Public Education, Manitoba 1910-1930." Unpublished thesis, University of Manitoba, 1974.

Martynowich, Orest T. "Village Radicals and Peasant Immigrants: The Social Roots of Factionalism among Ukrainian Immigrants in Canada, 1896-1918." Unpublished thesis, University of Manitoba, 1978.

McKillop, A. B. "Citizen and Socialist: The Ethos of Political Winnipeg, 1919-1935." Unpublished M.A. thesis, University of Manitoba, 1970.

Melnycky, Peter. "A Political History of the Ukrainian Community in Manitoba 1899-1922." Unpublished thesis, University of Manitoba, 1979.

Mochoruk, Jim. Untitled paper on the 1933 Flin Flon strike; in the possession of the Manitoba Labour Education Centre, 1983.

Mott, Morris. "The 'Foreign Peril': Nativism in Winnipeg 1916-1923." Unpublished thesis, University of Manitoba, 1970.

Milan, Robert. "Education and the Reproduction of Capitalist Ideology: Manitoba, 1945-1960." M.Ed. thesis, University of Manitoba, 1980.

Rowland, Douglas. "Canadian Communism: The Post-Stalinist Phase." Unpublished thesis, University of Manitoba, 1964.

Skene, Reginald. "Theatre and Community Development: Toward a Professional Theatre in Winnipeg, 1879-1958." Ph.D. thesis, University of Toronto, 1982.

Spector, David. "The Knights of Labour in Winnipeg." Unpublished essay, 1974.

Usiskin, Roseline. "Toward a theoretical reformulation of the relationship between political ideology, social class, and ethnicity:

a case study of the Winnipeg Jewish radical community, 1905-1902." Unpublished thesis, University of Manitoba, 1978.

Provincial Archives of Manitoba

John Bracken papers
The Chamber of Commerce papers
Michael Harris (Hrushka papers)
Labor Progressive Party papers
Manitoba Attorney General — miscellaneous papers
R. B. Russell papers
Joseph Zuken papers

Index

522